WITHDRAWN
UTSA LIBRARIES

The Committed Neutral

Published in cooperation with
The Swedish Institute of International Affairs,
Stockholm

The Committed Neutral

Sweden's Foreign Policy

EDITED BY
Bengt Sundelius

Westview Press
BOULDER, SAN FRANCISCO, & LONDON

Westview Special Studies in International Relations

This Westview softcover edition is printed on acid-free paper and bound in softcovers that carry the highest rating of the National Association of State Textbook Administrators, in consultation with the Association of American Publishers and the Book Manufacturers' Institute.

All rights reserved. No part of this publication may be reproduced or transmitted in any form or by any means, electronic or mechanical, including photocopy, recording, or any information storage and retrieval system, without permission in writing from the publisher.

Copyright © 1989 by Westview Press, Inc.

Published in 1989 in the United States of America by Westview Press, Inc., 5500 Central Avenue, Boulder, Colorado 80301, and in the United Kingdom by Westview Press, Inc., 13 Brunswick Centre, London WC1N 1AF, England

Library of Congress Cataloging-in-Publication Data
The Committed neutral.
   (Westview special studies in international relations)
   Published in cooperation with the Swedish Institute
of International Affairs, Stockholm.
   Includes bibliographical references.
   1. Sweden—Foreign relations.   I. Sundelius, Bengt.
II. Utrikespolitiska institutet (Sweden).   III. Series.
DL860.C56 1989   327.485   89-25067
ISBN 0-8133-7713-7

LIBRARY
The University of Texas
At San Antonio

Printed and bound in the United States of America

The paper used in this publication meets the requirements of the American National Standard for Permanence of Paper for Printed Library Materials Z39.48-1984.

10   9   8   7   6   5   4   3   2   1

Contents

Acknowledgments

As with most academic works, this volume is the result of collaboration among many individuals. *The Committed Neutral* was launched as part of the *New Sweden 88** campaign while I was still associated with the University of Washington. It was hoped that this project would result in one of the more enduring and concrete results from that massive information effort. The Swedish Institute granted the necessary funding. Ove Svensson and Christina Engfeldt provided valuable support throughout the project. Neither they—nor anyone else at the Swedish Institute— interfered with either the content or academic purpose of the project in any respect. Instead, they offered helpful assistance whenever it was requested. Bo Huldt of the Swedish Institute of International Affairs facilitated the project during its early phases. The volume is now published under the auspices of his institute.

The manifold contributions by Don Odom are gratefully recognized. The definition of his responsibilities as project assistant was stretched beyond any reasonable limits during our many Sunday afternoons in the questionable company of the preliminary drafts. Don prepared (coded and edited) the entire book and compiled the *For Further Reading* section of the book. If the book in front of you reads at all well, then it is the result of Don's careful and diligent polishing.

My most important lesson from this project is that commitment begins at home. Even more than before, I have come to admire the quietly practiced commitment that Julie personifies. To know her is to experience commitment.

Bengt Sundelius

---

*To commemorate the 350th anniversary of the first Swedish (and Finnish) settlers in the United States (the New Sweden Colony located in the area that is now Delaware), a massive celebration—*New Sweden 1638–1988*—was held in both countries throughout 1988. It included royal visits to the United States, a week of on-location coverage in Stockholm by the hosts of ABC television's *Good Morning America,* numerous museum exhibits, concerts, cultural exchanges, and countless workshops and lectures at American colleges and research centers. Although it is still too early to assess its lasting impact, the celebration certainly succeeded in highlighting many aspects of the kinship between the United States and Sweden.

1

Committing Neutrality in an Antagonistic World

Bengt Sundelius

The contemporary European security context can be defined in terms of two opposing alliances that seek to avoid a military confrontation through determined efforts to prepare for just such a situation. In this setting of allies concerned with coalition management and bloc balancing, a European neutral stands out as a deviant case. It is not easily integrated into the bloc perpectives of the two alliance leaders. The neutral's position can be misunderstood by either side as serving the strategic interests of the opposing side. For much of the postwar period, the United States remained skeptical concerning the efficacy of neutrality as a policy choice. As the postwar record shows, however, the United States was not alone in these misgivings.

> For the United States neutrality represented not only a discredited past and an undesired feature of the European system erected after the war but also an unhealthy sign of the potential future of that system. The Soviet Union was not much in disagreement with the United States about the past or the present of European neutrality, particularly as some of the defectors from the ranks of the WTO showed inclinations in that direction (Albrecht, Auffermann and Joenniemi, 1988:11).

Standing alone, a neutral state finds itself frequently forced to explain and defend its record. This is part of the never ending determination to build confidence—both at home and abroad—in its chosen position. In times of East–West tension, such as during most of the 1980s, this need to profess one's innocence becomes the daily task for the representatives of a European neutral. Many illustrations of this limited appreciation for neutrality among world leaders, as well as among the publics at large, can be given. In a 1976 dinner speech, Henry Kissinger expressed this sentiment well. He is quoted as having addressed his Swedish host as follows: "I think we can also agree that the neutrality of some is made possible by the commitment of others" (Pers, 1987:91). This skeptical view of neutrality is not a novel phenomena linked to the contemporary East–West divide in world politics. According to one student of neutrality, Efraim Karsh, for a long time "the general attitude towards the neutral state was one of intolerance and principled reluctance to recognize neutrality as a legitimate political option" (1988:14). To commit neutrality in an antagonistic world is not usually a popular policy choice with the combatants.

In this volume, five U.S. scholars give the reader the benefit of their outside perspectives concerning different facets of Swedish foreign relations. Through this mirror of U.S. interpretations of our reality, we can gain new insights into a subject that may be so mundane and familiar that its essence has been lost. To accentuate any discrepancies between these outside views and our self-image, the book begins with an essay by the distinguished Swedish diplomat Sverker Åström. In his chapter, the reader gets perhaps as close a reading as is possible (with the exception of official and often sterile policy declarations) of how the Swedish foreign policy establishment prefers to portray its position in world affairs. This chapter reveals as much from what is omitted or downplayed as from what is highlighted.

The extent to which the preferred Swedish image has penetrated U.S. scholarship can be noted in the writings of the other contributors and, especially, in the final chapter by Mikael Steene. Steene surveys the shifting views of Swedish foreign policy among prominent U.S. specialists as reflected in their writings over a period of seven decades (1929–1987). Certainly, the combination of perspectives chosen for this volume may be useful to students abroad who want to learn about our foreign policy. In addition, the material should be examined by the many Swedes who are trying to understand the seemingly contradictory elements of their *committed neutral.*

Before others can appreciate our international role, we must first understand it ourselves. The neutrality aspiration is ill-served by overly pessimistic interpretations of its limited value to our security or by grand illusions about the almost boundless opportunities for influence by a small neutral state. To assist in our continous self-examination, it is valuable to draw on the observations of outsiders. They may note aspects of our profile that have escaped us and provide insights into the established patterns that we have taken for granted.

An Enduring Commitment

In Chapter three, John Logue traces the lengthy tradition of Swedish neutrality and peace. Sweden has been spared involvement in any wars since 1814 and has aimed at a consistent policy of neutrality over at least 100 years. This recent record of peaceful external relations is often contrasted with the costly, and in the end futile, attempts during earlier centuries to play power politics through wars and alliances. The national interpretation of this heritage of successful neutrality was confirmed during World War II. The choice of neutrality in the postwar Great Power confrontation came easy to the government, and it has been widely supported ever since.

The war experiences also served to underline the importance of national defense for a credible neutrality posture. Subsequently, the Swedish government has been a traditional neutral with respect to reliance on the classic means of security—armed force. Even today, defense expenditures are considerable and higher, per capita, than those of most NATO countries. In addition, the comprehensive nature of national defense and the economic dimension of security have been stressed. World War II brought home the lesson that extensive stockpiles and industrial adaptability are vital components behind successful neutrality when it is challenged by conflicting parties.

Sweden shares strong economic links with the Western economies. Only around five percent of its trade is with Eastern Europe. Experiencing outstanding affluence throughout the postwar era and recognizing the importance of the Western economic channels for this prosperity, the official neutrality line has interfered only marginally with the private pursuit of commerce and finance. This liberal attitude toward international exchange has to some extent also included items of strategic significance, such as advanced technology, arms, and ammunition. Critics of Swedish policies often point to this aspect of foreign relations as evidence of the anachronistic nature of contemporary neutrality. Others see this aspect as proof of the flexibility and success of the government line.

In many quarters, Sweden is also viewed as a detached, impartial party in the resolution of international conflict. Providing noncontroversial meeting-grounds, offering good offices, initiating mediation, and giving humanitarian assistance in tense areas have become part of the international role of this small state. In this respect, Sweden has been widely admired and has established standards for other nations. Sweden shares with its fellow Nordic nations an inclination for marked visibility in global issues and arenas. Not content merely to adjust their foreign policies to international realities, the Nordic states hope to promote international change more directly. Such ambitions are evident both in North-South issues and in East-West negotiations. Sweden combines this diplomatic high profile with the traditional elements of neutrality. Critics point to the inherent tension between these two dimensions of Swedish foreign policy, while advocates of so called active neutrality regard this dualism as a comprehensive security strategy.

The classic definition of the Swedish foreign policy doctrine is "freedom from alliances in peace aiming for neutrality in war." Neutrality is a status defined in terms of open conflict and is regulated by international rules, such as in the Hague Conventions of 1907. The strategy of no alliances is a peacetime effort to enhance the credibility of the determination to remain outside an East-West confrontation. This doctrine forms the core of the national security posture. It is relevant to international conflicts that may involve the superpowers and that could then impact on the Swedish situation.

Sweden does not profess to be impartial to all conflicts around the world or to remain insensitive to injustices and violations of international norms. Rather, the government often chooses to speak out on controversial issues, even at the risk of offending other world leaders. In particular, the rights of small states have been defended when seemingly brutalized by stronger parties. Clearly, this concern with the faith of distant nations and with the preservation of international law, as symbolized in the Charter of the United Nations, relates to immediate security needs close to home.

Securing Independence

Joseph Kruzel addresses the question: How can Swedish security be maintained in a north European setting characterized by growing strategic significance? In a more polarized structure both alliance leaders may during peacetime try to strengthen their relative positions by including, at least informally, additional states into each bloc. At the very least, it would be vital to deny such arrangements between any neutral state and the opposing side. Invitations to some type of informal cooperation or demands for conformance with certain principles advocated by the superpower may be made. A passive acceptance of a new strategic order may be encouraged.

The major threat to the future security of Sweden may not come from the possibility of a major superpower confrontation involving it. Instead, the step-by-step pulling that may over time lead to new structural conditions for national security is a concern. Sweden follows with interest the negotiations for arms reductions in Europe well knowing that the results directly affect its future although the outcome lies beyond its influence.

A second strategic dimension addresses the direction of superpower interests in crisis or war. Regardless of the level of East-West tensions, technological developments and changing political circumstances may shift the focus of the alliance confrontation. During recent years, much attention has again been given to the North. Mutual interests in the North Atlantic and its surrounding land areas have been reflected in an increased military presence by both blocs.

Sweden is located within the orbits of the strategic interests of the opposing alliances. Thus a sense of exposed geostrategic vulnerability has developed. Although not directly involved in this East-West strategic posturing, Sweden is motivated by legal obligations and political convictions to ensure that its territory is not used by either bloc in this game. In this perspective, the ability to protect its territorial integrity in peacetime might seem paramount to the wartime credibility of a neutral. Certainly, both superpowers would find it useful to insist on such a linkage to reduce the potential advantages to the other side.

Securing Prosperity

Ebba Dohlman reminds us that Sweden is a small, highly trade dependent society with intense economic ties to the surrounding world. Its relative political aloofness, manifested in the neutrality doctrine, has been combined with considerable international economic involvements, particularly in the West. Although continuous prosperity is linked to this ability to participate in international economic exchanges, a dilemma has arisen to the extent that the superpower blocs increasingly link their economic policies to national security ambitions. During much of the 1980s, the traditional two-tier international structure, with distinct arenas for security and economics, in some respects has eroded. Terms such as strategic embargo, economic sanctions, and even warfare have returned to the vocabulary of international relations. Such activities are particularly problematic for states trying to stay politically unattached yet wanting to participate in economic relations.

On the one hand, continued access to the markets, resources, services, and high technology of the Western economies is a fundamental prerequisite for future economic success. On the other hand, one could argue that a comprehensive neutrality posture should also include a balanced economic profile with equally intimate links in all directions. For example, it must be difficult for a neutral state to deny technology transfers to the East with the argument that this flow would violate Western export regulations to which the neutral, per definition, does not subscribe. This dilemma has given some neutrals, like Austria and Sweden, the perhaps unfair reputation in the United States as particularly notorious channels for technology diffusion to the Soviet bloc. To remedy such a problem, the Swedish government in 1986 amended its export regulations and tightened controls of transfers of U.S.–based technology. According to both governments, this, at one time delicate, issue is no longer a matter of concern between the nations.

At the same time, one must note that the neutrality rules apply to states but not to the private sphere of society. Sweden's classic heritage forbids any forceful restrictions on the pursuits of private endeavors, even if these would undermine the widely supported neutrality doctrine. With intimate links between the public and the private sectors, such a differentiation serves as a complicating factor for any image-building efforts. How can one separate state policy from the acts of private citizens or firms? This issue may be particularly relevant as Sweden has been identified by many scholars as a society with well developed corporatist partnerships in most areas of public involvements, including international economic relations.

The overlap issue has appeared as one sensitive dimension of the dialogue with the U.S. government over high technology transfers. Recently the Swedish debate has shifted to arms exports and to the implications of these commercial activities for the official foreign policy posture. Similarly, the perennial issue over our ties to the European Community (EC) revolves around the distinction between private acts and state commitments. Today, relations with the EC are a topic of considerable concern in Sweden, and they are discussed by Sverker Åström in Chapter two.

Promoting Global Welfare

In Chapter six, Susan Holmberg discusses the Swedish tradition of generosity toward the Third World. The Swedish model of development assistance policy is generally characterized by annual aid volumes that— when measured as a percentage of GNP—are among the highest in the world. A sizable portion of this aid is free from any reciprocal purchase requirements. The least developed countries have received special consideration and rural projects with long-term development effects have been emphasized. Humanitarian assistance to national liberation groups in southern Africa and support of so-called "progressive regimes" has been granted. For good reason, the Swedish image has been one of a progressive, generous, and committed partner in the global development process.

In contrast to most prominent development assistance grantors, Sweden lacks a significant colonial heritage. Its unusually high aid commitment cannot be explained by a colonial background or by far-flung strategic interests. Rather, the domestic experiences of peaceful political development during the last century of rapid (and significant) socioeconomic change have heavily influenced current attitudes toward economic and social progress in less developed countries. The successful Swedish transformation from a poor rural society to a highly advanced post-industrial economy has helped to form dominant political attitudes toward global development problems. The strength and political prominence of the labor movement has also helped to shape government views concerning socioeconomic progress and international solidarity.

Today, the Swedish commitment to global welfare is less prominent than it once was in terms of the quality of bilateral assistance. Development assistance policy, a traditionally protected area, seems to have become more integrated with the overall economic and commercial objectives of the nation. Now, it is more accepted than in the past that resource transfers may also bring benefits to the donor. The net cost of these impressive programs is reduced considerably through the type of measures recently adopted. Perhaps such innovations are necessary to maintain broad popular support for the public expenditures required to uphold the famed one percent target.

Swedish support of the United Nations development effort is very significant compared to most states. Together with the other Scandinavian states, Sweden provides about one-fourth of the funds for the U.N. Development Program, as well as gives disproportionally high grants to the specialized U.N. agencies. The share of multilateral assistance, however, has declined in recent years. In international fora, Sweden often supports Third World positions, such as the proposal for a New International Economic Order (NIEO). The status of Sweden as a like-minded country was coined during the 1970s to accentuate its commitment to global welfare.

How durable is this heritage of international solidarity in the face of new economic and political pressures? The perceptive Swedish editor, Arne Ruth, has made a pessimistic prediction:

> But in all essentials, the myth of Swedish internationalism is bound to deflate under the impact of the real conflicts of interest between the old and new industrialized countries, between traditionally rich and hopelessly poor nations in the North and South (1984:75).

In Chapter five, Ebba Dohlman touches upon this tension between the support of global welfare and the demands of economic security at home.

The Kaleidoscopic Images of Neutrality

Sweden is a Western democracy with a pluralistic political and economic system. These features are shared with most members of the Atlantic Alliance. In this respect, Sweden is a world apart from the predominant political values and social orders of the East European nations. It is often stressed that the government is not neutral in terms of ideology but merely with respect to national security policy. The neutrality is not one of beliefs but of strategic choice. There is an element of expediency behind the national doctrine. Of concern is how this support of basic Western values can be combined with the equally firm commitment to neutrality in the political struggle between East and West.

This latent conflict between ideological preference and strategic necessity appears in much of the U.S. scholarship from the 1920s through the mid-1980s that Mikael Steene reviews in Chapter seven. The neutral strikes many in the West as a free rider. To many in the East, the neutral position may seem an envious one. Throughout the world, it is recognized as a policy of courage. Inside the European neutrals, one speaks more often of strategic necessity than of moral virtue. In one sense, however, a policy that can save people from the sufferings of war, or can offer the promise of freedom and democracy, may be seen as morally superior to any alternative that would risk these fundamental values.

Partly in response to such normative concerns, key political figures have from time to time stressed the virtues of representing a third, middle position in the East-West confrontation. By keeping a distance from both sides, the Swede indicates a commitment to impartiality in any political conflict between these sets of values. Through such reasoning, the neutral position can be justified in positive terms. It is said to provide a foundation for a unique and valuable international mediating role. The neutral stand is identified with a vital systemic function and in this way is transformed from a strategy of political necessity to a moral imperative. In such a perspective, a neutral democracy is clearly not morally compromised. On the contrary, it represents reason and a concern for the overriding interests of the international community. This favorable view of the potential contributions of neutrality as a positive option in world politics has recently been articulated by a group of European peace researchers.

> The aspirations for neutrality seem still to be too much dependent on the classical understanding that the state of war is neatly distinguishable from a state of peace, that governmental military behaviour is clearly distinguished from governmental non-military behaviour or that political alignment can be separated from economic intercourse. The traditional concept focusing

mainly on military neutrality seems to be by and large obsolete. Instead of non-alignment containing a commitment to non-participation in war neutrality has grown in importance as a peace-time policy. It is no longer to be seen mainly as a classical instrument of regulation and limitation of the generally accepted phenomenon of war but as a policy aiming at the prevention of war. In an increasingly interdependent world neutrality can no longer be based on autarchy and isolationism. For the most part the legalistic, formal and historically oriented concepts of neutrality that still float in the discussion are no longer adequate (Albrecht, Auffermann and Joenniemi, 1988:2).

Sweden's role in the East-West context as mediator, bridge builder, and impartial critic is widely recognized as having enhanced its national prestige and possibly its influence on world affairs as well. By contributing to a more stable environment with less propensity for conflict, national security interests may also be served. In addition to serving such national ends, the role function could also be of systemic importance. From time to time, even the superpower leaders recognize this valuable function in a divided world, full of issues that somehow must be managed. To grease the wheels of world politics is a vital part to play, especially when a machine breakdown could mean global disaster.

Committed Neutrality

The Finnish scholar Harto Hakovirta has recently reminded us that the two key resources for successful peacetime neutrality are the accumulation of credibility and respectability (1988:26). Drawing on the historical experiences of postwar European neutrality, Hakovirta concludes that

> The basic problem of contemporary neutrality lies in its inherent partiality and bias arising from the neutral states' Western values and ties. In terms of value premises and dependencies, this is not neutrality, but Western neutrality, or a paradoxical effort at maintaining a neutral image and label despite Western starting-points and predispositions. . . . In Eastern eyes the credibility of Western neutrality is of course chronically questionable, and this together with the basic Marxian class view tends to lower its respectability, too (1988:249).

In his authoritative overview of Swedish neutrality policy in Chapter two, the distinguished diplomat Sverker Åström shows how its credibility builds upon the confidence placed in it by others and the commitment to it by the Swedish people. Closely associated with the Swedish government for over forty years, Ambassador Åström's personal interpretation of the major elements and crucial tests of Swedish neutrality policy can be read as a unique example of the lines of thought that occur among public officials within the innermost circles of Sweden's foreign policy establishment. Many individuals, including Swedish diplomats and journalists, regard Sverker Åström's speeches and articles as providing authoritative guidelines for the proper interpretation of Swedish neutrality.

To an extent, the themes of Chapter two also reflect the image that the Swedish state wants to present abroad. In another context, Ambassador Åström stressed the importance of presenting the *correct* view when addressing Swedish foreign policy. In 1987, he wrote:

> One of the most important objectives for Swedish security policy is to shape abroad an image of Sweden that corresponds with our own view of it, as a mid-size, peace-promoting, fairly decent nation which is determined and capable of defending itself against demands, incursions, and attacks. . . . The information work in this area must not be limited to effective distribution of knowledge about what Sweden does and says. In addition, a special effort is required to explain and justify the policy to governments and public opinion in other nations (1987:109–10; my translation).

Clearly, the Swedish conception of neutrality includes aloofness but it is not restrained by a passive and reactive approach to foreign policy. Ambassador Åström is likely to agree with Karsh's assessment that

> . . . the successful pursuit of this policy requires the most finely tuned foreign policy instruments. . . . It appears exceedingly naive, therefore, to argue that neutrality will be preserved through 'lying low and escaping notice'. Without extended preparations—often carried out in peacetime— and without adopting a policy of initiative and vision, capable of giving an operative dimension to this jurisprudential concept, neutrality will remain a dead letter in the tombs of international law (1988:32–3).

The Swedish statement of Chapter two can be compared to the independent perspectives provided by the U.S. scholars in the other chapters. To Åström, credibility is at the heart of successful neutrality, and, indeed, several of the independent observers also address this issue. In fact, some cite potential problems in this regard, but all agree that the credibility component is of vital importance to the Swedish policy of neutrality. In his recent analysis of wartime neutrality, Karsh echoes the conventional wisdom by observing that "through deriving its *raison d'être* from the state of war and having its ultimate political, as well as only legal, significance in warlike situations, the successful implementation of neutrality requires meticulous preparatory work in peacetime" (1988:108).

Curiously enough, Karsh limits his definition of successful wartime neutrality to the ability to avoid so-called external violations, such as loss of independence or territorial integrity. He argues that the "instances where the neutral state has succeeded in remaining outside the circle of war, even at the cost of committing an internal violation, will be considered the success of neutrality as a foreign policy instrument" (Karsh, 1988:25). It is unclear if his acceptance of domestic accommodation to external pressure as a viable instrument toward credible neutrality is also extended to peacetime conditions. On this controversial point, Sverker Åström seems to hold to a stricter interpretation of the requirements of credible neutrality, which is more in accord with the views of the U.S. contributors to this volume.

The other basic dimension of successful neutrality—respectability—is less directly addressed by Åström. However, his essay is obviously colored by an attempt to enhance the "prestige, respect, regard, and appreciation that the state's position and policy enjoy in the eyes of . . . the leading world powers and other neutral states" (Hakovirta, 1988:29). In this ambition, Åström reflects a widely felt Swedish yearning for international respectability and, perhaps, even appreciation.

In official policy declarations, the credibility aspect of Swedish neutrality is often explicitly mentioned. It has become part of the official liturgy that the credibility of neutrality must be maintained and, if possible, continuously strengthened. A closer study of Swedish arguments reveals, however, that the respectability aspect of neutrality has just as often been the focus of concern. The potential peacetime contributions by a north European neutral have been stressed as a way of justifying the Swedish wartime choice.

Certainly, the relationship between these two resources of peacetime neutrality is complex. Often it is assumed that the respected neutral is also the credible neutral. Thus, it follows that one should build respectability so as to strengthen credibility. Without going into a detailed discussion concerning the logic of this assumption here, one can still note that strategies to strengthen one dimension do not necessarily enhance the other. For example, measures to improve respectability abroad may also serve to undermine the certainty that a self-serving neutral stand will be pursued during an acute crisis affecting shared values. Similarly, clear articulations of the egocentric objectives of neutrality may help to strengthen its credibility, but they also serve to reduce its respectability both at home and abroad.

Obviously, the Swedish government is faced with two potentially conflicting policy requirements. Ideally, the designated policy line should simultaneously strengthen both the credibility and the respectability components of neutrality. With usual political skill, a conceptual solution for this balancing act has been found in the formula of *the committed neutral.*

This term conveys a clear signal concerning Sweden's unshakable commitment to wartime neutrality, no matter what the cost in other policy areas. The concept also underscores Sweden's peacetime commitment to a just world order, the plight of the weak confronting the strong, the principle of democracy, and the value of human rights. Sometimes, it is even inferred that Sweden's contribution in the latter sphere is contingent upon (or at least facilitated by) its uncompromising neutrality. The two dimensions—credibility and respectability—would appear, then, to be inseparably intertwined and mutually supportive.

The conceptualization of Sweden as the committed neutral also reflects domestic sentiments. To many Swedes, neutrality is a dogma as embedded in the national character as democracy. To question its utility as a security strategy would be political suicide for any aspiring leader. Like the sacrosanct welfare system, this notion offers protection for a people that have been characterized as obsessed with individual security. Neutrality offers the promise of again escaping the perils of conflict even as the surrounding world crumbles. At the same time, the concept serves not only as a means toward such a self-centered security objective, but it is also widely associated with aspirations to international prestige and with national pride.

The commitment to a just and equitable world order in many ways reflects the salient features of Swedish domestic life. Clearly, the hope for global understanding, nonviolent solutions to security dilemmas, and adherence to principles of international law and organization is inspired by the comparatively tranquil domestic and regional developments of the last century. The quest for global solidarity parallels the ideals of the influential labor movement. The belief in managed market solutions to international economic problems draws upon successful experiences at home that have combined economic growth with shared affluence. The international bridge-building aspirations reflect the dynamics of national consensus formation, whereby sector demands are transformed into broad coalitions composed of leading parties and interest groups. The domestic sources of Swedish foreign policy are obvious and offer one explanation for its international role as the *committed* neutral.

Diplomacy, like politics, thrives on finding workable formulas that integrate contradictory interests into one common policy that fits the needs of all parties. In this regard, the Swedish government seems to have been highly successful in its choice of foreign policy profile. Happily, Harto Hakovirta concludes his seminal analysis of European neutrality on a positive note:

The overall credibility of European neutrality is inherently questionable, but this problem remains largely latent due to the relative satisfaction of the West, the limited leverage of the East, and the fact that, currently, neutrality is principally evaluated within the domain of peace. Besides, this problem is being overshadowed by the increased respectability of neutrality resulting from a combination of favorable environmental developments and the neutrals' own performances (1988:259).

The prospects for the committed neutral, then, appear to be promising. In the event that Swedish leaders and people have been blinded by their own time-tested success, however, the outside critical perspectives provided in this volume may be illuminating. Historical experiences often turn into national myths, where the boundary between fact and fiction becomes blurred.

By locking onto a specific foreign policy course—making it its *raison d'être*—a state runs the risk of ignoring the dynamics of the external setting, and in certain circumstances is liable to find its policy totally cut off from its environment (Karsh, 1988:37).

After all, what matters most with regard to the credibility and the respectability of our neutrality is not what we Swedes believe, but more what skeptics abroad sense to be the essence of our position.

References

Albrecht, Ulrich, Burkhard Auffermann, and Perti Joenniemi. (1988) *Neutrality: The Need for Conceptual Revision*. Occasional Papers, No. 35, Tampere: Tampere Peace Research Institute.

Åström, Sverker. (1987) "Sverigebilden och säkerhetspolitiken," in *Sverigebilder: 17 svenskar ser på Sverige*, Statens Offentliga Utredningar, No. 57, Stockholm: Allmänna Förlaget.

Hakovirta, Harto. (1988) *East–West Conflict and European Neutrality*. Oxford: Oxford University Press.

Karsh, Efraim. (1988) *Neutrality and Small States*. London: Routledge.

Pers, Anders. (1987) "Färre 'wild cards' i utrikespolitiken," in *Sverigebilder: 17 svenskar ser på Sverige*, Statens Offentliga Utredningar, No. 57, Stockholm: Allmänna Förlaget.

Ruth, Arne. (1984) "The Second New Nation: The Mythology of Modern Sweden," *Daedalus*, Vol. 113, No. 2, Spring, pp. 53–96.

2

Swedish Neutrality: Credibility Through Commitment and Consistency

Sverker Åström

Credibility

On 9 August 1914, most of the Russian Baltic fleet steamed out of Helsinki harbor headed for the island of Gotland. Its commanding officer was Admiral von Essen, whose intention was to search out and attack those units of the Swedish fleet he presumed were assembled in the Fårö Channel. He left behind a liaison officer in Helsinki who was to keep in touch with the Russian naval command in St. Petersburg. When he was halfway, von Essen received counterorders. The naval command in St. Petersburg was not quite sure whether or not Sweden would actually join forces with Germany, nor was it sure of the accuracy of reports that Swedish and German men-of-war were joining up in the Baltic for the purpose of launching an attack on Russian naval units and harbors. Yet the Tsarist government strongly suspected that Sweden might relinquish neutrality. Least of all could they ignore the ambiguous statement made by K. A. Wallenberg, the Swedish foreign minister, to the British, German, and Russian ministers a few days earlier. Wallenberg had pointed out that if Great Britain went to war against Germany, it would be difficult for Sweden to keep out of the conflict on account of anti-Russian sentiments at home.

I refer to this historical event in order to illustrate one important aspect of Swedish neutrality policy. The chosen course must be firmly and consistently pursued. It is dangerous to give room for doubt as to the likely stand the country will take. In other words, one has to avoid raising vain hopes in one quarter and causing groundless fears in another. In this sense, the policy must gain the respect of other nations. This has become one of the basic principles directing our policy of neutrality.

As we see it, this policy today serves two basic purposes. The first is to create the best possible conditions for allowing Sweden to stay outside a military conflict in Northern Europe. We evidently do not believe that neutrality is a guarantee *per se*. We know very well that when the great military powers decide their strategies in wartime they base their decisions mainly on military and technical considerations. With regard to Sweden, this means that two types of questions are being studied by the general staffs of the leading powers. The first concerns the use that they themselves could make of our territory. The second is focused on the risk that a potential adversary might want to make use of Swedish territory.

Certainly, the attitudes and the declared policies of the small country in question are also factors that the great powers have to take into account when planning their strategies in wartime. If the small state—and I think here of Sweden—shows clearly that it is determined to pursue a policy of neutrality in wartime, that it is prepared to resist threats, and, if attacked, to repel aggression from whatever quarter it may come, then one of the reasons for involving that country in the war would disappear, namely the suspicion that the country may, after all, join forces with the adversary or be an easy prey to threats or blandishments. It is equally important that none of the great powers be given any reason to believe or to hope that the small state is secretly willing to help it.

In brief, we want to create such a situation that we are not drawn into a war on false assumptions. We believe that a consistent policy of nonalignment and neutrality in peacetime should and, indeed, does influence the strategic planning of the great powers and serves as a deterrent against aggression.

We are well aware that if the policy is to fulfill its purpose it has to be underpinned by military forces that make a war against Sweden costly. Thereby, a forceful argument against an attack on us (whether motivated by calculated advantage or misunderstanding) is formed.

It should be added here that Swedish neutrality, unlike that of some other European countries, is not constituted or guaranteed by any international arrangements, nor confirmed in the Swedish constitution. For Sweden, neutrality is a self-chosen policy. Its interpretation is the sole responsibility of the Swedish government.

The second purpose of our neutrality policy is to serve the cause of stability in Northern Europe. It is a fact—and a very positive fact—that the security pattern in Northern Europe as it emerged a few years after World War II has stood the test of time and has served its purpose well. While various political crises and military conflicts have struck so many parts of the world—from Korea, the Soviet-Chinese border, Afghanistan, and Iran to Central Europe and Berlin—Northern Europe has existed in a state of relative calm. The reason must be that none of the great powers has found it in its interest to challenge the present pattern of security in the North or to make any moves that would aim at, or result in, a change in the status quo. We believe that both sides would consider it unfortunate if we abandoned our course. We are confident that such attitudes will also prevail when the member countries of the European Communities ponder the question of future relations with Sweden. They cannot conceivably have an interest in isolating Sweden or in forcing a choice between neutrality and welfare.

National Determination

Our neutrality policy must, of course, be seen in the context of Swedish history. Adhering to this policy, we have been spared involvement in two world wars. Obviously, it was not neutrality alone that saved us, but also—and mainly—strategic and political circumstances largely beyond our control. No one, however, can deny that a deliberate policy of neutrality was *one* of the requisites for keeping Sweden outside these two major conflicts. In any case, neutrality has won the full support of the nation. Almost instinctively, the Swedish people feel it represents a safety net and a guarantee of peace. Every chance to preserve peace is felt to be that much more precious in an era when a war can threaten the survival of an entire people. Sweden's policy of neutrality is deeply rooted in the minds of all Swedish citizens. Foreign powers cannot play on differences of opinion inside Sweden concerning foreign policy. This is a source of strength.

The second main premise behind our policy, besides the weight of history, is—of course—Sweden's geographical and strategic position. Sweden is not Chad or Uruguay, nor is it China or the USA. Sweden is a medium-sized democratic country in northern Europe, with strong economic ties to the Western world, at the crossroads between major strategic interests, and in the immediate proximity of areas of vital demographic, economic, and military importance to one of the superpowers. Being so situated, it stands to reason that Sweden should have two aims—the one, to avoid coming under the influence of the nearby superpower, and the other, to avoid becoming the menacing outpost of the other superpower. A policy of neutrality is the obvious answer.

It is sometimes suggested that there is something disreputable about taking into account the security interests of the neighboring superpower— the Soviet Union. After all, isn't this a kind of dependence? We have no reason to view the matter this light. By basing our policy on a rational assessment of reality, as we see it, we serve our own interests. After we have set up the framework, it is up to us to decide the content of our policy. The content of our doctrine must be decided from case to case in light of the main purpose of our security policy—to safeguard our national independence and our democratic society and to improve the chance of saving Sweden from war.

Sweden's security is a basic motive for our neutrality policy. There is also another, but nonetheless secondary aspiration. This policy has given Sweden a particular profile on the international scene and has made it easier for us to pursue an active, independent policy in a number of fields such as development cooperation, environmental protection, laws of war, disarmament, and others. We are not immediately suspected of running errands for any superpower. Neutrality inspires a certain confidence in our independent jugement. Certainly, these spinoff effects are all to the good, and they enhance the value of our neutrality policy. They are not, however, the basic motives for it.

The Limits of Neutrality Policy

Proceeding from the premises given above, the limits of neutrality can be discussed in two parts. The first aspect is that *no commitments* must be made in peacetime that prevent us from fulfilling the obligations of a neutral power under international law in a war between other states. The second is that in peacetime we must pursue a policy that inspires and *sustains the confidence* of the rest of the world in our determination and ability to remain a neutral and independent state in wartime. This is no easy task in an era of increasing global interdependence in all fields.

There are no rules of international law governing how a neutral state must *act in peacetime*. Yet it is logical that nonparticipation in alliances is the fundamental requirement—so fundamental that the really correct definition of our policy is "nonparticipation in alliances in peacetime aiming at neutrality in the event of war." In a war situation we have to take the Hague Conventions of 1907 and 1912 into account. They are based on century-old experience of what cannot be tolerated by belligerent states and what may lead them to regard a neutral state as a legitimate target for countermeasures, perhaps even war. This applies, for example, to the obligation to refuse the transit of troops, the duty to intern belligerent troops entering the neutral country, and, if bans are imposed on exports of military equipment, the nondiscriminatory application of such bans to all belligerents. On the other hand, these rules say nothing about general nonmilitary trade, even if neutral states themselves often apply a principle of "normal trade."

The second part of the problem is concerned with the confidence that the rest of the world places in our will and ability to remain neutral in war, primarily, the confidence of the superpowers. If they get the idea that we are not really serious about our neutrality or that it only needs a little pressure to get us to throw in our lot with either of the blocs, then neutrality is worthless as an element of our policy. This is why the government states that we must seek to remove groundless fears and hopes about our policy. Likewise, we must stand firm even under "strong external pressure."

This problem has many facets. First and foremost, the fact that we want to keep out of war may seem obvious to everyone, but we must expect great suspicion. The strongest proof of our will to remain neutral is our refusal to join alliances. This is combined with a determination to make considerable sacrifices to maintain a strong defense, as far as possible supported by our own resources. Should the Swedish government secretly entertain the idea of making common cause in the event of war with one of the superpowers, our military budget and our defense organization would look quite different. As I see it, our defense policy in peacetime clearly signals our determination to remain neutral. Thus, it is an important prerequisite of a neutrality policy that really intends to serve its main purpose.

If we wish to retain the confidence of other countries in our neutrality we must avoid all engagements that would reduce our freedom of action on the international scene and would alter our "profile." We cannot take part in cooperation that makes an illusion of our ability to remain neutral in the event of war. There must be no doubt about our determination to be independent.

The confidence of other states not only in our determination but also in our ability to keep out of a possible war is crucial to our security. The main points here are the arrangements for military defense and economic preparedness.

It is, of course, impossible to say exactly how strong our defense must be to meet this requirement. But some principles are important. It must be strong enough to make resistance worthwhile, at least to certain types of attack. We have, of course, no real protection against nuclear attack. The structure of defense must not be such that it can obviously only be used in one direction. It must be organized and equipped in such a way that it is self-supporting, without help from abroad, for a certain length of time. If there are gaps that can only be filled from certain quarters, making it impossible to defend ourselves in the initial phases of an attack, then the credibility of our neutrality policy will be pretty threadbare. This is one of the motives behind the support given to domestic production of military equipment.

The same reasoning applies to the economy. We must try to organize the planning of emergency supplies as well as the structure and orientation of production so that we can survive a blockade situation for a reasonable period of time, whether a war has broken out or not. This is a very serious problem that becomes more and more complicated with every day that passes—because of the great and constantly increasing dependence on foreign trade inherent in our type of economy. We are dependent on outside sources for raw materials, fuels, technology, and a great range of finished goods, and we must therefore count on the possibility of being subjected to pressures in emergencies and wartime. The stockpiling of goods and our preparations for sustaining production should we be cut off from the outside world are the means we use to reduce this dependence.

Obviously, it is here that Swedish security policy meets one of its most serious problems. This is more than amply confirmed by the experiences of two world wars. Still, the situation is in no way hopeless. We cannot be prepared for every contingency. Certainly, even a radical reduction in the standard of living during a war is better than war itself.

At times one hears the view that neutrality also must include efforts to remain ideologically neutral and unbiased in our opinions. The first point against that view is that such a requirement has no legal basis. And, what is more, everyone knows where we stand ideologically—in the Western democratic, cultural community. The right to express our solidarity with this cultural community, to criticize phenomena that are contrary to our democratic principles and to basic human rights, to demand respect for international law and for the interests of the small nations, is one right we refuse to relinquish.

Yet there may still remain the lingering question—do we act at variance with the prime purpose of our policy by actually exercising this right? The answer could be affirmative if the positions we take are determined by pressures from some great power or if they were the manifestations of some fundamental political opposition to a particular great power. This, however, is not the case.

We must assume therefore—and historical experience points in this direction—that even strong declarations by a neutral state, based on principle and ideology, are not in themselves causes of military attack against that country. Such action is determined by weightier—essentially strategic and economic—factors.

If these arguments are sound, we obviously have no reason for nervously weighing the force and frequency of our criticisms of phenomena in different foreign countries, in the East and in the West. From the neutrality point of view, the essential point is that we act with consistency and according to firm principles over a long period of time.

When we say that if our neutrality is to fulfill its purpose, it must enjoy the respect and confidence of the great powers, we must be quite clear about what we mean by this subjective element. There is a pitfall here. The great powers may think along these lines:

Splendid! We maintain that a certain decision made by Sweden is not compatible with neutrality and that this reduces our confidence in their policy. Then, according to its own doctrine, the Swedish government must attach importance to what we say and change its policy, that is, if it wishes to preserve the credibility of its neutrality policy.

The temptation to try to influence us in this way may be strong in certain situations. Therefore, we must thoroughly analyze all that is said about us abroad to find out if it is merely tactical move or reflects a serious concern. We must constantly ask ourselves how rational political and military leaders in the great powers will reason, according to our best judgment. We must shape a trustworthy policy in light of these concerns. We must not gear our conduct to tactical moves or outbursts of anger.

Earlier, I said that the aim of our policy is to preserve and strengthen the chance of being spared from war in Europe. We thus assume that there is a chance, and that it is worth taking. Still, when making our plans, we must never forget that the assumption may be wrong. A great power may argue:

Of course we have all the confidence in the world in Sweden's will and—at least to a certain point—in its ability to remain neutral, but it so happens that we have a definite military reason for occupying part of Sweden. Therefore, if war comes we shall do just that.

Should such a situation arise, our neutrality policy will have no function, and we shall have to rely on our defense alone, its power to deter or, if we are attacked, to offer resistance.

Neutrality in Practice

Having concluded this general review of our guiding principles, a few examples can be given of actual situations where the Swedish government has had to weigh conflicting considerations in the light of the overriding necessity of preserving the chance of peace. The experiences surveyed here are also part of my personal involvement with the pursuit of Swedish neutrality over the last fifty years. In my experience, Swedish policy has, over a long period of time, passed the test of external challenges.

World War II

During the World War II, Sweden made great efforts—supported by constantly mobilized, relatively strong defense forces typically called "the neutrality guard"—to demonstrate both its determination and its capability to uphold its independence and neutrality. In no way was Sweden the passive victim of neutrality violations that could have led either to futher aggression or to counterattack from the other side. We had a sufficiently strong defense to make our claim to independence credible. Aircraft that violated our neutrality were shot or forced down. Their crews were interned.

At the same time, there is no doubt that in order to achieve our main objective—to keep out of the war—we made a few not insignificant concessions to the belligerents, sometimes in violation of legal commitments as a neutral state. I refer, for example, to the transit of German soldiers on leave through Sweden during the first years of the war and the passage of the so-called Engelbrecht Division from Norway via Sweden to Finland in the summer of 1941. In the latter case, the government made it quite clear that this was a one-time concession. One motive behind the government's stiff attitude was that our credibility in the West and in the East would not stand the strain of further concession— we might have been regarded as a co-belligerent. The other motive was our own self-respect and the Swedish people's confidence in the government. It would have been impossible to officially declare that we pursued a consistent policy of neutrality and at the same time to deviate, albeit in single cases, from the rules of neutrality.

Membership in the United Nations

After the war, the question of our membership in the United Nations arose. We were obviously interested in joining an organization that had collective security and peaceful cooperation on its program. Still, there was a snag. In one important respect, adherence to the U.N. Charter is theoretically incompatible with a policy of neutrality. Should the Security Council decide that peace is threatened or aggression has taken place, it may decide to impose sanctions on a particular country. There has been one case of this kind—the resolution to impose economic sanctions on former Rhodesia; a resolution that we have strictly implemented.

A hypothetical waiving of neutrality, however, is of no practical importance. We pursue a policy of neutrality in order to prevent being automatically drawn into a war between the great powers, and because the great powers must be in agreement before the Security Council can make a decision to apply military or other sanctions, we run no risk of being ordered by the Security Council to declare war on either of them. Thus, we could become a member of the United Nations.

The fact that without departing from our policy of neutrality, we can participate in sanctions decided by the Security Council is one thing. It is quite another question whether we can—unilaterally and without a decision of the Security Council—impose sanctions on a state that acts in contravention of international law and whose policies we strongly disapprove of. The answer to that question is, in principle, negative. We have consistently acted in accordance with this principle and thus have not taken any such measures, e.g., as regards our trade, even in cases where we have strongly condemned the conduct of a state, such as the Soviet Union's occupation of Afghanistan.

A sole exception is our recent stand against the South African regime, in which our policy follows the intent of numerous resolutions by the U.N., including those taken by the Security Council, which describe the situation in Southern Africa as a threat to peace. The unilateral measures have taken the form, first, of a prohibition for Swedish companies to make investments in South Africa and then, in 1986, of a total prohibition of trade between the two countries. In certain cases, exceptions can be made such as for humanitarian reasons. We keep this law under close review in order to ensure that it serves its purposes.

Scandinavian Military Defense Union in 1948

Toward the end of the 1940s, the Cold War confronted all the states of Europe with new security problems. In 1948, Sweden invited Denmark and Norway to join a military defense union. Sweden's main reason for this proposal was simply to show Denmark and Norway that there was an alternative to military affilation with the West. However, as it turned out, Norway (which played the leading role) did not choose the Swedish alternative but the Atlantic Alliance instead, and Denmark followed suit.

The Swedish offer of a binding defense union implied that Sweden would go to war if Norway was attacked at Nordkap (North Cape) or if Denmark was attacked in Sønderjylland (South Jutland). This was an innovation in Swedish foreign policy, and, quite understandably, there were widespread political doubts in Sweden. Some muttered about adventurous policies. No one could deny that this was a departure from our traditional policy. At the same time, however, it was quite clear that one prerequisite would be that the proposed union would pursue a common consistent policy of neutrality vis-à-vis the rest of the world and would formulate its own defense policy.

Negotiations with the European Communities

The general line of Sweden's postwar policy in relation to Europe has been on the one hand to encourage and to participate in economic and cultural cooperation whenever possible and, on the other hand, to keep away from any military discussions and political obligations in pursuance of the chosen policy of neutrality. Thus we have been quite active in such organizations as the Organization for Economic Cooperation and Development (OECD) and the Council of Europe.

We followed the slow process of the creation of the European Community with some distraction and a great deal of disbelief and distrust. We underestimated the strength of the political forces for unity at work in the continental states and their importance for the emergence of a new Western Europe where centuries old rivalries and brutal confrontations gave place to relationships that make another war between these states unthinkable. It is natural for a Northern observer to make the parallels with the situation in Northern Europe.

It was the Messina Conference in June 1955 that compelled us, like Great Britain, to consider in more concrete terms exactly what cooperation between the six could mean for us. The UK reaction was strongly negative. On 1 July 1955, the Danish and Norwegian ambassadors in London, together with the Swedish *chargé d'affaires,* were invited to the Foreign Office to be received by Lord Reading, then Minister of State. Lord Reading read us (I happened to be the Swedish *chargé d'affaires*) a stern lesson on the dangers of the Messina plan. Her Majesty's Government had "the most serious objections against practically all proposals discussed at Messina and did not want to contribute to the creation of any new organisation for discussion of questions that had already a forum in the OECD." It was true that Her Majesty's Government had decided to be represented at a meeting in Brussels under the chairmanship of Mr. Spaak, but exclusively "in order to present objections, hindrances and doubts."

When Messina—in spite of the UK opposition—led to the reality of the EEC, the UK attitude changed fairly quickly, because of a series of political and economic reasons. When the UK applied for membership in 1961, Sweden limited itself to seeking association. The reason given was that the political goals and the partly supranational institutions of the EEC were incompatible with neutrality. In 1967, after the renewed British application, Sweden changed its stand to include the possibility of membership. The motive advanced was that the Luxembourg compromise and the halting evolution of EEC cooperation in general had created a new situation. It was argued that Sweden's profile as a neutral state would not ncessarily be compromised in case of membership.

Finally, in 1971, Sweden reversed its stand taking the position that membership and neutrality were, after all, incompatible. There were two reasons given by the government. They clearly indicate where a Swedish government sets the limits as to how far a neutral state can go. The first reason concerned political cooperation. We would have been drawn into institutionalized cooperation in foreign policy that, although initially not formally binding, aimed at the formulation of a common foreign policy. This was impossible to accept for a neutral state.

The other reason was the then existing plan for an economic and monetary union that would have deprived member states of an essential part of their national sovereignty, as far as their right to make decisions about their economies and budgets was concerned. We were, and are, well aware that our extremely heavy dependence on the rest of the world obviously limits our freedom of action. Still, there is a difference between recognizing this fact and determining the nation's policy accordingly, on the one hand, and committing the nation to programmatic economic cooperation designed to achieve a union that entails a depreciation of national sovereignty, on the other.

So there were two strong motives. Their importance was further enhanced by a political situation at home that had made the question of membership extremely controversial. It would have caused a domestic battle that could have split the nation even more than in Great Britain, Norway, and Denmark.

In 1972, we concluded a Free Trade Area Agreement with the EEC providing for the complete abolition of all tariffs on industrial products. This agreement has served us well and seems to have functioned to the full satisfaction also of the EC members. A new chapter of challenge and response in our relations with the EC has now opened. We have to decide what attitude to take to the White Paper on the Internal Market and to the Single European Act. I shall return to this issue at the end of the Chapter.

A Nordic Nuclear-Weapons-Free Zone

None of the Nordic countries has nuclear weapons on its territory. In its peace treaty with the Soviet Union, Finland has undertaken not to manufacture nuclear weapons or to permit the stationing of such weapons on its territory. Denmark and Norway do not allow nuclear weapons on their territory in peacetime. Finally, Sweden has decided not to manufacture or possess nuclear weapons and, obviously, not to allow others to station nuclear weapons here. All these states have also signed the Non-Proliferation Treaty. Consequently, the Nordic area is *already* a nuclear-weapons-free zone, a fact that undoubtedly contributes to the calm and stability typical of the security situation in Northern Europe.

Many ask themselves if the Nordic countries could take any further measures to reduce the friction between the great powers and increase the likelihood of their escaping the destruction of war. What they have in mind is that the Nordic countries should in some way commit themselves to remaining nuclear-weapons-free in both peacetime and wartime. In return, the nuclear-weapons powers would undertake in the first place not to employ nuclear weapons against these countries. It should be pointed out, however, that the promises already given in various forms by the nuclear-weapon states not to employ nuclear weapons against non-nuclear states apply in the case of Sweden.

One of the difficulties of an arrangement of this kind is that Denmark and Norway would have to change their policy so that not even in the event of war or threat to the peace could they permit the stationing of nuclear weapons on their territory. The present nuclear-weapon option is regarded by NATO as an important element in these two countries' membership of that organization. Judging by Danish and Norwegian official statements, a decision to change current policy would require the proximate nuclear-weapons power—the Soviet Union—in addition to promising not to use nuclear weapons, to also withdrawing some of its nuclear weapons from extensive areas in its northwestern region. A further requirement is that the nuclear-weapon-free zone should be part of a more comprehensive European agreement on disarmament.

For its part, Sweden has long asserted that one condition of such an agreement must be that nuclear weapons in its vicinity mainly intended for use against targets in the Nordic area must be withdrawn. We have also said that any undertakings that the nuclear-weapons powers may take upon themselves not to employ nuclear weapons against Swedish territory must be formulated in such a way that they cannot in any form be used for exerting pressure on Sweden or for interfering in our internal affairs. Our ability to pursue an independent, active foreign policy and to maintain our neutrality in the event of war or in crisis situations must not be jeopardized. These questions are still being discussed both within and between the Nordic countries. No agreement is yet in sight.

Alien Submarines in Swedish Waters

On 27 October 1981 a Soviet submarine of the Whiskey class nosed its way into Swedish territorial waters near the Karlskrona naval base in southern Sweden. The submarine ran aground and was unable to get afloat under its own steam. Certainly, the intrusion was an extremely serious violation of Sweden's sovereignty and territorial integrity. The captain of the submarine was questioned. A special investigation revealed that there was a probability bordering on certainty that uranium-238 was present onboard, and that this uranium was very probably contained in one or several nuclear charges. The Swedish government lodged firm protests in Moscow against "this deliberate violation of Swedish territory for the purpose of pursuing illegal activities."

The Soviet government demanded to be allowed to send its own vessels into Swedish territorial waters in order to tow out the submarine. The seriousness of this demand (which was refused by the Swedish Government) was underscored by the concentration of a Soviet naval force in the waters outside Karlskrona. After nine days, the submarine was permitted to leave. It was towed out to international waters by Swedish ships.

This incident attracted worldwide attention. Of particular note was the fact that throughout the intensive negotiations with the Soviet Union, the attitude of the Swedish government was firm and determined but was in no way provoking. Thus, the handling of the incident served to confirm the credibility of Sweden's intention to protect its sovereignty and territorial integrity in peacetime as well as in the event of war. Therefore, our standing as a neutral state should have been strengthened.

No one would seriously dispute the importance of the situation in the Baltic Sea to both Soviet and Swedish security. It is not surprising that the Soviet navy and air force are on constant alert in the area—and that NATO monitors Baltic developments closely. Evidently, the Swedish coast on the Baltic is kept under close observation by both sides. This we must accept. What we cannot accept, however, are attempts at observation that take the form of intrusions into Swedish territory—whether these violations occur in the air, on or under the water, or on land.

For a number of years, we have experienced numerous violations of Swedish territory. In addition to the 1981 incident, there were a series of incursions near the naval base at Hårsfjärden in 1982. After Hårsfjärden, a government committee was appointed to look more closely into the matter. On the strength of strong and concordant evidence, the committee reported that the intruding submarines were Soviet, and a strong protest was personally lodged by Swedish Prime Minister Olof Palme on 26 April 1983.

During the ensuing years, more intrusions have been observed and reported. Despite thorough investigations and careful appraisal of all available evidence—occular, radar, sonar, etc.—the Swedish authorities have not been able to establish the nationality of the intruding submarines to the degree of certainty necessary as a basis for a diplomatic *démarche*. Certainly, we do not want to accuse any other government of such grave offenses without being able to refer to conclusive evidence, such as in the 1981 and 1982 cases.

It is not surprising, however, that inasmuch as the incursions in 1981 and 1982 were identified as undertaken by Soviet submarines, large parts of Swedish public opinion assume the subsequent violations to be of the same origin. This means that even if the suspicions are entirely unfounded—as long as the incursions continue without identification as to the nationality of the submarines—there exists an element of uneasiness and uncertainty in Swedish public opinion regarding the Soviet Union. Evidently, this is not in the interest of either of the two countries.

In Sweden, there is constant debate as to the reasons for the incursions—whatever single power or military alliance is responsible for them. Some have speculated that the intruding party wants to intimidate or frighten the Swedish people or perhaps to try and weaken the Swedish national will to resist. This scenario seems highly unlikely. In any event, the effect has been exactly the opposite. Indeed, the determination to combat the incursions by all available means has been strengthened. Additional financial resources have been allocated to upgrade the technical capability of the Swedish navy to detect, force to the surface, and to destroy intruding submarines. Instructions to the navy have been made more strict.

Some attempt to explain the rationale for the intrusions from a standpoint of military strategy. Whether they come from the East or the West, the intruders apparently wish to know more about the configuration of the Swedish coast in order to facilitate its use—either offensively or defensively—in the event of war. The exact answer, of course, is unknown.

What we do know is that if we succeed in identifying a submarine—either by forcing it to the surface or by destroying it—there will be a very serious crisis between the home state of the submarine and Sweden. It would be a crisis of no short duration and would likely affect public opinion for many years to come.

If the intruder is one of the superpowers, an additional factor has to be taken into account. Both President Gorbachev and President Reagan clearly declared in conversations with the Swedish Prime Minister that their respective states would never violate Swedish territory and that measures had been taken to avoid such occurrences. Should a violation take place and the intruder be identified as either Soviet or American, the situation would become so much more critical because the personal credibility of one or the other of the leaders would be at stake. In Sweden, we certainly have no interest in such a development. We also hope and believe that this sentiment is shared by General Secretary Gorbachev and by Mr. Reagan's successor, President George Bush.

The most obvious step available to remove the dark shadow of this unwanted scenario from the national security agenda in Sweden would of course be a political decision abroad to refrain from any intrusions. Surely, the political cost of this type of activity must outweigh any conceivable military benefits. At the White House in September 1987, Prime Minister Ingvar Carlsson explained our position on this issue to then President Reagan. In April 1986, he discussed the matter with

General Secretary Gorbachev, who reiterated the view that the Soviet Union did not intend to engage in any underwater activity in Swedish territorial waters. Similar assurances were given by Prime Minister Nikolai Ryzhkov during his visit to Stockholm in January 1988.

If a violation were to occur and if the intruder was clearly identified as one of the superpowers, then a very serious political situation would arise. Reactions in Sweden would be highly charged. We must base our security policy on the assumption that such a crisis would so severely damage the credibility of the offending state that any potential military advantages from the incursion would seem negligible. If this assumption is correct, then we can face the future with guarded optimism.

Neutrality in a Changing Europe

The account put forth here of Sweden's attitude in international affairs may have given the impression that our policy is unchangeable and static. If so, this may be due to the fact that I have so strongly stressed the necessity of asserting the main principles of our security policy with consistency and firmness if our neutrality is to serve its purpose. Nevertheless, I hope that I have made it equally clear that our neutrality policy certainly does not imply isolation and that it gives us greater scope for action than is often assumed both here at home and abroad.

I should add that the impression of unchangeability is, perhaps, strengthened by the fact that the government cannot launch into a debate about a possible revision of neutrality policy. That would give rise to speculation and doubts about the steadfastness of the policy. But, of course, everyone knows that the external context in which Swedish foreign policy functions is constantly changing. Allow me to mention just a few trends and phenomena that may become important.

Our economic dependence on the rest of the world is constantly growing. The difficulties of securing necessary supplies in the event of war or blockade will increase. We may be confronted with new and trying problems of striking a balance between economic benefits and firm adherence to our traditional foreign policy. Holding our defense forces at top-level technological standard demands not only the unfailing willingness of the Swedish people to make sacrifices but probably also intensified international cooperation for military research and development.

The security pattern in Europe may change. Its main feature now is that most states are affiliated to military blocs having the powerful support of one or the other of the superpowers. Many states have accepted foreign allied troops being stationed on their territories. Some states pursue a policy of neutrality. There is no guarantee that this pattern will remain unchallenged to the end of the century. The reverse is more likely.

It is not unreasonable to hope that the thirty-five states, which at the Helsinki Conference on Security and Cooperation in Europe so solemnly repudiated the use of force, may eventually find it in their common interest to provide for their security in more modern and more rational ways than by enormously costly armaments and constant, extremely expensive military preparedness.

The contours of a new order that may emerge as a result of these various factors cannot yet be discerned. Still, it is obvious that it must be based on a political rather than a military concept of security, that is, be founded on greater mutual trust, a readiness on the part of states to search for agreed solutions and never get to the point of using force or the threat of force. Is this Utopia? Yes, of course it is if we talk about the near future and if we include the totality of the geographic area represented by the countries present at the Helsinki Conference. There is far too much national, ideological, and social dynamite around for quick results.

Against this background of some improvement in the all-European security setting, the public debate in Sweden over our relationship with Western Europe and the European Community has become intense. Industrial and labor organizations have mobilized their best brains. Old arguments are being brushed off and new ones advanced. Politicians are compelled for a moment to think less about childcare and privatization of railways and to try to come to grips with such esoteric matters as technical obstacles to trade, international harmonization of taxes and participation in supranational decision making. Media are filled with news and running commentaries on Sweden's place in the integration process. Even the man in the street is showing signs of interest and concern.

To characterize the debate it may be useful to start with the official position as reflected in a 1988 decision by Parliament, the Riksdag. It is clearly stated that Sweden has a vital interest in participating to the full in the realization of all goals indicated in the White Paper except those that have to do with foreign policy and defense. No preliminary conditions or reservations are put forward. Sweden shares the underlying assumption that the continued well-being of the European peoples and the assertion of their rightful place in the world economy are linked to the completion of this great work.

The statement that we are anxious to associate ourselves with all aspects of EC activities, with the sole exception of foreign policy and defense, should also be seen as a rebuttal of the often heard argument that Sweden intends to pick the plums out of the cake or to choose Europe *à la carte*.

Whether Sweden's participation in the creation of the Internal Market is achieved through agreements with the EC or through one-sided adaptation to EC rules, we shall not insist on special conditions or privileges. Any arrangement that can be reached will have to be based on a balanced system of mutual advantages and concessions. We do not see it as a zero sum game.

In this connection it might be useful to indicate that over half of Swedish foreign trade is with the EC. The EC countries on their side sell more to Sweden than to an economic giant like Japan. Sweden is the third EC market and the eighth market for UK exports. Postwar experience has shown that the EC countries are keenly interested in the contributions that we can make in the field of research and industrial development. We are shameless enough to think that the inclusion of Sweden in the Internal Market is in the economic interest of the EC countries as well.

With regard to Sweden's institutional links with the EC it is argued in the Riksdag decision that if Sweden were a member of the EC and participated in European Political Cooperation (EPC) this "could influence confidence in our policy of neutrality." The reason given is that the EPC is a form of mandatory, institutionalized cooperation on foreign policy aimed at finding common positions. It is added curtly that membership is not a goal for the discussions with the EC that are *now* forthcoming. This is all.

The decision of the Riksdag is the result of long discussions in committee rooms. It is a compromise position reflecting the usual Swedish tendency to unite whenever really important national interests are at stake.

Behind the Riksdag formula there is a plethora of differing interpretations of Sweden's choices for the future. It is characteristic that a minor debate has flared up concerning the correct interpretation of the words that "membership is not a goal for the discussions that are *now* forthcoming." Some argue that this statement leaves the door open for membership after 1992. Others, and this includes the government, maintain that hindrances due to neutrality may well persist after that date. The dispute resembles the one about the sex of the angels. Only in case of a highly unlikely practical test will the truth be revealed.

It is probably safe to assume that the unspoken reasoning behind the lapidary formula just quoted runs somewhat along the following lines: Title III of the Single European Act states that the member states "shall endeavor jointly to formulate and implement a European foreign policy." They are to "increase their capacity for joint action in the foreign policy field," and they "shall endeavor to adopt common positions on the subjects covered by this Title." Amongst such subjects one finds "closer cooperation on questions of European security." It is added that the member states are "ready to coordinate their positions more closely on the political and economic aspects of security."

Although the Single European Act carefully avoids mentioning of military matters, it is obvious that participation in discussions of the kind just mentioned would raise problems for a neutral state. Doubts and uncertainty concerning the sincerity and firmness of its neutrality policy would arise.

We assume that Title III forms an integral part of the total EC legal system and that a neutral state wishing to seek membership cannot reasonably expect to stay outside the EPC framework. We are perfectly aware that, although participation in the work of the EPC is compulsory, adherence to the words and deeds decided upon in the course of the consultations is not obligatory.

However, a neutral member state may, and probably would, want to reserve its position more often than other member states. This would raise questions in the rest of the world about the real differences of opinion and the reasons for them. The situation would be uncomfortable to the EC as a group no less than for the neutral state concerned.

It should be said that, as to substance, Sweden could have consented to most, if not all, words and deeds resulting from the EPC work so far. In the case of voting in the United Nations, Sweden more often than not supports the same positions as the other Western European states. The communality of values and interests is such that the exceptions are few.

Even if Sweden considers itself prevented from participating in a system like the EPC, we nevertheless are keenly interested in following, as closely as possible, the development of this process. We would appreciate having the opportunity to make our views known on matters of particular interest to us. It is too early to say whether practicable arrangements to this effect are feasible. In any case, Sweden is not a country to push its way into confidential deliberations within a group of other states.

So the debate is on in Sweden among various interests. Not surprisingly, leading industrialists consider membership the only acceptable ultimate solution. There is in their view no other method of guaranteeing non-discriminatory treatment of Swedish products and services on the Internal Market or access on equal terms to public purchasing.

With considerable grumblings and many reservations they have accepted, for the time being, the government's approach, but they are fairly convinced that it will fail. This attitude will hardly influence the character of our forthcoming contacts with the EC. It may, however, have serious consequences if it means that some highly important economic decisions (e.g., investment) will be made on the assumption that Sweden will be excluded from the Internal Market. This may result in industry deciding to place its bets inside the EC walls. If the assumption is proven wrong, Swedish economy will be the worse off.

More unexpected than the industry position are some reactions in the labor movement, both in its political and trade union branches. Twenty years ago there was strong opposition by the Swedish Left and Center against too close an association with the EC, in whatever form. One spoke of the dangers of the *four C's*—capitalism, conservation, colonialism, and catholicism—to Swedish independence and to the Swedish way of life.

The climate of the debate on the Swedish Left has changed dramatically since then. The only reservations, besides neutrality, formulated on the Left have to do with the possible risk that Sweden would somehow have to lower working environment standards. A new positive interest in Europe that has been expressed by the Left is the hope to contribute to the development of "a social dimension" in the work of Western European integration.

Behind these changing attitudes lies a deeper, albeit less tangible, motive. Today, it is possible to detect in Sweden a growing sense of community with the other Europeans, an awakening feeling of solidarity with Europe, and a corresponding willingness to take part in the exciting endeavor to construct a strong and united Europe that is able to play its proper role on the world stage.

We believe that it is this spirit of constructive solidarity that will also inspire the EC leaders when they look upon Sweden and its role in the Europe of the twenty-first century. We believe that the 1984 joint Luxembourg Declaration on an European Economic Space, adopted by the EC and European Free Trade Association (EFTA), indicates that such is, indeed, the case.

One aspect of our formal relations with the EC which is often forgotten in the domestic debate concerns the attitude of the EC members themselves. It is obvious that none of them are willing to answer hypothetical questions about membership as long as there is no application. In fact, such questions seem to be little appreciated. We see no signs that the EC and its member states would welcome membership application from an EFTA country at the present time. To the contrary, in a period when all efforts are concentrated on deepening the collaboration within the EC it is more likely that the member states will be inclined to discourage such potential applications. In any case, they may very well hold them on ice until after 1992. As we see it, one would be unwise to try to rush the timetable and to create a situation that might embarrass the EC states.

3

The Legacy of Swedish Neutrality*

John Logue

. . . the increasing military pressure on the Nordic area following the end of superpower detente is likely to reduce the credibility of international action as a means toward furthering Swedish security. Swedish foreign policy stands the risk of going through a similar process of contraction such as occurred before 1939: from the solidaristic internationalism of the twenties, to an attempt to formulate a regional concept of security following the breakdown of the sanctions system of the League of Nations, and finally, in the neutral isolation of the war years, to an interpretation of the national interest so narrow that even Sweden's Nordic neighbors felt a sense of betrayal.

—Arne Ruth, Editor-in-chief of
Dagens Nyheter, 1984:75

On October 28, 1981, astonished Swedish fishermen discovered a Soviet "whiskey class" submarine beached just outside Sweden's sensitive naval installation at Karlskrona. During the aftermath of the "whiskey on the rocks" incident, Sweden's security policy of "nonalignment in peace aiming for neutrality in war" has been the subject of unaccustomed foreign scrutiny and intense domestic discussion. Developed during the aftermath of the Napoleonic Wars, Sweden's policy has rested on an unusual degree of realism about the relative military capacities of small powers. Swedes have long maintained that self-protection requires at least a rough parity with that of potential attackers. This has prompted Sweden

---

*This chapter draws on "Swedish Neutrality Between Isolationism and Internationalism," a paper prepared for the Lemnitzer Center for NATO Studies conference "National Security Policies of Neutralist and Non-Aligned Countries of Europe," at Kent State University in April 1986. A rather different version of this paper appeared in S. Victor Papacosma and Mark R. Rubin, eds. (1989) *Europe's Neutral and Nonaligned States: Between NATO and the Warsaw Pact.* Wilmington, Del.: Scholarly Resources. Reprinted with permission. I appreciate the comments, suggestions, and criticisms provided by Michael Lytle, Bernt Schiller, Bengt Sundelius, and Krister Wahlbäck.

to maintain a relatively large military establishment. For example, Sweden currently has more than *twice* the number of military combat aircraft than Denmark and Norway *combined*. Compared with Britain and the Federal Republic of Germany, Sweden maintains approximately two thirds as many aircraft as each of these countries.

Coupled with a strong military capability, Sweden simultaneously pursues an active role in the promotion of international disarmament. Most Swedes find no incongruity in this situation. Although armed neutrality has saddled Sweden with a proportionally heavier military burden than that of its Nordic neighbors, the policy has served the country well. Sweden's last war was in 1814.

This chapter will assess the development, foundations, and nature of Sweden's policy of "nonalignment in peace aiming for neutrality in war." First, it examines Sweden's transition to neutrality from the great power bellicosity of the reigns of Gustav II Adolf and Karl XII.[1] Second, it traces the development of Swedish neutrality from the end of the Napoleonic Wars. Third, it examines the reaffirmation of the Swedish policy during the aftermath of World War II and the onset of the Cold War. Finally, the chapter explores the viability of the traditional Swedish policy within the current context of an accelerated arms race that followed the breakdown of detente.

Before beginning that discussion, three basic aspects of Swedish nonalignment should be mentioned. The first—Sweden's placement on the periphery of Europe—is obvious. The Scandinavian peninsula that Sweden shares with Norway offers no high road to conquest and, indeed, much of it is impassable. Undoubtedly, Sweden's location has been the principal factor that has sustained Swedish neutrality through the years. An attack on Sweden yielded few strategic benefits. With the increased importance of the "high north" in superpower calculations, however, the traditional strategic view of Sweden may well be changing.[2]

Second, Swedish neutrality differs from that of other European neutrals such as Switzerland, Austria, and Finland in that it is not based upon international treaties or bilateral agreements. The Swedish policy of "nonalignment in peace aiming at neutrality in war" is the country's self-proclaimed and self-maintained security policy. As such, it is grounded in a sense of realism that seems almost cynical to outsiders. Although other powers have clearly benefited from it, the policy has evolved out of Sweden's perceived interests, not those of its neighbors. Yet, if it is to serve as a guarantee of the so-called "Nordic balance" (the political configuration between NATO and the Soviet Union on the northern flank of Europe), the policy must be credible. This credibility is based not only upon military strength, but political will as well. It rests in no small measure upon massive popular support. After the successful

Normandy invasion during World War II, it might have seemed an opportune moment for Sweden to join the Allies. Polls, however, indicated a reaffirmation by Swedes to neutrality by a margin of ninety-six to one percent (Håstad, 1950:228-9). The preservation of Swedish neutrality is a basic tenet of Swedish policy on which all political parties and nine-tenths of the voters seem to agree.

Third, although Sweden has repeatedly avoided military conflict since 1815, its policies toward that goal have been far from constant. The outward reach of Swedish neutrality has waxed and waned in response to international and domestic pressures. At its peak, Swedes sought to extend neutrality to the Nordic countries generally and took an active role in the promotion of international cooperation and disarmament outside the region. At its ebb, Sweden's neutrality was isolationist with the feeling that the country's responsibilities stopped at the border. The reason is apparent enough. Although Swedish neutrality after World War I (with the triumph of the democratic popular governments) had clear moral overtones, the main objective was consistent with the neutrality of pre-democratic times: to keep Sweden out of war.

The Prehistory of Swedish Neutrality

Once, Sweden was as bellicose as any other great European power. From the Swedish rebellion against Denmark under Gustav Vasa in 1521 until the Treaty of Nystad in 1721, Sweden was at war as often as not. In the period from 1630 until Karl XII's defeat at Poltava in 1709, Sweden was numbered among the great European powers. During that three-quarters of a century, the Baltic was little more than a Swedish lake and Sweden was frequently entangled in alliances. From the Treaty of Nystad until the end of the Napoleonic Wars, Sweden's dreams of recovering the lost empire continued to sporadically shape the country's policies. That 1815 would mark the beginning of 170 years of uninterrupted peace could not have been predicted on the basis of prior Swedish behavior.

The Swedish state that entered the European military arena under the leadership of Gustav Vasa was centered around Stockholm and its southern areas, and included Dalarna, Bergslagen, Västmanland, and the coast of Finland. The west coast of Sweden and the fertile provinces of Skåne, Blekinge, and Halland in the southern part of the peninsula remained Danish territory until 1658. Despite the small population and relative backwardness, the Swedish state had several notable advantages. The feudal legacy in Sweden was weak. Almost half of the land in 1520 was owned by peasant farmers. The new state's establishment coincided with the Reformation. Although Sweden adjusted slowly to the religious side of the Reformation, the more secular goals were accomplished in 1527 when Gustav Vasa stripped the Church of its secular power and lands. The crown was the principal beneficiary. This helped to place state finances on an even keel and to provide the spoils necessary to solidify secular loyalty to the new regime.

In order to consolidate his power, Gustav Vasa had to build a new state. He undertook a series of administrative and military reforms which laid the foundation for what was—at the time—a modern state administration. The three sons who succeeded Gustav Vasa (with the exception of Karl) permitted the administration to decline. Militarily, however, Sweden expanded into the power vacuum in the Baltic (caused by the decline of the Hansa and the Teutonic Order) and acquired Estonia in the 1580s. It was in his grandson, however, that Gustav Vasa had a worthy successor. Gustav II Adolf's reform of the state administration gave Sweden what Michael Roberts described as "one of the best-developed, most efficient, and most modern administrations in Europe" (quoted in Scott, 1977:184).

Some of the reforms, including the establishment of a land survey office in 1628 to map the country and to provide a firm basis for taxation, were innovations that other European countries would eventually follow. The reform of the court system and of local administration under Gustav Adolf expanded the scope of the central government's authority. The fact that the Swedish Estates General included a representative assembly for the farmers (the Fourth Estate in the Riksdag) reflected the relatively egalitarian pattern of landholding that existed. Sweden held a virtual monopoly on European copper production and its customs duties on the Russian (and after the 1620s, the Polish) Baltic trade provided a firm financial basis for the Swedish state.

The relative efficiency of the Swedish state administration and its openness to new ideas and technology[3] explain much of Sweden's military prowess in the century between Gustav II Adolf's accession to the throne in 1611 and Karl XII's defeat at Poltava in 1709. Although the population of the Swedish state in 1630 was only about 1.5 million,[4] Sweden was able to muster a *conscripted* army of some 70,000 men that were supplied by a highly efficient state-sponsored defense industry at home.[5] Although Gustav Adolf used mercenaries to good effect in Germany, he was convinced of the superiority of national troops. The Swedish conscription system, which required considerable efficiency in administration, grouped all eligible men by tens. One in ten was inducted and the others were required to outfit him. Miners and munitions plant workers were exempted. The reform of the conscription system under Karl XI (king 1680–1697) produced a regular army of about 40,000 and a navy of about 11,000. Karl XII (king 1697–1718) would use it to raise numerous armies. The Karlskrona naval base, made famous by the grounding of the Soviet submarine, was inaugurated during the reign of Karl XI.

Despite of the general backwardness of the Swedish economy and society, the Swedish advantage in administration and military production gave competent kings the means by which to make Sweden a great power for almost a century. In time, however, Sweden's opponents (notably the Russians under Peter the Great) undertook their own reforms. By the time of Poltava, the relative size of the populations took its toll. Whereas Karl could raise new armies, so too could the Russians and from a much larger population. In spite of defeat, Swedish administration proved to be sufficiently strong to continue to raise troops for a king who had not been in the country for fifteen years. The Swedish edge, however, was gone. It would take the Swedes a century to learn that fact.

The Legacy of Empire

The Peace of Nystad in 1721 crowned the Swedish defeat in the Great Northern War. Sweden was forced to surrender its Baltic provinces. Besides the core of the kingdom in Sweden and Finland, it retained control of only a small part of Pomerania. Karl XII's wars had left the country battered and impoverished. War casualties, Russian raids, and starvation had cost Sweden and Finland one-eighth of their population. The obvious disaster of Karl XII's military adventures convinced the nobility of the need to avoid a repetition. Upon Karl XII's death in 1718, they took steps to establish a constitutional regime. For half a century, the royal fixation on the recovery of Sweden's losses to the east—the legacy of a lost empire—was stymied by a strong parliament and foreign intrigue. The "age of freedom" as this period of parliamentary supremacy was known, lasted until Gustav III (king 1771–1792) staged a royal coup d'état in 1772 immediately after ascending to the throne.

The attempts by Gustav III and by his son (Gustav IV Adolf) to replay their predecessors' foreign wars began in farce and ended in tragedy. In 1788, Gustav III took advantage of the outbreak of Russo-Turkish hostilities to take Sweden to war against its eastern neighbor. He circumvented the Riksdag's prohibition against waging aggressive war by outfitting a detachment of Swedish troops in Cossack uniforms (borrowed from the Royal Opera) and attacking one of his own border positions in Finland. Gustav III achieved the war he sought, but produced a virtual mutiny among Finnish officers. His reaction in attacking the nobility led to his assassination in 1792. The war was badly managed, but Sweden escaped disaster by winning a major naval victory at Svensksund off Finland in July 1790.

Gustav III's successor, Gustav IV Adolf (king 1792–1809) also attempted to emulate Gustav II Adolf and Karl XII and was easily drawn into the war on the Continent. He marched his army out of Swedish Pomerania in 1805, but was defeated in 1806 by French Marshall Jean Bernadotte. The worse, however, was still yet to come. Within months after the meeting with Napoleon at Tilsit provided him a free hand, Tsar Alexander turned on his erstwhile ally and attacked Finland. Although capable of fielding an army in Finland that was not notably inferior to the Russian forces in the area, Sweden lost Finland through disastrous mismanagement. Gustav's response was to degrade his officers and to continue the war with stubborn incompetence. Before the end, Russian troops took the Åland Islands and parts of northern Sweden. Finally, in desperation, Georg Adlersparre (one of the Swedish commanders on the Norwegian front) reached an agreement with the Danes (who were fighting on the Russian side). After marching on Stockholm, Adlersparre deposed Gustav IV Adolf, reestablished a constitutional regime, and made peace.

Toward Neutrality

The military coup d'état of 1809 changed more than just the personnel of government. A new constitution, hastily drawn up under the pressures of war, divided power between the monarchy and the Estates General. Gustav IV Adolf's uncle, Duke Karl (king 1809–1818) served as regent until the constitution was approved and was, thereupon, elected king. Although he would reign until 1818, Karl XIII was old and feeble. Furthermore, he lacked an heir. To sercure a new dynasty, the Swedes turned to Danish prince Christian August (commander of the Danish forces in Norway) who had tacitly supported the overthrow of Gustav IV Adolf. He was proclaimed to be the crown prince in 1809, but died the following year of injuries suffered from a fall from his horse. Although the fall was apparently caused by a stroke, many people at the time suspected poisoning. Thereafter, the Estates General then elected as crown prince the French marshall Jean Baptiste Bernadotte (king, as Karl Johan, 1818–1844). The choice of Bernadotte was a dramatic break with tradition.

In large part, Bernadotte's selection was dictated by the desire for a French alliance to recover Finland. That, however, was not to be. Bernadotte demonstrated the flexibility that made him the only one of Napoleon's relatives to retain a throne. He converted to Lutheranism while passing through Denmark en route to Sweden. Bernadotte took the name Karl Johan and was adopted by Karl XIII. Because he did not share his predecessors' preoccupations with the historical boundaries of Sweden-Finland or with Sweden's possessions in Germany, Karl Johan moved quickly to reverse the Swedish orientation from east to west. Using the January 1812 French occupation of Pomerania as an excuse,

Karl Johan denounced the Swedish-French alliance and negotiated instead a pact with Tsar Alexander that promised Norway (a part of Denmark since 1380) to Sweden. After Napoleon's defeat in Russia, both Prussia and England (in order to persuade Karl Johan to join in the battle on the Continent) were induced to recognize Sweden's claim to Norway. The campaign culminated at Leipzig in October 1813 where Karl Johan led one of the three allied armies against his former commander. Turning north, he forced Denmark (still an ally of Napoleon) out of the war. Under terms of the Treaty of Kiel (1814), Sweden took Norway in exchange for Swedish Pomerania and the Norwegian portion of the Danish national debt.

The Norwegians, who had not been consulted, demonstrated little enthusiasm for the Swedish plan. They drafted their own constitution (proclaimed May 17, 1814), elected Kristian Frederik (a Danish prince who was also Statholder of Norway) as king, and prepared to resist the planned unification with Sweden. Karl Johan, however, moved rapidly against Norway. After a brief campaign, he made a generous settlement which established a loose union in which the rights of the king were restricted (relative to the Norwegian parliament) far more than in the Swedish constitution.

Although Karl Johan escaped the obligation to cede Pomerania to Denmark (by arguing that the Danes had not surrendered Norway peaceably), Karl Johan had the prescience to sell Pomerania promptly to the Prussians. The loss of Finland and the sale of Sweden's continental outpost removed the two principal sources of Sweden's involvement in foreign wars from 1660 to 1815. Now, Sweden-Norway occupied the entire Scandinavian peninsula. Its one remaining land border (with Russian Finland in the north) was in a thinly populated area that made it an unlikely source of conflict. The stage was now set for neutrality.

The Development of Swedish Neutrality

From Neutrality by Accident . . .

From the conclusion of the Napoleonic Wars until today, Sweden has successfully avoided participation in war. In Europe, this remarkable record is matched only by Switzerland. Indeed, Sweden's neutrality policy is a sanctified by more than 170 years of success. It has become so much a part of the national tradition as to be virtually beyond political dispute. Among significant Swedish policies, neutrality particularly enjoys the broad-based support of all of the political parties and major interest groups. This development, however, was hardly a foregone conclusion in 1815. Indeed, the century and a quarter of nonalliance and peace that preceded World War II was largely the result of caution and opportunism of Sweden's leaders combined with a healthy dose of good fortune, rather than any vision in policy.

From a military standpoint, Karl Johan was the most experienced Swedish ruler since Karl XII. After 1815, it may be said that he was also the most cautious. The military weakness of his new kingdom was perhaps more obvious to him than to either of his immediate predecessors. He had an equally realistic basis for judging the strength of potential adversaries. It is not surprising that Karl Johan was also insecure in his crown. He was a foreigner of bourgeois background on a throne from which two of his recent predecessors had been assassinated or overthrown. Although Karl Johan was pacific neither by background nor inclination (he had, after all, used his military victories in 1813–14 in order to solidify his position), he was careful to avoid endangering his rule through foreign adventures. He balanced judiciously between Britain and Russia, which were the major powers of the day. When the Near East crisis of 1834 threatened war between them, Sweden proclaimed its neutrality.[6]

Karl Johan's son and successor, Oscar (king 1844–1859), demonstrated similar caution toward the same powers. During the Crimean War (1853–1855), Sweden proclaimed its neutrality. It was, however, a neutrality that clearly tilted toward Britain and France, which made full use of Sweden's ports to attack Russian positions in Finland (the Russians had Baltic ports of their own). Although wooed by the British and the French, the Swedes never joined them as a belligerent. This was apparently based more on the fact that the allies would not guarantee the restoration of Finland to Sweden, than any Swedish commitment to neutrality. In any event, Sweden successfully dodged the war and the possible subsequent Russian war for recovery.

In 1848, Oscar's response to the entreaties of the Danish king Frederik VII for aid against his rebellious subjects in Holstein (who had invaded Schleswig) and their Prussian supporters was somewhat more bellicose. Although Frederik himself was in no small measure responsible for the rebellion, his appeal to a rising pan-Scandinavian sentiment seemingly struck a responsive chord in the north. The Swedish and the Norwegian parliaments agreed to provide troops for the defense of Denmark proper. Whereas a Swedish-Norwegian expeditionary force was stationed in Fyn, a substantially larger army was held in reserve in Skåne. After the armistice of 1849, Swedish troops were stationed as a peace-keeping force in Schleswig. Although British and Russian pressure eventually forced the Prussians to withdraw from Holstein, it did nothing to settle the clash between the dynastic claims (the Danish king was also duke of Schleswig and of Holstein, which were partly and entirely German, respectively) and the rising tide of nationalism.

That clash finally came to a head under Oscar's successor, Karl XV (king 1859–1872). Less cautious than his father, Karl XV promised Frederik full Swedish military support. There was discussion that Frederik might adopt him, thus offering the prospect of reestablishing a single Scandinavian state. Karl, however, had promised too much. Frederik overplayed his hand by again seeking to merge Schleswig in to the Danish kingdom in 1863 through a constitutional revision. Upon Frederik's death (just two days after the constitutional changes were promulgated), the Prussians had a perfect opportunity for intervention. The protested both the incorporation of Schleswig, as well as Christian IX's title to the duchies. When Karl sought to deliver his promised support, the Swedish government balked. The Norwegian parliament had long opposed his commitment to the Danes. While the Swedes sought French and British help, the Danes were left to fend for themselves on the battlefield against the Prussians and Austrians. Denmark lost not only Holstein, but Schleswig (including its substantial Danish-speaking population) as well.

Sweden's failure to aid the Danes deflated pan-Scandinavianism, reduced Danish confidence in assistance from the North, and discouraged royal interventionism. Karl and his brother Oscar, who acceded to the throne in 1872 as Oscar II (king 1872–1907), refrained from any effort to intervene in the Austro-Prussian and Franco-Prussian wars. If they had such inclinations, the response in 1863 had made it clear that foreign adventures had little domestic backing. In time, Oscar came to admire the new German state and Swedish neutrality (during the last quarter of the century) took on a decidedly pro-German cast. The Germans reciprocated by offering aid against the threatened Norwegian rebellion which finally came to a head in 1905 after some two decades of rising tensions. Again, the threat of war was a very real one. On June 7, 1905, the Norwegian parliament acted unilaterally (and unanimously) and declared that the union with Sweden was dissolved. There was strong sentiment in Sweden to use its superior military force to reestablish the union. The Norwegians, however, mobilized and, again, caution prevailed. Crown Prince Gustav (king, as Gustav V, 1907–1950) urged recognition of Norwegian independence and the Social Democrats threatened a general strike if the government resorted to force. The Swedish government (under strong domestic pressure to concede Norwegian independence, to democratize elections to the Swedish parliament, and to introduce universal suffrage) eventually decided against the military option. The eventual dissolution of the union, ratified by a Norwegian vote (368,208 votes for and only 184 against independence), called for a demilitarized zone between the two countries.

Through the nineteenth century, the development of Swedish security policy reflected some very basic changes in military perceptions. At the beginning of the century, the possibility that Sweden might win a war against Russia (assuming that the latter was fighting on some second front) lay within the bounds of sane calculation. Although the Swedes *were* badly defeated in 1808–09, it was more the result of incompetence than of numerical inferiority. It should be noted that Sweden fielded an army that was essentially the equal of the one committed by the Russians. Sweden's successful avoidance of war with Russia was not the result of adherence to a principled neutrality. Instead, it resulted from royal caution in the face of superior Russian strength. After the German unification, the Swedish attitude toward military conflict with Prussia similarly changed. Not only was the 1848 commitment of Swedish troops to defend Denmark's borders not matched in 1864 (despite royal wishes), it was not even suggested subsequently. Clearly, the military equation had shifted against Sweden. Further, the loss of Finland and the sale of Pomerania had removed the territories that were the traditional bones of contention with Russia and Prussia, respectively.

In the latter half of the nineteenth century, the domestic political equation changed as well. Although Sweden remained backward industrially relative to the Continent, the same sorts of social forces were building up and the same types of political demands were being made. The government's refusal to support the King blocked Swedish intervention in the war between Denmark and Prussia/Austria in 1864. The replacement of the old Estates General with a modern bicameral parliament in 1866—together with the rapid growth in representation for the Liberals and subsequently for the Social Democrats—increased domestic pressure to avoid military adventures. The Liberals, as well as the Social Democrats, opposed increased military spending which in their view strengthened the hand of the dominant Conservatives. Whereas the Swedish military might not be very useful against the Russians or Germans, they feared that it might be against the Social Democrats. The impact of the Liberal/Social Democratic pressure from below is most visible in 1905. Then, the threat of a general strike (against the possible use of military force in Norway) played a significant role in deterring the use of Swedish armed force. By the turn of the century, the power to determine the issues of war and peace had passed out of the hands of the king and his Conservative advisors and into a far broader circle of interests.

During the twenty years that preceded World War I, the debate concerning military preparedness was entangled in the struggle for political democracy. Despite a long constitutional and parliamentary tradition, Sweden was not a democracy. Suffrage was restricted and the upper house of the parliament was elected indirectly in a system that provided multiple votes to property owners. This, in effect, guaranteed political power to a tiny, well-to-do minority. In 1901, it briefly seemed as if the Conservatives would accept broader suffrage in return for Liberal support for defense measures. Universal military service, however, was legislated in 1901 without a grant of universal suffrage. At the turn of the century, Conservatives got fortifications in the north of the country and, a decade later, obtained a major naval construction program. In 1911, a Liberal government succeeded in stopping the so-called "F-boat" battleship program. Indeed, the battleship *Sverige* was finished by popular subscription. Both the left and the right mobilized massive demonstrations to support their respective views in defense matters. In fact, Prime Minister Karl Staaff, a Liberal, was forced from office during the aftermath of a Conservative demonstration in 1914. If consensus existed in any area of Swedish politics, defense policy was not it.

. . . to Neutrality by Design

Between 1815 and the turn of the century, Sweden avoided war more by luck, accident, and inertia than by principle. If there is any common denominator for Swedish declarations of neutrality during that period, it is that neutrality was the opportune choice. However, the rapidly growing strength of the left produced a sea of change in the early years of this century. The benign acceptance of Norwegian independence was a harbinger of things to come—the promotion of neutrality even when military adventures might have seemed opportune.

In 1912 (during the intermittent crises in the Balkans and North Africa that preceded World War I), Sweden joined Denmark and Norway in affirming a commitment to neutrality. When World War I began in 1914, Sweden reaffirmed its neutrality unilaterally first on August 3 and, next, together with Norway on August 8. Even so, Sweden barely escaped the war. On August 9, the Russian Baltic fleet sailed from Helsinki to attack the Swedish fleet. The Russians placed little faith in Swedish protestations of neutrality and perhaps suspected that such declarations were probably a cover to prepare a common action with Germany. In any event, the Russian fleet was recalled at the halfway point. Perhaps it was thought better to wait and see, rather than guarantee Swedish involvement on the German side through a preemptive strike.

The Russians' fears were not entirely groundless. On the one hand, pro-German sentiment in Sweden was strong among the nobility and seems to have been shared by Gustav V. Germany was the bastion of conservative values not unlike their own and, after all, was not Russia the hereditary enemy? Furthermore, an alliance with Germany held out the possibility of restoring Finland to Sweden. On the other hand, domestic opposition in Sweden was also strong. Although the Conservatives trounced the Liberals in the first election in 1914, the Social Democrats continued to gain strength. In fact, during the second election of 1914, the Social Democrats overtook both the Conservatives and the Liberals to become the largest party in the lower house.

As the war on the Continent raged, the tide in Sweden swept to the left as food shortages and interruptions of normal economic activity took their toll. In the election of 1917 (*before* universal suffrage was implemented) the Conservatives lost one-third of their seats in the lower house. In fact, a revolutionary left socialist party polled one vote in twelve. The pressure, then, for Sweden to enter the war on the German side failed in 1915. It would fail again in December 1917 when the Bolshevik revolution offered the Swedes a free hand in the Åland Islands.[7]

Sweden came through the war years with its productive capacity intact and with substantial export earnings. Sweden had also rearmed, because the outbreak of the war had put an end to the attempts to link defense to electoral reform. After the Russian, German, and Austrian revolutions of 1917–18 put the handwriting on the wall for all but the most recalcitrant conservatives, Sweden also achieved full political democracy. The reforms of 1918–1921 finally established universal and equal suffrage in the elections to both houses of parliament. The consequence of these changes was to tilt the balance of political power to the popular forces (the Liberals, Agrarians, and Social Democrats) who were anti-militaristic by tradition. To them, neutrality was not only an opportune course, but a preferred one as well.

In that crucial period in which the modern political system was being established in Sweden, the cultural nationalism of the democratic movement (liberal, farm, and labor) came into conflict with the military nationalism of the old ruling class. The democratic popular movements feared, perhaps realistically, that the army was actually more suitable for use against domestic opponents than foreign enemies. The democrats claimed nationalism for their own and derided the delusions of chauvinistic military grandeur that presumably still filled the minds of some conservatives.[8] To the left, patriotism, common sense, and democratic aspirations all argued for neutrality and disarmament. To the right (from the vantage point of hindsight), neutrality had been an astounding success. The apparently realistic alternative (an alliance with Germany) would have brought almost certain defeat and, perhaps, even a revolution in its wake. The lesson was reasonably clear.

Politically, Sweden had passed quickly from the control of a conservative non-democratic regime into an egalitarian Social Democratic one with only a brief Liberal interlude. Whereas the first purely Social Democratic government lasted only a matter of months in 1920, the party achieved greater stability during the governments of 1921–23 and 1924–26. Indeed, from 1932–1976 (with the exception of two months in the summer of 1936), the Social Democrats remained in power alone or in coalition— a record of unparalleled longevity in democratic government. For Swedish Social Democrats (like their party comrades elsewhere at the time) the promotion of disarmament and international cooperation—while at the same time avoiding capitalistic alliances—were the cornerstones of the proper working class foreign policy.

Sweden began the interwar period with an early version of what has since become known as the policy of *active neutrality*. This policy, which represented the maximum extension of Swedish neutrality, sought to modify the international environment through the promotion of a re-laxation of tensions and an increase in international cooperation. It was thought at the time that the goals of Sweden's isolated neutrality were better served through the collective security of the League of Nations. This position, however, was not easily adopted, at least initially. The vote on League membership was divided. The pro-League group won, at least in part, because of the erroneous assumption that membership by the United States (the neutral giant of the day) was inevitable.

Initially, there was a fear that League membership would commit Sweden to military sanctions. The League, after all, had grown out of a wartime alliance. In 1924, Sweden specifically ruled out military sanctions. That the League would prove incapable of military action was not foreseen. The Social Democrats were quick to grasp the opportunities presented by the League and dispatched top-flight delegates. Hjalmar Branting, the party's leader and Prime Minister, represented Sweden in the League until 1925. He was followed by Östen Undén who served for twenty-five years in the cabinet, principally as foreign minister (1924–26 and 1945–62).

The new Swedish policy also supported international arbitration as a means to settle disputes between states. The first example of international arbitration that Sweden experienced, however, was hardly reassuring. The Åland Islands, which control the entrance to the Gulf of Bothnia, had been a part of Sweden until the loss of Finland to Russia in 1809. The islands were of strategic importance to both Sweden and to newly-independent Finland. The population, however, was entirely Swedish. In 1919, when the issue of reunification with Sweden was put to a vote, no fewer than ninety-five percent of the votes cast were in favor. Finland responded by sending in troops.

A crisis was averted when Sweden and Finland both agreed (the former enthusiastically and the latter reluctantly) to binding international ar-bitration by the League of Nations. After the League's special commission awarded Åland to Finland, the Swedish disappointment in the decision was unconcealed.[9] Despite the adverse ruling, Sweden continued to provide strong support for the League and its efforts to settle disputes through peaceful means. After all, Swedish leaders argued, what real defense did small nations have other than a strengthening of international law? In fact, when Conservative Foreign Minister Carl Hederstierna advocated a Swedish-Finnish defense agreement directed against the Soviet Union in 1923, he was forced from office.

If only the rest of the world had been like the Nordic area (Denmark and Norway also accepted international adjudication concerning the ownership of East Greenland[10]) the interwar period would have been far more peaceful. That, however, was not the case. The League's collective security system collapsed when the organization proved to be unable to apply effective sanctions against aggressors. When the Scandinavian states withdrew in 1938, the League's hopes for maintaining peace were in shambles.

After the Nazis assumed power in Germany in 1933, the Swedish government gradually retreated from the multilateral arena and began to explore other, more narrow alternatives. One such plan, proposed by Denmark, called for the creation of a Scandinavian defense union. Denmark, of course, was greatly concerned with developments south of its border at the time. In addition, possible Finnish-Swedish cooperation to protect the Åland Islands also became the subject matter of serious discussions. In the face of rapid German rearmament, however, the Danish government withdrew its support of a Scandinavian defense pact in 1937. Prime Minister Thorvald Stauning, who had made the original proposal, now referred to it as a utopian idea that was likely to decrease Danish security, because of the implicit threat such an arrangement might pose to Germany.

Instead of collective security, then, the Scandinavian states reaffirmed their individual neutralities in a jointly drafted declaration in the spring of 1938. The pressure, however, quickly increased. In the aftermath of the Austrian *Anschluss* and the Munich agreement, the Nazis pressured all of the Scandinavian states for nonaggression pacts. Denmark signed such an agreement. Its Social Democratic/Radical Liberal government had long reasoned that Denmark was indefensible. Norway may have been more defensible, but it was equally unprepared. Only Sweden and Finland were in any way prepared. They had both undertaken rearmament during the 1930s after the sharp arms reductions of the 1920s. Even so, the proposed Swedish-Finnish defense pact for the Åland Islands foundered in 1939 largely as a result of Soviet opposition.

The Ribbentrop-Molotov nonaggression pact of August 1939 freed the Soviets to improve their defensive perimeter in the west. In September, the USSR forced the Baltic states to agree to the location of Soviet bases on their territory. Finland, however, rejected similar demands for Soviet military bases (in return for Soviet territorial concessions) in October. The three Scandinavian states offered Finland rhetorical support, but after the Soviets invaded late in November, both Denmark and Norway proclaimed their neutrality in the conflict. Sweden, however, stopped short of a declaration of neutrality and, instead, proclaimed itself to be a "non-belligerent." Sweden, thereupon, pursued a policy that one director of the Swedish Institute of International Affairs would later describe as "nonbelligerent interventionism" (Åhman, 1950:277). Sweden resupplied the Finns from Sweden's own military stockpiles and gave permission for Swedish volunteers to join in the conflict. However, the Swedish role (which the Soviet Union bitterly protested as being anything but neutral) was still one of caution. Whereas Sweden permitted the transit of British and French weapons to Finland, they rejected, on March 3, 1940, a query from Britain and France as to whether the transit of troops would be permitted. The rationale was to prevent Scandinavia (and, of course, Sweden) from being a theater of war for outside powers.

The threat the Winter War posed to Swedish neutrality was removed by the peace of March 1940. However, another serious threat to Swedish security promptly followed. On the morning of April 9, German troops invaded both Denmark and Norway. Denmark capitulated quickly, but the Norwegians fought on for two months in the north with the help of British aid. Again, public sentiment in Sweden demanded assistance. Again, the government equivocated. The danger of a Nazi invasion was perceived to be imminent.

Despite the rapid Swedish rearmament of 1939 (Swedish defense spending increased to eight times the 1938 level), Sweden's ability to defend against a possible German invasion was strictly limited.[11] After the fall of France, Sweden's interpretation of neutrality was flexible as well as pro-German. During the first years of the war, the Swedish government permitted German troop transports to sail through Swedish territorial waters and German airplanes flew over Swedish air space. Swedish industry supplied Germany with key war materials, as well as civilian goods, and extended economic assistance and credits to Finland.

Wilhelm Carlgren observes that the Swedish neutrality of the time "covered all measures which served to keep Sweden out of war, whether or not they were consistent with the rules of neutrality in international law" (1977:5). Sweden, in fact, became a route for resupplying German troops in northern Norway. After June 22, 1941, Finland (using the opportunity provided by the German invasion of the Soviet Union) reopened hostilities to recover what had been lost in 1940. This time, Sweden not only permitted German supplies to be transported across

Sweden to the Finnish-Soviet front, but allowed an entire German division to cross from Norway to Finland as well.

This issue sparked immense controversy within Sweden's national unity coalition government which included the Conservatives, Liberals, Agrarians, and Social Democrats. The Social Democrats were generally opposed, but bowed to the wishes of their coalition partners and to King Gustav's threat to abdicate "rather than risk war by saying no" (Hadenius, *et. al.*, 1972:157). Although the Swedes rationalized the act as being a one-time-only concession to Germany (in order to support the Finns), it was remarkably similar to what they had earlier refused the British. The difference now, however, was the realistic fear that the alternative was a German attack on Sweden.

Only after the German defeats in 1943 in North Africa and at Stalingrad did the Swedish position begin to change. Sweden reduced her trade with Germany, provided sanctuary for Norwegian and Danish resistance groups, and—as the end of the war approached—trained Danish and Norwegian security forces that would play a role in the liberation of their respective countries. Swedish humanitarian aid included the sheltering of the entire Danish Jewish community, some 35,000 Estonian refugees, and about 70,000 Finnish children. Toward the end of the war, Count Folke Bernadotte arranged the transportation of some 19,000 Danish and Norwegian concentration camp prisoners to Sweden.

The German surrender in May 1945 brought a national collective sigh of relief. Although Sweden's interwar pursuits of international collective security and, subsequently, of a regional defense pact had been in vain, its policy of isolated neutrality had successfully evaded the war and its destruction. Indeed, the national industrial base had expanded and, at the end of the war, a new era of unparalleled prosperity (derived in no small measure from Swedish exports to a devastated Europe) had begun. It was not difficult to draw the obvious conclusion. Neutrality had served Sweden well and it had been preserved by a combination of military preparedness and policy flexibility.

A Neutral Norden?

The Nordic world of June 1945 was very different from that of June 1939. To the east, Finland had fought two wars against the Soviet Union. Although the first had been forced upon Finland, the second had been decided in alliance with the Germans. Finland may have lost both, but it had preserved independence through a successful effort to stop the Soviet offensive in the summer of 1944 and by a timely separate armistice (encouraged by Sweden which served as an intermediary) in September 1944. Finland's scope for independence in foreign and military policy, however, was strictly limited by the terms of the armistice which included the stationing of Soviet troops as the Finnish base at Porkkala. To the west and south, Norway and Denmark had been occupied despite their neutrality and had become unwilling participants on the Allied side. Iceland, which had been part of Denmark since 1380, had used the opportunity presented by the British and American occupation to declare its independence in 1944. The various resistance groups that had been formed in Norway and Denmark had close ties either to Great Britain or to the Soviet Union. Neutral Scandinavia had been caught in a web of foreign entanglements neither of its own making nor choosing. Only Sweden had escaped.

During the immediate aftermath of the war, Sweden sought to restore the nonaligned *status quo ante* in the Nordic area within an expected new world order and, in 1946, followed its Scandinavian neighbors into the United Nations. Sweden's hope—shared by other countries—was that this broadening of the wartime Allied alliance would be able to maintain the peace as the League had been unable to do. After all, this time the United States was a member. Sweden enthusiastically gave its support to the United Nations in part because Trygve Lie (the Norwegian Social Democrat) served as the U.N.'s first general secretary. Sweden, thereupon, took an active role in the early United Nations's efforts to reduce tensions.[12]

With the rise in tensions in 1946–47, idealistic postwar hopes dissipated. The proclamation of the Truman Doctrine, the formulation of the Marshall Plan (and its rejection by the East), and the hardening of positions in Germany were disturbing events. The parallels to the prewar period were frightening. After British Foregin Secretary Ernest Bevin suggested the need for a European alliance extending beyond Britain's closest neighbors in January 1948, he ignited a major foreign policy debate in the Scandinavian countries. Should nonalignment be maintained? Östen Undén, the Swedish foreign minister, replied with alacrity in the Riksdag that "we do not want, through prior commitments, to deprive ourselves of the right and possibility of remaining outside a new war."[13] Denmark and Norway initially pursued a similar course. However, the Communist *coup d'état* in Czechoslovakia at the end of February 1948, together with increasing Soviet pressure on Finland (which resulted in the Finno-Soviet Treaty of 1948), made the maintenance of neutrality by individual countries seem increasingly precarious. Furthermore, the signing of the Brussels Pact between France, Britain, Belgium, the Netherlands, and Luxembourg on March 17, 1948, marked the formal resurrection of the old system of military alliances.

On May 1, 1948, the Social Democratic party leaders (then in power in Denmark, Sweden, and Norway) gave the traditional May Day addresses.

Danish Prime Minister Hans Hedtoft stressed the need to preserve a common Scandinavian foreign policy. In Sweden, an independent Scandinavian defense arrangement (in private communication to Denmark and Norway) was proposed. The Swedish aim was essentially to adapt the Swedish policy of nonalignment into a wider context. Unarmed, isolated neutrality had demonstrated its limits on April 9, 1940. Armed neutrality, however, had kept Sweden out of war. Although Swedish doubts concerning the defensibility of Denmark apparently ruled out a separate Swedish-Danish pact in 1949, a reasonably armed Swedish-Norwegian arrangement might have protected Norway in 1940. Indeed, a Scandinavian pact might keep all three out of war. Sweden had emerged from the war with substantial military capability. For example, Sweden's air force was second only to Britain's in Europe. Therefore, it seemed plausible that an expansion of Swedish armed neutrality to a regional context might be a viable mechanism to confine East-West tensions to occupied central Europe and to lessen the likelihood of serious Soviet pressure on Finland.

In the effort to create a Scandinavian defense pact, the chief protagonists were the Norwegian Labor and the Swedish Social Democratic governments. Although their domestic policies, ideologies, and bases of support were similar, their wartime experiences were fundamentally different. The Norwegian experience (occupation, resistance, and a London-based government-in-exile) had left Norway's labor government with a healthy respect for Great Powers—as friends as well as enemies. Sweden emerged from its wartime experience with the conviction that neutrality could be sustained, provided that the government was astute and that country was well armed.

The negotiations between the Scandinavian states in the fall of 1948 took place under outside pressure. Denmark and Norway were given to understand that they would be invited to join an Atlantic pact. The discussions between the three countries began without a public avowal of the Swedish premise that neutrality was the *sine qua non* of a Scandinavian pact. The Norwegians were not eager to compromise themselves regarding a possible membership in an Atlantic Alliance. Denmark supported a Scandinavian agreement. It was even suggested to Bevin that an invitation to join the Atlantic Alliance was untimely while negotiations on a Scandinavian pact continued. For its part, Norway continued to be dubious of the viability of such an agreement in a world divided between East and West with Scandinavia in between.

January 5–6, 1949, the prime ministers (together with the foreign and defense ministers) of the three countries met in Karlstad, Sweden. The proposal before them called for the establishment of a regional defense pact within the framework of Article 52 of the U.N. Charter.

The agreement proposed a military buildup of both Denmark and Norway, the modernization of Swedish forces, and the coordination of defense planning and production. A résumé released by the Danish Foreign Ministry in 1968 divulged that the basic premise of the negotiators was that the pact would have a deterrent effect, both by making potential aggressors consider the power of the pact and by making outside support more likely in the event the group was the target of aggression.[14]

During the Karlstad meeting, the Swedish government insisted that none of the members of the proposed pact should be linked to any other alliance. Foreign sources of weapons, however, were vital to the military viability of the project and on January 14, the United States announced that countries that were formally allied to the U.S. would have first priority in obtaining American weapons. During the formal negotiations in Copenhagen January 22–24, 1949, the Norwegians insisted that Scandinavian security should be approached within the context of the general question of Western defense. In their view, a Scandinavian pact was viable *only* if linked to the Atlantic Alliance. The latter point was unacceptable to Sweden and the negotiations collapsed. In February, Norwegian Foreign Minister Halvard Lange visited Washington to discuss Norway's membership in NATO and Denmark's foreign minister soon followed suit. In April, they were back, this time to sign the North Atlantic Treaty. A general Scandinavian neutrality was now a thing of the past.[15] Once again, Sweden found itself in splendid, isolated neutrality between the blocs.

Maintaining Neutrality

The new Nordic configuration featured Norway and Denmark in NATO and Finland (through the 1948 Treaty of Friendship, Cooperation and Mutual Assistance) in a security arrangement with the Soviet Union.[16] Only Sweden remained completely nonaligned. Whereas the Nordic countries had pursued parallel courses before the war, now there were three divergent paths.[17] Although the Nordic countries had accommodated themselves to a bipolar world, they still retained a strong degree of community even in diversity and a considerable loyalty to their traditional nonalignment which Swedish policy sought to encourage. Thus, Norway (although an eager founding member of NATO) rejected the stationing of foreign troops on Norwegian territory. In 1953, Denmark followed Norway's lead. Both countries rejected the positioning of nuclear weapons on their territory and renounced nuclear arms development. Sweden has also done the same.

Whereas Norway is the only NATO country to share a border in Europe with the Soviet Union (and that border is close to the key Soviet naval installations on the Kola Peninsula), Norway maintains only minimal forces in the area. Svalbard, which is part of Norway, is demilitarized under the treaty of 1920. Although Svalbard is under Norwegian administration, it has a substantial Russian community. After the war, Norway required that the U.S. vacate its radio station on Jan Mayen, another Arctic island. The Åland Islands are demilitarized by the international agreement of 1921. Although the Faeroe Islands (which are part of Denmark) maintain a radar station that is part of NATO's early warning system, no foreign NATO personnel are present.

The Soviet Union has also demonstrated restraint in the region. The Red Army liberated both northern Norway and the Danish island of Bornholm from German occupation, but then withdrew. Although the armistice of 1944 provided the Porkkala naval base to the Soviets and, after 1948, Finland was linked to the Soviet Union by treaty, the Soviets relinquished Porkkala in 1955 and have had no troops in Finland since. When the Soviets pressed for military consultations with Finland in 1961, President Kekkonen argued against the idea. Backed by Swedish rhetoric and Norwegian threats to permit stationing of foreign troops on Norwegian territory in peacetime, Kekkonen invoked the need to preserve the *Nordic balance*.[18]

The idea that has come to be referred to as the Nordic balance refers to the fact that, from the beginning of the Cold War, the Nordic area has been one of low tension and relatively low force levels. During the early part of the period, this condition may have resulted from the marginal importance of the region to both the U.S. and the USSR and the substantial military force that Sweden was capable of fielding. More recently, the importance of the area has increased dramatically with the Soviet naval buildup on the Kola Peninsula. Although there has been an accompanying increased level of Soviet ground forces in the area, their number and armaments seem more appropriate to the defense of the Kola naval facilities than to offensive purposes.[19] The Soviet Kola facilities, however, would permit the rapid deployment of significant offensive forces. The area's past low force levels certainly provide no guarantee that future troop build-ups will not occur.

The so-called Nordic balance rests upon three interrelated factors. First, there is the common interest of the Great Powers to maintain the region as one of low tension. The Soviet Union seems to have more to lose than it would gain through the promotion of a military build-up in the north, because that would threaten its vital naval installations. Whereas that development, presumably, would be to NATO's advantage, there is no Norwegian interest in encouraging an arms race on its own territory that might endanger its own security. Nor is there any desire to reduce Norwegian links to the Alliance.

The second factor is the extraordinary political stability of the Nordic countries. Domestic stability guarantees no sudden changes of alliance or reversals that could endanger the balance in the north. Finally, the linchpin of the arrangement is the crucial role played by Sweden's policy of armed neutrality. Sweden provides a buffer between NATO and and Finland that offers the reasonable confidence that an independent Finland poses no threat to the Soviet Union. Indeed, the credibility of Sweden's nonalignment and neutrality may well provide the guarantee that permits continued Finnish independence. Swedish officers speak of Swedish armed neutrality as being "a strong stabilizing factor in the North" (Lyth, 1977:23) In fact, Sweden's policy also receives what seem to be sincere accolades from the Soviets.[20]

Swedish Security Policy

Swedish nonalignment rests on the military credibility of Swedish defense forces. It is also supported by civil and economic defenses and self-sufficiency in military materiel. Although the current status of those three issues is the subject of Joseph Kruzel's chapter in this volume, some changes in the Swedish doctrine during the postwar period are worthy of note in this historical survey.

When Sweden began its rearmament during the late 1930s, Swedish strategic doctrine proposed matching potential aggressors in every way possible. The Germans never really put the Swedes to the test, but as far as the 1942–45 period is concerned, Sweden could justifiably attribute this to the deterrent effect of its rapid rearmament. In particular, the Swedish air force became a potent force. By the end of the war, it was second only to the RAF in Europe.

The strategy of unlimited defense remained in the foundation of Swedish military thinking into the 1960s. Its realism, however, was affected by two developments: the proliferation of nuclear weapons and changing Swedish perceptions of the nature of the military threat. During the first decade of the Cold War, Swedish defense planners conceptualized an isolated attack along the lines of the Finnish-Soviet Winter War. Meeting any potential aggressor on an equal footing required a Swedish nuclear force. "All military considerations speak unanimously and strongly for acquisition of atomic weapons," judged the military high command in 1957, "so long as we must reckon that an attacker could use them."[21] Despite the fact that nuclear weapons were considered to be vital to insure a credible neutrality in wartime, the costs of developing and maintaining a serious nuclear force was problematic. After all, Sweden was a small power, even though it was a technologically advanced one. Developing a nuclear force sufficient to be credible against a Soviet attack would be extraordinarily expensive. Furthermore, it would make sharp cuts in Swedish conventional forces almost unavoidable. In turn, that might even increase the likelihood of a conventional attack and decrease (rather than increase) Swedish security unless Sweden were prepared to meet a conventional attack with an immediate nuclear response which would almost certainly be suicidal. Ultimately, it was the air force itself which (principally out of concern with the impact of the cost of an atomic weapons program upon vital modernization of its capacity) opted against going nuclear.[22]

During the 1950s, Sweden basically regarded nuclear weapons as only quantitatively different from conventional arms. As time passed, however, it became increasingly clear that there was a qualitative difference as well. The escalation of a conventional war to a nuclear one threatened the very existence of civilization. Therefore, the first use of nuclear weapons became a political and not a military choice. By 1968, the government's defense committee reasoned that a Swedish nuclear force offered no improvement in Swedish security. If Sweden would not be the first to use nuclear weapons, then such weapons could not be used to deter a conventional attack. It was also highly unlikely that Sweden would be the target for another country's first use of nuclear weapons (against which a Swedish nuclear force might actually be a deterrent). Further, it was reasoned that a Swedish nuclear force could not be an effective counter to a massive exchange in a general nuclear war. Therefore, Sweden put its signature on the non-proliferation treaty in 1968. Subsequently, Sweden has been an advocate of successive proposals for the establishment of nuclear-free zones in the Baltic area which would restrain the deployment of such weapons by the nuclear powers.

In fact, by the early 1960s, Sweden's perceptions of the potential military threat had apparently changed. After the development of the ICBMs, the usefulness of Swedish territory to either Great Power had diminished. The likelihood of facing alone a Great Power bent on improving its defensive perimeter seemed increasingly remote. Instead, Swedish defense planners reasoned that the only realistic military threat would occur in the context of a general European conflict to which an attacking power could only devote a small portion of its resources to the Swedish campaign. Under these circumstances, Swedish strength should be sufficient to make an attack on Sweden more costly for a potential aggressor that any benefits that might accrue. The Swedish assumptions are apparently based on the idea that Great Power objectives can be achieved without the use of Swedish territory. The control of Swedish territory and air space would certainly be a convenience, but not an overriding necessity. Thus, Sweden's aim is to keep the cost of acquiring that convenience far above its true value.[23]

The military is backed by a substantial civilian defense effort that includes a civil defense and evacuation program that is sometimes referred to as "the most extensive nuclear shelter program in the world" (Roberts, 1986:102). In addition, Sweden maintains a program of economic defense that is designed to ensure that Sweden can neither be brought to its knees nor forced into a conflict through economic pressure. Although the principle of economic self-sufficiency may have once been realistic, the rapid growth of international trade after World War II has undercut the viability of Sweden's "stand-alone" strategy.

Today, the policy of economic defense proposes the stockpiling of vital supplies that could be cut off in war. For example, Swedish oil stocks are designed to last a year with rationing. Again, the stress is on the maintenance of a credible Swedish neutrality in wartime. That, of course, requires Sweden to have the ability to survive an economic blockade. Although the stockpiles may assist the country in negotiating a brief crisis, it is clear that an extended crisis would call for a degree of belt tightening that would test the mettle of even the most determined among the Swedish population. Ultimately, it may be the Swedish people's willingness to sacrifice which supports the credibility of an economic defense.

Finally, the Swedish policy of neutrality is based not only on Sweden being able to field a substantial military force, but also on the ability to supply that force independently during wartime. Because Sweden has traditionally been dependent on foreign supplies of raw materials and fuel, it has never been completely self-sufficient in military production. Until World War I, however, Sweden's defense industry (including Bofors and state foundries) was more than adequate to meet the country's needs.

The sweeping changes in military technology and strategy during the interwar period undermined Swedish capacity and led to dependence upon foreign suppliers for tanks and aircraft. In fact, one of the key problems in Swedish rearmament (especially between 1938 and 1942) was how to create a production capacity in these two areas.[24] Although the production problem was largely solved during the latter part of the war, the accelerating postwar changes in military technology (with the accompanying rapid increase in both sophistication and costs) has threatened continued Swedish self-sufficiency.

To date, the most striking example of the difficulties in combining self-sufficiency and high performance with affordable cost has been the decade-long discussion of whether Sweden should build its own replacement for the *Viggen,* its chief combat plane, or purchase another fighter from abroad. The decision, made ultimately in 1982, was to replace the *Viggen* with another Swedish-built aircraft, the all-purpose *JAS-39 Gripen.*[25] However, the *Gripen* severely strains Swedish capacity both technologically and financially. Almost a third of its components will be foreign-made, despite the efforts to design the strongest Swedish consortium possible. Estimates of the total cost of the program run as high as thirty billion Swedish kronor and it is likely to force budget cuts in other areas of defense spending.

Costs could be lowered if the production run were longer, but that, in turn, would require substantial foreign sales which Sweden, as a neutral country, finds difficulty in justifying. Although Sweden could get more planes for the money by purchasing them abroad, the domestic defense production capacity continues to be a vital part of the credibility of the country's neutrality. Sweden does not want to risk another wartime embargo such as the one the United States imposed against Sweden in 1940.

Nonalignment: More Than a Military Matter

Security policy is only one facet of Swedish nonalignment. Throughout this century, Swedish nonalignment has also encompassed support for international organizations and, in particular, their efforts to promote disarmament and to reduce tensions. Since the establishment of the League of Nations, Sweden has played a significant role in the various functional organizations of the League and its successor, the United Nations. In particular, Sweden has been extremely active in recent years in the promotion of Third World development. Sweden, through the development and expansion of extensive multilateral and bilateral aid programs, has put substantial resources behind its rhetoric in this instance.

Sweden has attained a leading role in international organizations not least because it performs the role of honest broker between East and West and, increasingly, between North and South. Although Sweden's enthusiasm for the United Nations was tempered by its realism (which arose from the disappointing performance of the League), Sweden has consistently been a pillar of the U.N. It is no accident that Sweden has furnished more that its share of United Nations leaders, including Dag Hammarskjöld, and that Swedish troops have been regular participants in various U.N. peace-keeping forces. The commitment to the United Nations remains one of the cornerstones of Swedish foreign policy. This is the case not because Sweden is unrealistic about the U.N. and its role, but because it represents one of the few avenues of hope for small, neutral states. Sweden's efforts in the promotion of arms control and confidence-building measures also fall into the same category, as does the willingness to attempt to mediate the most intractable disputes, such as the attempt by Olof Palme to mediate the Iran-Iraq war.

Considerations of nonalignment have also shaped Swedish relations to regional organizations. Sweden has been an active participant in the

Nordic Council since it was formed in 1952 on Danish initiative. In 1955, Finland was able to join during the relaxation in the aftermath of Stalin's death. The Nordic Council has created a common labor market (1954), passport union (1954), a technology and industrial development fund (1972), and an investment bank (1975), among other measures of functional integration. The Nordic Council, however, involves no military commitments. Sweden rejected the idea of membership in the European Community as irreconcilable with neutrality, but neither the European Free Trade Association (EFTA) nor the abortive attempts to establish a Nordic Common Market has offered a permanent alternative to association with the European Community. Finally, Sweden did negotiate a trade agreement with the European Economic Community.

The long, involved discussions concerning the sort of relationship with the EEC that is compatible with the policy of neutrality is a fairly extreme example of Sweden's concern with the maintenance of a neutrality that is credible. It is fairly obvious that full EEC membership does not place many restrictions upon the foreign policies of France or Britain or even neutral Ireland. However, the peacetime reality has had less effect on Swedish policy than possible crisis scenarios. Because the Soviet Union judged the EEC to be dangerous company for neutral Finland (which ultimately led to the Finns establishing comparable ties to both the EEC and to the Council of Mutual Economic Assistance or CMEA), it would be difficult for Swedish-EEC relations to be considered without regard to this fact.[26] The credibility of neutrality, much like beauty, is in the eyes of the beholder.

In the last quarter of a century, Swedish neutrality has increasingly focused on the Third World. Because of its nonaligned status (taken seriously in the Third World in no small measure because Sweden was, among industrial democracies, the most outspoken critic of the U.S. policy in Vietnam), Sweden has been able to serve as a bridge between North and South. Sweden is one of the few countries to provide development assistance at the level mandated by the U.N. Although it may be true that Swedish companies have followed in the wake of Swedish development programs, Swedish aid has, to a remarkable degree, been focused on grassroots development. More than any other area of foreign policy, development assistance has been influenced by the basic Social Democratic preoccupation with the creation of popular organization from below. It is indeed fitting that (at least in official Social Democratic pronouncements) the solidarity of the neighborhood and the trade union local, extended to include the whole nation during the war, is also extended to encompass Third World countries. It is also characteristic that Sweden has provided assistance to revolutionary movements and regimes (including the MPLA in Angola, Frelimo in Mozambique, PAIGC in Guinea-Bissau, and the Sandinistas in Nicaragua and to on-going liberation movements such as the African National Congress), as well as to firmly established, moderate governments.

Maintaining Neutrality Today

Swedish neutrality certainly has a past, but does it have a future? There is no question that the rapid growth of the Soviet navy and the concomitant importance of the Kola peninsual installations have made Swedish territorial waters and air space of greater interest. Indeed, the submarine incursions may be related to that fact. From a historical perspective, however, the submarine violations are minor, though blatant, irritations. Certainly, there have been equivalent threats (with some regularity) to Swedish neutrality in the past. Although one should never overestimate one's security while living on an international fault line, Sweden has indeed been clearly fortunate.

Many Swedes would argue that good fortune accrues to those who help themselves. Swedish neutrality has been an armed neutrality. Obviously, that has not been enough to deter submarine incursions, but that particular sort of peacetime violation was not foreseen. The focus of Swedish defense spending is not to keep submarines out of its territorial waters in peacetime, but to enable Sweden to withstand an attack or invasion during a war among the big powers. The aim was simple enough—to make the cost of an attack on Sweden far outweigh the potential benefits for any aggressor.

The regular probing of Swedish waters by submarines in the 1980s has induced a degree of hysteria among journalists who came to see the violations as pressure to "Finlandize" Sweden. If that were the Soviet aim, then the choice of means reflects exceptional miscalculation. The result of the submarine incursions has been increased government spending for anti-submarine warfare and a surge in popular support for increased defense spending. Far from being intimidated, opinion polls suggest that the Swedish people today possess a higher will to resist militarily than in the 1970s—a higher will, incidentally, than the citizens of either the United States or Great Britain.[27]

Given the importance attached to mobilization and in-depth territorial defense in Swedish military thinking, a high level of popular support is vital to the credibility of Swedish security policy. Indeed, the government has sought to promote that idea through the maintenance of as high a degree of consensus on defense as possible. Within the context of the sharp disagreements on defense policy that existed prior to World War II, the relatively consensual nature of postwar defense policy is the more impressive. The concept of neutrality itself has also been contested in the past, but today, hallowed by tradition and consecrated by success, Swedish neutrality has acquired the status of an immutable dogma, not least because it, too, is deeply embedded in popular opinion.

The pressure of the 1980s has not been sufficient to induce Sweden to retreat from its active role toward that of a more isolated neutrality. There remains a tension between isolationist and internationalist aspects in Swedish neutrality. This perhaps reflects the fact what while Swedish neutrality stems from Sweden's own self interest, the self interest of small countries today requires a far more internationalist orientation than was true in the past. Sweden's disproportionately prominent role in international affairs stems from this interpretation of nonalignment. Sweden's pursuit of an active neutrality through Nordic cooperation, international organizations, and development aid policies reflects that basic truth. It also may reflect the search for a "middle way" between the Great Powers in international affairs much like the "middle way" in domestic policies that Marquis Childs found during the 1930s.[28] Sweden's neutrality is independent, but not isolationist. The pessimism of Arne Ruth that was expressed earlier in this chapter seems unconfirmed by events. If Sweden's international profile seems lower under Ingvar Carlsson than under Olof Palme, then it is more a difference of person and of style than of policy.

Can Sweden's military capability actually deter a marginal attack? Fortunately, Sweden has not been put to the test. Indeed, the guiding principle in Swedish neutrality has never been to deter as much as to avoid the need to deter. Today, that requires not the maneuvering of monarchs, but the credibility of Swedish nonalignment in peace and neutrality in war. That is provided by a reasonably strong defense, a stable national consensus for neutrality, and a consistent government effort to assure any potential belligerent that, first, Sweden is not going to enter the conflict on the other side and, hence, need not be attacked and, second, that an attack on Sweden costs much more than it is worth. It is the consistency and credibility of this policy that has created the Nordic balance and that balance, in turn, has created a low tension area around Sweden in which neutrality is easily maintained. In no small measure Sweden has achieved the aims of minimizing Great Power confrontation in the Nordic region—the intent of the abortive Nordic Defense Pact—through its unilateral action.

Notes

1. Gustav II Adolf and Karl XII both played sufficiently prominent roles on the world stage to have their names anglicized as Gustavus Adolphus and Charles

XII, respectively. That has not been the case for other Swedish kings. For the sake of consistency, I have used the Swedish names throughout.

2. See Joseph Kruzel's chapter in this volume.

3. From a military point of view, perhaps the most notable was the importation of Dutch and Walloon craftsmen under Gustav II Adolf to develop a munitions industry. Willem de Besche and Louis De Geer opened cannon factories in Finspång and Norrköping, respectively, that supplied Gustav with advantageous light artillery during the Thirty Years' War. In fact, the quality of Swedish cannon—proved through field use—made them an export item. Franklin Scott (1977:176) describes De Geer as "the Krupp of his day." Between 1655 and 1662, Sweden produced 11,000 cannons and exported 9,000 of them.

4. Population figures for the period should be taken with a grain of salt. The first official Swedish census was in 1750.

5. In 1629–30 (as Gustav II Adolf prepared his German campaign), the royal munitions works—managed by De Geer—produced 20,000 muskets, 13,670 pikes, and 4,700 suits of cavalry armor. Gustav Adolf's expeditionary force consisted of 10,000 infantry and 3,000 cavalry (Scott, 1977:175–89).

6. Krister Wahlbäck (1986:7–12) traces the origin of Swedish neutrality to Karl Johan's memorandum of 4 January 1834 to the British and Russian governments proclaiming Sweden's neutrality in this conflict.

7. Swedish forces briefly occupied the islands in 1918 to supervise the withdrawal of Russian troops and to prevent the spread of the Finnish civil war to Åland. Swedish troops were withdrawn in May 1918 after German troops landed and the victorious Finnish Whites dispatched troops to the islands. See Krister Wahlbäck (1986:28–9).

8. For an example of the Social Democratic position, see Höglund, Sköld, and Ström (1913, 1979). They argue that "profit is the fatherland of the rich, just as it is their god. It is only the fatherland they will defend . . . (T)he only patriotism worthy of the name is that of the working class" (1979:127).

9. For a detailed treatment of the Åland dispute, see Barros (1968).

10. The dispute came to a head after Norwegian expeditions occupied portions of East Greenland in 1930 and 1931. It was taken to the International Court which awarded sovereignty over the disputed area to Denmark in 1933.

11. Swedish defense spending in 1939 was increased to *eight times* the 1938 level.

12. Perhaps the most notable case was the Swedish role in mediation in the Middle East where Gustav V's nephew Folke Bernadotte, who as head of the Swedish Red Cross had transported Danish and Norwegian prisoners from the German camps to Sweden, was assassinated by Jewish terrorists in September 1948. See Sune Persson (1979) for an analysis of Bernadotte's mission.

13. Speech to the Riksdag, February 4, 1948, as quoted by Haskel (1976:41).

14. Udenrigsministeriet (1968), as quoted in Haskel (1976:45–6).

15. For accounts of the efforts to establish a Scandinavian defense union, see Haskel (1976), Lundestad (1980), and Wahlbäck (1973). Bernt Schiller argues provocatively that this attempt—like others to achieve Nordic unity in the military and economic fields—was a product of *incipient* outside pressure and failed (like the others) when the outside pressure became manifest (1984:221–38).

16. Designed to prevent a repetition of the Continuation War, this treaty commits Finland to defend her territory against Germany or any state allied with Germany that seeks to attack the Soviet Union through Finland (with the aid of the Soviet Union, if needed) and requires Finnish–Soviet consultations when such an attack is threatened.

17. See Holst (1973) and Andrén (1982).

18. For a good summary of the discussion of the concept of the Nordic balance, see Tomas Ries (1980:5–24).

19. See Lellenberg (1985). Lellenberg was Director, Northern Region (European and NATO Policy) in the Office of the Assistant Secretary of Defense for International Security Policy at the time he wrote this piece. According to the International Institute for Strategic Studies (IISS), the Soviet forces regularly stationed on the Kola Peninsula have a capacity for only "a limited attack against targets in Finnmark (the part of Norway bordering the USSR) . . . (which) would give such modest military advantages that it is doubtful that it is worth the risk for the Soviet Union in terms of countermeasures from NATO" (1985:139).

20. O. K. Timashkova's comment that "Sweden's non-alignment policy favourably influences the foreign–policy actions of other Nordic countries. For example, though Denmark and Norway are NATO members, they rejected the deployment of nuclear weapons on their territory largely under the influence of their neighbours' peaceable policy" (1981:193). For an examination of changing Soviet views, see Bo Petersson (1986).

21. As quoted by Jervas (1983:58). For a magisterial discussion of changing Swedish policy toward nuclear weapons, see Wilhelm Agrell (1985).

22. See Agrell (1985:289–330)

23. For a concise discussion of Swedish threat perception and the "marginal attack doctrine," see Nils Andrén (1984:89–99). The marginal attack doctrine has been repeatedly reaffirmed by the parliamentary defense committee reports. For a critical analysis of Swedish defense doctrine and capacity, see Joseph Kruzel's chapter in this volume.

24. See Ulf Olsson (1982)

25. Current problems of Swedish defense procurement are considered by Joseph Kruzel in this volume. The debate concerning the manufacture or purchase of a successor to the *Viggen* is the subject of a case study in defense policy making by William Taylor (1985:127–86). The decision to manufacture the *Viggen* represented a comparable commitment in research, development, and government spending. It is the subject of a detailed study by Ingemar Dörfer (1973).

26. This point of view, incidentally, also had the signal advantage that it enabled Swedish Social Democrats to escape the bloody battles about European Economic Community (EEC) membership that wounded their Danish and Norwegian equivalents in 1971–72. One should not ignore the value of neutrality in domestic party politics.

27. See *Nordisk säkerhetspolitik i utveckling* (1983:65), and Taylor (1985:150–51).

28. See Marquis Childs (1936).

References

Agrell, Wilhelm (1985) *Alliansfrihet och atombomber: Kontinuitet och förändring i den svenska forsvarsdoktrinen från 1945 till 1982.* Stockholm: Liber.

Andrén, Nils (1982) in Bengt Sundelius, ed. *Foreign Policies of Northern Europe.* Boulder, Colo.: Westview Press, pp. 73–103.

Andrén, Nils (1984) *Säkerhetspolitik.* Stockholm: Utrikespolitiska Institutet.

Åhman, Brita Skottsberg (1950) in Henning Friis, ed. *Scandinavia Between East and West.* Ithaca, NY: Cornell University Press.

Barros, James (1968) *The Åland Islands Question: Its Settlement by the League of Nations.* New Haven, Conn.: Yale University Press.

Carlgren, Wilhelm (1977) *Swedish Foreign Policy during the Second World War.* London: Ernest Benn.

Childs, Marquis (1936) *Sweden: The Middle Way.* New Haven, Conn.: Yale University Press.

Dörfer, Ingemar (1973) *System 37 Viggen: Arms, Technology and the Domestication of Glory.* Oslo: Universitetsforlaget.

Hadenius, Stig, Björn Molin, and Hans Wieslander (1972) *Sverige efter 1900: En modern politisk historia.* Revised edition. Stockholm: Aldus.

Haskel, Barbara (1976) *The Scandinavian Option: Opportunities and Opportunity Costs in Postwar Scandinavian Foreign Policies.* Oslo: Universitetsforlaget.

Holst, Johan Jørgen, ed. (1973) *Five Roads to Nordic Security.* Oslo: Universitetsforlaget.

Håstad, Elis, ed. (1950) *"Gallup" och den svenska väljarkåren.* Uppsala, Sweden: Hugo Gebers Förlag.

Höglund, Zeth, Hannes Sköld, and Fredr. Ström (1979) *Det befästa fattighuset.* Reprint of 1913 Original. Lund: Arkiv.

International Institute for Strategic Studies (IISS) (1985) *Militaerbalansen 1985–86.* Oslo: Det norske Atlanterhavskomité.

Jervas, Gunnar (1983) in Bertel Heurlin, ed. *Kernevåbenpolitik i Norden.* Copenhagen: Det Sikkerheds—og nedrustningspolitiske Udvalg.

Lellenberg, Jon L. (1985) "The Military Balance," in Johan Jøorgen Holst, Kenneth Hunt, and Anders C. Sjaastad, eds. *Deterrence and Defense in the North.* Oslo: Universitetsforlaget.

Lundestad, Geir (1980) *America, Scandinavia, and the Cold War 1945–1949.* Oslo: Universitetsforlaget.

Lyth, Einar (1977) *Den nordiska balansen.* Stockholm: Utrikespolitiska Institutet.

Nordisk säkerhetspolitik i utvekling. (1983) Stockholm: Centralförbundet Folk och Försvar.

Olsson, Ulf (1982) "The State and Industry in Swedish Rearmament," in Martin Fritz, et. al. *The Adaptable Nation: Essays in the Swedish Economy during the Second World War.* Stockholm: Almqvist and Wiksell.

Papacosma, S. Victor and Mark R. Rubin, eds. (1989) *Europe's Neutral and Nonaligned States: Between NATO and the Warsaw Pact.* Wilmington, Del.: Scholarly Resources.

Persson, Sune (1979) *Mediation and Assassination: Count Bernadotte's Mission to Palestine.* London: Ithaca Press.

Petersson, Bo (1986) "Changes of Wind or Winds of Change? Soviet Views on Finnish and Swedish Neutrality in the Postwar Era," *Nordic Journal of Soviet and East European Studies.* Vol. 2, No. 1, pp. 61–85.

Ries, Tomas (1982) *The Nordic Dilemma in the 80s: Maintaining Regional Stability Under New Strategic Conditions.* PSIS Occasional Papers, No. 1, Geneva: Programme for Strategic and International Security Studies.

Roberts, Adam (1986) *A Nation in Arms.* Second Edition. New York: St. Martin's.

Ruth, Arne (1984) "The Second New Nation," *Daedalus.* Vol. 113, No. 2, Spring, pp. 53-96.

Schiller, Bernt (1984) "At Gun Point: A Critical Perspective on the Attempts of the Nordic Governments to Achieve Unity after the Second World War," *Scandinavian Journal of History.* Vol. 9, No. 3, pp. 221-38.

Scott, Franklin (1977) *Sweden: The Nation's History.* Minneapolis: University of Minnesota Press.

Taylor, William (1985) "Sweden," in William Taylor and Paul M. Cole, eds. *Nordic Defense: Comparative Decision Making.* Lexington, Mass.: Lexington Books.

Timashkova, O. K. (1981) *Scandinavian Democracy Today.* Moscow: Progress Publishers.

Udenrigsministeriet (1968) *Dansk Sikkerhedspolitik 1948-66.* Vol. 2., Copenhagen.

Wahlbäck, Krister (1973) *Norden och blockuppdelningen 1948-49.* Stockholm: Utrikespolitiska Institutet.

Wahlbäck, Krister (1986) *The Roots of Swedish Neutrality.* Stockholm: The Swedish Institute.

4

Sweden's Security Dilemma: Balancing Domestic Realities with the Obligations of Neutrality*

Joseph Kruzel

An unobtrusive sign in the Swedish Army Museum reminds the visitor that Sweden has not always been the peaceful nation it is today. From 1521 to 1814, the sign proclaims, Sweden fought a total of 48 wars. During those three centuries the country was more often at war than at peace.[1]

The sign is a pointed reminder that Sweden was at one time an assertive great power quite willing to defend its empire with a formidable military establishment. Gustav Adolph, whose achievements are prominently displayed in the Army Museum, was one of the great military innovators of all time, revolutionizing infantry tactics and establishing the first national standing conscript army in Europe. Sweden's aggressive great power past stands in marked contrast to its peaceful small power status of today, and how Sweden managed the transition from one status to another is an interesting and instructive story.

During the eighteenth century Sweden repeatedly attempted to regain territory it had earlier lost, and it was only after the definitive defeat of 1809 at the hands of Russia and the subsequent installation of the French Marshall Jean Baptiste Bernadotte as king that Sweden began to reconcile itself to a more modest role in international relations.[2] The aftershocks continued to be felt well into the nineteenth century. Karl

*The author gratefully acknowledges the helpful comments of Ingemar Dörfer, Bo Hugemark, and Bengt Sundelius on an early draft of this chapter. These scholars and friends labored diligently to correct my factual mistakes; any remaining errors, particularly those of interpretation, are entirely my own.

Johan's son and grandson both entertained ambitions of regaining Finland and restoring Sweden to great power status, and it was only gradually and grudgingly that Swedish leaders and people accepted the new geo-strategic reality. The adaptation to a new role in world politics took over a century to take hold in the national psyche.

Old mindsets are difficult to change, but once Sweden accepted its more modest role in world affairs it did so with great enthusiasm. The country would pursue an active policy of peace and neutrality. Sweden would play a dominant role in encouraging international peace and disarmament. Sweden would also take all military preparations necessary to defend itself against attack, but avoid any action that might give concern to other states. These tenets have been the foundation of Swedish security policy since the early years of the twentieth century.

Swedes are proud of saying that their country has never been invaded, a singular achievement among European states over the past 200 years, and Sweden's delivery through two world wars when conflict raged all around her borders makes her security policy a *prima facie* success. There is an understandable reluctance to tamper with such an impressive record, but the conditions on which Swedish defense policy were based during the 1950s and 1960s changed significantly in the 1970s and 1980s. They will continue to change in the years ahead. The challenge for Sweden is to understand and adjust to new geostrategic realities as it heads into a new century. As it did in the nineteenth century, Sweden will have to tailor its security policy to changing geopolitical circumstances. This time the leadership is unlikely to have a century to make the change.

Sweden is a country of paradoxes. The most vocal elements of its population often seem more interested in North-South than East-West issues, more concerned with Vietnam, Afghanistan, and Nicaragua than with activities in their own territorial waters. Its dominant political party is unenthusiastic about defense spending, but at the same time is vehemently protective of the practice of military conscription. Sweden prides itself on maintaining a sophisticated arms industry, but Swedes are distinctly uneasy about the sale of arms to other countries, a practice that is essential to the survival of the domestic arms industry. It is a country with virtually no standing army, but it can mobilize three-quarters of a million troops within three days. Sweden is a state that spends more on defense than any other neutral, but it stood almost alone among European states, neutral and aligned, in not raising defense spending during the 1970s and 1980s.

Swedish security policy rests on two pillars: an ability to defend the country against external threats and a policy of non-alignment that strives to reduce the risk of Sweden becoming entangled in international conflict. The two pillars are mutually reinforcing. Strong defense adds credibility to neutrality, and a policy of neutrality serves to assure other states that Sweden will not undertake aggression itself or allow the country to be used by other powers for such a purpose. While recognizing the relationship between these two pillars, this chapter will concentrate on the military aspect of Swedish security policy, leaving to others the task of elaborating neutrality policy.[3]

In the remaining years of the twentieth century, four problems will be at the top of Sweden's security agenda. The most pressing problem (although to most Swedes, perhaps not the most serious one) is how to respond to the peacetime threat posed by continued incursions of foreign submarines into Swedish territorial waters. The second is how to react to the changing wartime threat brought about by the increasing strategic importance of the High North. A third problem, certain to grow more serious in the future, is how to maintain an indigenous high-technology defense industry in light of increasing costs and restrictive arms export policies. Finally, there is the enduring question of how to maintain the level of defense spending necessary to meet the external threat when demographic pressures, public opinion, and the cost of social services are likely to restrict the funds available for defense.

Neutrality and National Defense

Sweden's "armed neutrality" is longstanding and self-imposed. It is not guaranteed by international convention, as is the case for Switzerland and Austria, nor conditioned by any agreement of cooperation with a powerful neighbor, as is the case for Finland. Strictly speaking, Sweden is not even a neutral state. Its posture is freedom from alliances, a literal translation of the Swedish phrase *alliansfrihet*. This stance aims at preserving the ability to be neutral in wartime. Swedes are quick to stress that they are neutral only in security policy, not in ideology, culture, or economic life. Politically and socially Sweden is well established as a western democracy.

Peace and reconciliation are important objectives for Swedish security policy, and their priority explains why the country has maintained such a high profile on arms control and other efforts to promote *detente*. Sweden played an important role in the Conference on Security and Cooperation in Europe (CSCE), and has always valued membership in the United Nations. Dag Hammarskjöld, the second secretary general of the United Nations, was a Swede. In addition, Sweden has actively sought out opportunities for mediation and peacekeeping and has taken a leading role on North-South issues, particularly on the question of aid to developing countries. A central feature in Swedish foreign policy is an emphasis on territorial integrity, on non-interference in the affairs of other states, and on self-determination—principles that axiomatically put Swedish sympathy on the side of any small state in a dispute with a large power, even when the particulars of the dispute might suggest a more measured allocation of blame and sympathy.

In official Swedish policy, neutrality is not seen as an end in itself, but rather the means through which the country's independence can best be maintained. In the Swedish public mind, however, there is a tendency to see neutrality as sacrosanct, as the cornerstone of security policy. Neutrality has served the country well, particularly through two world wars, and it enjoys overwhelming popular support today. Nevertheless, a clear tension seems to exist between the view of neutrality as an intrinsic value and that of neutrality as a means to an end. It is the difference between neutrality as something fixed in all situations and neutrality as a means of keeping options open in a crisis. Everyone agrees that if any outside power attacks Sweden, the country would no longer be bound by any dictates of neutrality. But in the future it may be difficult to determine when a country is under attack.

Would repeated overflights of Swedish territory constitute an attack? Would an economic embargo? In the gray area of contemporary international security, there is no clear dividing line between war and peace, a fact that significantly complicates the posture of a nation desiring to be neutral. Tolerating "minor" transgressions may allow a state to hold on to neutrality, but at the risk of being seen by others as having compromised its position. By focussing on the threat of military conflict, neutrality might itself become neutralized by non-military factors (Danspeckgruber, 1986:273). Short of unambiguous attack, however, Sweden is extremely unlikely to give up a policy that has served its interests so well for so long a time.

The Evolution of Swedish Defense

In the years after World War I Sweden followed, and indeed encouraged, the general European trend toward substantial reduction in armaments. In 1925 the Riksdag passed a resolution effectively reducing the army by half. By the mid-1930s, however, the original dream of detente had been dashed. The idea of progressive disarmament leading to increasing international stability, so avidly embraced in Sweden, found little support in Sweden's two most important neighbors, Germany and the Soviet Union. In response to the rearmament of these potential adversaries, Sweden began a slow military buildup that accelerated with the outbreak of the Winter War between Finland and the Soviet Union and the German invasion of Denmark and Norway. By 1941 Sweden was spending almost 12 percent of its gross national product on defense. This military buildup was based on the classical tradition of a conscript army that could be rapidly mobilized. The militia army was supplemented by a growing Swedish Air Force, established as an independent service in 1926 and which by the end of the war had become one of the strongest in Europe.[4]

Although surrounded throughout World War II by German troops, Sweden was the only Nordic country that managed to stay out of the conflict. It is a matter of historical debate whether this was the result of good fortune, circumstances beyond her control, or Sweden's own policy of armed neutrality, but the popular Swedish view clearly supports the last interpretation. Neutrality worked as a strategy for staying out of the war in the early stages, and Sweden's growing defense capability ensured her neutrality in times when Germany might have been tempted to consider attack. Neutrality backed by arms became the cornerstone of postwar security policy.

Isolated neutrality was not Sweden's first choice at the end of World War II. In the early postwar years Sweden took the initiative in attempting to form a wider Scandinavian zone of neutrality that would include Norway and Denmark as well as Sweden. Negotiations continued into 1949, but collapsed largely over disputes about whether the Scandinavian security system should have any connection with a broader Western security alliance, a linkage that Sweden resolutely opposed.

Despite an insistence on noninvolvement in alliances and on building a *défense à tous azimuts*, Sweden's defense planning throughout the late 1940s and 1950s was based quite openly on the objective of being able to hold out against an aggressor until foreign military assistance arrived. A 1947 report prepared by the Supreme Commander defined the mission of the Swedish armed forces as being to "delay the advance of the aggressor sufficiently long as to give time for allied assistance."[5]

Although no government official ever identified which country was regarded the most likely aggressor and which other nations would be likely to provide assistance, the implicit assumption within the Swedish military was that the threat came from the Soviet Union, not from the West, and that Western military assistance could be hoped for if Sweden were attacked. Eventually the notion of waiting for outside military aid was dropped as a formal defense objective because it could be seen as undermining the commitment to nonalignment.[6] After the early 1960s there is no explicit reference to this mission in Swedish defense doctrine, and threat assessments in the 1980s consistently emphasize the need to prepare for attacks from all directions without any need for external assistance.

The 1950s saw the evolution of a Nordic "balance" (although equilibrium would be a better word). To Sweden's west and south, Norway and Denmark joined NATO, with the condition that they not be required to provide permanent basing for foreign troops or to have nuclear weapons stationed on their soil during peacetime. To the east, Finland developed a special relationship with the Soviet Union. Sweden came to view its role as that of a pivot point of this Nordic "balance," a perception that prevails to the present time.

There are no explicit links between Sweden and the other Nordic countries on defense policy; peacetime defense cooperation, even at the level of staff talks, would be inconsistent with neutrality. But there are frequent and lengthy meetings of all Nordic defense ministers, and it would be surprising if these conversations did not entail frank and serious discussions of mutual security interests. Certainly the Nordic countries themselves understand the interrelatedness of their security postures, and each state is careful not to take actions that would upset the defense calculations of its neighbors.

Sweden is well known for its opposition to nuclear weapons and civilian nuclear power, and many people may be surprised to learn that in the 1950s Sweden seriously considered the acquisition of nuclear weapons.[7] In abstract terms, nuclear weapons might seem to provide the ideal defense for a small neutral state constrained by its size from building a conventional force equaling that of its larger neighbors, and precluded by its policy from relying on the nuclear strength of an ally. The acquisition of nuclear weapons could provide the "great equalizer" for such a state, the ultimate deterrent. At least this was the argument put forward in Sweden in the 1950s by a variety of civilian strategists and military officers, particularly those in the Air Force.

In 1959 the Swedish government decided to defer the development of nuclear weapons, and by the early 1960s a number of factors had turned Sweden entirely against a decision to go nuclear. One important consideration was cost. Nuclear weapons would be so costly that their acquisition might severely constrain the modernization of conventional forces. The Army had consistently opposed nuclear weapons for precisely this reason; even the chief of the Air Staff joined in opposition when the magnitude of the cost, and its implication for conventional force structure, became apparent.

Another reason for opposition to nuclear weapons was political. The nuclear issue threatened to split the ruling Social Democratic party. In addition, a broad segment of the Swedish public felt that keeping open the nuclear option was inconsistent with a foreign policy putting great emphasis on nuclear disarmament.[8]

A final consideration was strategic. By 1960 there was a growing belief that Sweden was unlikely to be atacked with nuclear weapons, or even by a large conventional force. Given the country's limited strategic significance, Swedes thought their state would probably be a marginal factor in the calculations of the two military blocs.

Giving up nuclear weapons meant giving up massive retaliation and abandoning the idea of an ultimate deterrent. Without nuclear weapons, Sweden was forced to rely on conventional forces, which could never hope to match in numbers those of its potential adversaries.

The decision to abandon nuclear weapons led Sweden to adopt the concept of "marginality" as a basis for defense planning. This is the idea that Sweden would only be a marginally important strategic goal, and that any adversary contemplating an attack on Sweden would therefore devote only a marginal part of its military strength to such an endeavor. On its surface, this seems a plausible assessment. There are no natural or manufactured resources unique to Sweden, and therefore no great material advantage to be had from possession of Swedish territory. And since any state attacking Sweden would be involved in a conflict with its opposing military alliance, there would be a far greater claim on its military resources than the invasion and occupation of relatively unimportant Sweden.

In sum, the marginality thesis argued that the greatest threat to international stability was a war between the superpowers; that in such a conflict, neither side could afford to use significant forces against a third party; and Sweden's policy should therefore be to prepare to defend the country against marginal forces of the military blocs.

There was some debate about the concept of marginality before the abandonment of nuclear weapons, but once the nuclear option was dismissed, the issue was settled for all practical purposes. Without the doctrine of marginality, no affordable Swedish defense posture would have made strategic sense.

Paradoxically, the adoption of the marginality thesis improved the prospects for Swedish defense without changing the force structure at all. What seemed inadequate under one set of assumptions suddenly appeared to be quite sufficient, perhaps even more than necessary. In a way, the marginality thesis provided the justification for the gradual decline in Swedish defense spending that lasted from the late 1960s until the late 1980s.

Even today the marginality hypothesis is so central to Swedish defense planning that it is rarely discussed and debated, at least in public. In private, however, many analysts are increasingly doubtful concerning Sweden's continued marginality. Although an isolated bolt-out-of-the-blue attack on Sweden is not considered a serious possibility, it is possible that one military bloc or the other could see Sweden as such a strategic prize that significant military resources might be devoted to an attack.

In a rare display of official candor, this possibility was explicitly noted by the 1984 Defense Commission:

> By virtue of her geographical position in the north European area, Sweden could be involved in the operational planning of both blocs in an early stage of a conflict. Sweden's territory might attract the attention of either side as a possible short-cut for air operations, as a transit area, and as a base primarily for air combat forces and forward-based surveillance.[9]

The control of Sweden and its use as a military base of operations might be so attractive as to make it a high and immediate priority in the event of a European war (Agrell, 1985:210). Pushing such a scenario too far, however, could undermine Swedish defense posture and its critical reliance on mobilization, which depends on a number of days of worsening political crisis to provide essential strategic warning.

Contemporary Threat Perceptions

In the late 1970s and 1980s two new security problems confronted Sweden, and raised doubts about the low strategic value defense planners had hitherto assigned to the country in an East-West conflict. The first was the heightened potential threat of being dragged into war by the growing strategic significance of the European "High North." The second was the real peacetime threat to neutrality policy posed by continuing military violations of Swedish territorial waters and airspace.[10]

From the end of World War II until the early 1970s the northern flank was seen as a peripheral area of marginal utility to both East and West. It was the forgotten flank, what former Defense Minister Anders Thunborg called "the quiet corner of Europe" (1984:2). This perspective began to change in the 1970s as the Soviet Union developed into a major maritime power and transformed the Kola Peninsula, its part of the Nordic region (geographically if not politically), into the most heavily armed territory in the world. NATO took a number of steps to counter the Soviet buildup: by prepositioning supplies and improving air bases for reinforcement in northern Norway, by the U.S. deployment of sea-launched cruise missiles, and by the elaboration of an aggressive American maritime strategy that envisioned challenging the Soviet Union in the Norwegian Sea during the earliest phase of a superpower war.[11] This heightened strategic significance forced a rethinking of the most plausible circumstances for Swedish involvement in a bloc-to-bloc conflict.

Three plausible scenarios for attack on Sweden are (1) a Soviet violation of Swedish ground or airspace en route to seizing and occupying the NATO airfields in northern Norway; (2) a Soviet amphibious landing on the Baltic coast and a march across the country en route to securing the southern tip of Norway; and (3) the "air scenario," in which one military bloc or the other would grab Swedish air bases for use in waging the battle of the Atlantic.[12]

A Soviet invasion of northern Norway might be attempted by land, sea, or air. If an attack were to come over the difficult terrain of Lapland, then Finnish as well as Swedish territory would be involved. This would provide strategic warning for Sweden and a hostile terrain through which an invading army would have to advance before encountering Swedish troops.

There is considerable debate among Swedish defense experts about how seriously to reckon the threat of a Soviet attack across northern Sweden. While the Soviets have significantly increased their air and naval forces based in the Kola region, there has been no commensurate increase in ground forces. The Soviet Union could reinforce their units, but new troops would be unfamiliar with the terrain and unlikely to be equipped to fight in such difficult conditions. Bringing in additional forces would also provide Sweden with warning time for mobilization. In any case, the road network in northern Sweden is not conducive to an east-west transit, making the prospect of such an attack a logistical nightmare for Soviet planners. With regard to this scenario, perhaps the "marginality thesis" still holds.

Another issue of great concern to Swedish analysts is the strategic value of the southern part of Norway. Command of this region controls access to, and egress from, the Baltic (Heginbotham, 1985:19–27). If the Warsaw Pact sought to occupy southern Norway it would have to do so after an amphibious landing and march across southern Sweden. This is not a scenario that NATO planners believe at all likely, but the low probability derives in part from the fact that a strong Swedish defense would impede a Warsaw Pact transit, thus giving Norway valuable strategic warning. Under the most optimistic scenario, Swedish military forces could effectively block an invasion or inflict such serious attrition that Norway could cope with the forces that survived the transit.

The third scenario sees Sweden's primary strategic utility to the two military blocs in its airfields and the unimpeded use of its airspace.[13] It is not inconsistent with either of the two scenarios described above. In any East-West war of more than a few days' duration the North Atlantic will be a critical theater of operations. NATO will be forced to rely on the shipment of personnel and equipment from the United States to Europe. Without that successful resupply effort NATO would almost certainly lose the war. The most important line in this battle of the Atlantic connects Greenland, Iceland, and the United Kingdom—the so-called GIUK gap—where maintenance of air superiority will be crucial to the outcome of the war. Here the Swedish airfields come into play. Possession of such bases would allow either side a considerably improved ability to operate in and around the GIUK gap. Gunnar Jervas estimates that operating out of air bases on Swedish soil would double the fighting capacity of attack aircraft involved in the battle of the Atlantic (Jervas, 1986:17). Swedish bases would also improve the occupying power's ability to give fighter protection to antisubmarine warfare, airborne warning and control, and bomber operations.

For NATO forces, Swedish air bases would provide an important additional attraction. Their use would aid immeasurably in waging the battle against Warsaw Pact forces in Central Europe and in launching air strikes against the Soviet homeland. Even if the air bases themselves were not occupied, control of Swedish airspace would greatly facilitate NATO air operations. For precisely these reasons, the Soviet Union would be quite interested in denying to their adversaries the use of Swedish airspace and base facilities.

For its part, Sweden wants to ensure that no outside power feels any apprehension about its commitment to remain neutral in time of war. This was the real issue behind the cruise missile controversy of the late 1970s and early 1980s. The Swedish government was never worried that NATO cruise missiles would wreak havoc and destruction on Stockholm, but rather that the prospect of U.S. forces violating neutral airspace might give the Soviets cause to seek early warning sites and perhaps even airbases on Swedish territory. The possibility of the Soviet Union responding to the cruise missile threat in such a manner was extremely remote, but the entire episode demonstrated Swedish sensitivity to the possibility of an outside power establishing a *droit de regard* over its security policy. The cruise missile controversy is also a good example of Western, particularly American, misunderstanding of the security predicament of neutral states. Most Americans who followed the issue simply could not understand the nature of Swedish concern.

The Special Problem of Submarine Incursions

For most of the postwar era there have been reports of unidentified foreign submarines, some likely armed with nuclear weapons, intruding deep into Swedish territorial waters. Such incidents became more frequent and far more brazen after 1980.[14]

In 1981 a "Whiskey" class Soviet submarine ran aground near the Karlskrona naval base, one of Sweden's most important naval facilities. Even more serious was a September 1982 incident at Hårsfjärden close to a major naval base near Stockholm. Numerous other incidents have occurred since that time. Although the "Whiskey on the rocks" and the

Hårsfjärden intruder were the only two vessels specifically identified as to national origin, the others are generally assumed to be Soviet as well.

These recurring intrusions into Swedish territorial waters prompted official protests by the Swedish government as well as considerable naval effort to bring the submarines to the surface but not to damage them.[15] Predictably, the Kremlin responded to Swedish diplomatic protests by emphasizing that the real threat to good Soviet Swedish relations was not posed by the activity itself, for which Moscow in any case was not responsible, but by unseemly Swedish accusations and protests. For a few years the submarine affair was a matter of considerable discussion and debate within all sectors of Swedish society. It continues to be a major issue of discussion within the small group of professional Swedish security analysts, and it seems to have touched off a wave of tough-mindedness within the community. A few scholars not previously known for their hawkish writings have taken a central role in examining the submarine incursions and have adopted a new and more realistic tone toward security issues.[16]

Among the general public there seems to be a divided attitude. On the one hand, Swedish public opinion has turned sharply against Moscow. A poll of nine West European countries taken in the summer of 1987 showed that Swedes were more negative about the Soviet Union than any other population in the survey.[17] On the other hand, there seems to be a growing sense of resignation and fatalism about the submarine incursions, and the entire issue has became the subject of jokes as much as of serious public discussion.

The Soviet Union paid a considerable diplomatic price for its underwater intimidation. The campaign undermined the 20-year Soviet peace offensive in Scandinavia intended to weaken the bonds between the Nordic NATO members and the other members of the alliance.[18] The Kremlin obviously calculated that with the military correlation of forces moving in its favor, intimidation was a more effective long-term strategy than amiability.

Sweden's inability or unwillingness to stop the submarine incursions has raised serious questions in the minds of many observers about the depth and strength of the Swedish commitment to armed neutrality. As the Soviets continue to mount underwater intrusions, many fear that the sense of public outrage in Sweden will continue to fade, eventually to be replaced by the insidious notion that a successful neutral must learn to adjust to geopolitical reality, that the interests of a neighboring superpower must be taken into account in peacetime as in war. The renewed Swedish interest in the diplomatic history of World War II, a time when Swedish diplomatic acumen counted for more than military capability, suggests a growing national apprehension that such conditions may await Sweden in the future.

With its activist and moralist foreign policy, Sweden continues to be watched closely by the rest of the world as it attempts to deal with its submarine problem. By the mid-1980s the Swedish Navy was evidently operating under orders to "take whatever action necessary" to force any intruding submarine to the surface and bring it to port. This was an encouragingly explicit amendment to the more equivocal orders hinted at in the *Report of the Submarine Commission,* but it still fell short of a specific order to try to destroy one of the intruders.

There was a long and essentially irrelevant debate in Sweden over Soviet intentions with respect to the submarine incursions. Were Soviet objectives primarily political or military? Were the submarines simply carrying out routine training missions, or actually preparing for amphibious attack—or was the motivation more psychological, aimed at intimidating Sweden into accepting subservience toward the Soviet Union? The debate was irrelevant because there was no need to choose among these possible objectives. Obviously all of these objectives were served by the intrusions. Moscow was able to gather valuable military intelligence, conduct realistic training maneuvers, and mount an unremitting psychological campaign in the bargain.

An important question for the future of Swedish security policy is how the country will deal with this continuing assault on its territorial integrity and the credibility of its commitment to armed neutrality. An argument that is frequently heard in Stockholm is that the issue of submarine incursions is relatively unimportant and that excessive attention to them will divert money and concern from the real problems in Swedish security. Indeed, there was even some speculation that the real Soviet intention behind the submarine intrusions was to heighten Swedish concerns and thereby to divert money into anti-submarine warfare programs and thus away from Swedish airpower, the real concern of Soviet planners. Such analysis cautioned against trying to win the battle of the submarines at the risk of losing the war of overall defense preparedness (Alford, 1985:73-81). Most Swedish security analysts consider this an extremely improbable explanation because it credits the Soviets with a strategem that was at once too subtle and too likely to backfire. The implication of the argument—that Sweden should concentrate on more important security problems—underestimates the corrosive effect on the Swedish commitment to defense through the failure to deal decisively with the problem of underwater incursions.

Swedish security analysts talk incessantly about perceptions and credibility, and these factors are precisely the issues at stake with the submarine incursions. To much of the outside world, the submarine threat is the defense news about Sweden and what may seem to the Swedish government as a preference for quiet diplomacy over rash military action may seem to others as hypocrisy and pretense. Indeed, the effectiveness with which Sweden deals with this problem may be regarded as a litmus test of just how determined the country really is to meet the obligations of armed neutrality.

Military Responses and Force Posture

Compared to the military forces of nations in the two military blocs, Sweden's force is numerically large relative to its population base, and relatively under equipped, particularly with respect to heavy weapons. But this is a misleading overall comparison. Given the particular circumstances of Sweden—large size, difficult terrain, often inhospitable weather—its defense forces are really quite impressive. Swedish military defense can be conceptualized as three concentric rings or layers, each with a different type of preparation for defense against military attack.[19]

The first and outermost ring is power projection, the ability to hit assaulting forces once Sweden is at war, but before enemy forces have actually penetrated Swedish land, airspace, or territorial waters. Second is perimeter, or shell, defense of the nation at the border. The objective of perimeter defense is to impose a high entrance cost on a potential attacker. The third ring is territorial defense, sometimes called defense in depth or defense with staying power. Territorial defense is resistance by military and other means even after an attacker has breached Swedish territory. The most notable proponent of territorial defense is the former Army commander-in-chief Gen. Nils Sköld, who has long touted the notion of a "people's army" equipped with inexpensive weapons but capable of extracting a high cost of occupation, and thereby serving as a powerful deterrent to a potential invader.

Sweden's defense posture is an interdependent combination of forces structured to fight at each of these three tiers. Each level reinforces and supports the other two. The result is a synergistic and effective combat force. While it would be a mistake to see each of the three levels as a competitor to the other two, each does require a particular type of force, and each carries with it a set of particular benefits and liabilities.

In the Swedish military, projection forces basically take the form of high-performance tactical strike aircraft.[20] Projection forces may be the most effective deterrent to military attack, and having such forces gives Sweden not only an ability to influence regional events but also some basis in force structure for acting as the central figure in the maintenance of Nordic military stability. Projection forces are the weapons that count on the world scene. On the other hand, they are also very expensive, and they can be seen by other states as provocative offensive weapons. They may also be very difficult forces for a country so manifestly nonaggressive as Sweden to use in a first strike. In *Red Storm Rising,* Thomas Clancy's best-selling novel about war in Europe, the Western alliance uses evidence of Soviet-directed sabotage as justification for the decision to launch a preemptive air attack against Warsaw Pact targets. Sweden would be hard pressed to act in similar fashion and use its power projection forces preemptively. And unless there is a credible threat that such forces would be used early in a conflict, they lose much of their utility as a deterrent.

Perimeter defense forces are less expensive and less threatening, but by themselves they cannot prevent an enemy from massing forces outside Swedish territory and mounting an invasion from a protected sanctuary.

Territorial defense is the least expensive level because it does not require complex equipment or lengthy training. At the same time there are serious questions about the war fighting capability and deterrent value of such forces. Many advocates of territorial defense have used the examples of guerrilla warfare in Yugoslavia and Vietnam, but the relevance of such experience to the Swedish case remains in doubt. No one knows how effectively and enthusiastically a citizen army could be expected to hold out after the country had been invaded and occupied.

The three layers of Swedish defense are intended to be mutually reinforcing, but in reality the connection between the various rings is not so direct and supportive. There is a continuing debate in Sweden about the priority which each of these levels should receive. Not surprisingly, each of the military services supports that layer of defense promising to give it the greatest role in national defense and the largest share of the military budget.

The Air Force is unabashedly in favor of power projection. The Navy, having been forced to abandon its power projection role in the 1960s, now emphasizes perimeter defense, preferably with reliance on anti-invasion ships. The Army favors both perimeter defense and territorial defense. In fact, it could be said that Army promotes the popular concept of territorial defense while remaining institutionally committed to a perimeter defense based on tanks and armored personnel carriers.

Sweden's military defense is based almost entirely on a system of mobilization. While virtually the entire Air Force and many naval units operate on permanent alert, the Army in peacetime is effectively a training cadre. At any given time, only a few officers and NCOs, and a few units undergoing basic training or refresher exercises, are on active duty. Such a force posture, relying almost entirely on mobilizable militia and reserve forces, is common to the European neutrals, and poses a special problem for them. The system is vitally dependent on adequate warning time for mobilization. Sweden recognizes this, and has designed a mobilization system that disperses equipment and units around the country, and has redundant channels of communication.

Once mobilized, the Swedish Army can field a force of over 700,000 troops. This includes five armored brigades, five special Norrland brigades equipped for fighting in northern Sweden, 18 mobile infantry brigades, and scores of independent battalions for specialized service such as air defense and coastal artillery, and local defense forces.

There is a broad national consensus in Sweden—one could say almost an ideological conviction—in support of a "people's army." The principle of universal male conscription has broad support throughout the country; very few politicians even question the notion. The Social Democrats, the least enthusiastic about defense spending in general, are perhaps the most enthusiastic proponents of conscription. Among other social and political virtues, conscription is thought to ensure civilian control over the military.

The cornerstone of the Air Force is the JA-37 Viggen multi-purpose fighter, with about 300 in the active inventory. The aging Viggen will be replaced in the 1990s by the new Gripen multi-purpose fighter. The quality of the Swedish Air Force, both in terms of personnel and equipment, is high, but the number of aircraft has declined significantly as the per-unit cost of modern fighters has skyrocketed. This decline has taken place over the past two decades, a period during which the number of foreign aircraft that can reach Swedish territory has increased over tenfold.

For the entire postwar era the Swedish Navy has been a service in search of a mission. Growing out of the experience of World War II, the role of the Navy in the early postwar years was to prevent a seaborne invasion and, equally important, to keep open the sea lines of communication to the Western powers along which essential supplies and assistance would have to pass. In the 1950s as the conviction grew that surface combatants—cruisers and destroyers—would be extremely vulnerable in a future war, the Navy's fortune began to wane. The 1958 defense decision set a course of fundamentally restructuring the Navy, moving to the concept of a "light fleet" composed of smaller craft with improved firepower. The primary mission of maintaining sea lines of communication was dropped; the Navy was directed to concentrate on its anti-invasion responsibilities. By 1970 Sweden had decommissioned the last of its destroyers and significantly reduced the number of operational submarines. The net effect was a drastic reduction in antisubmarine warfare capability, which was not regarded as a significant loss at the time since the need to protect convoys along the SLOCs was no longer regarded as an important mission. The contemporary mission of the Navy is to stop a seaborne invasion. Operating with the Air Force, the

Navy will harass troop ships and force escort ships to protect mine-clearing efforts.

Interservice rivalry over roles and missions, particularly between the "blue" services (the Air Force and Navy) and the Army is almost certain to grow in the constrained fiscal environment of the future. This rivalry is evident in the fact that officers of the Air Force and Army, services with more political influence than the Navy, have not been particularly vocal in expressing concern about the underwater intrusions. Doing so would pose a bureaucratic risk, since the more serious the submarine threat, the more likely it would be that funds would be diverted to the Navy from the Army and Air Force budgets. To look at another major procurement issue in interservice terms, the Army and Navy were unenthusiastic about the decision to proceed with the new Gripen fighter for the Air Force because that decision meant relatively less money for the other services.

The most serious force structure problem for Sweden concerns the Army and the future of universal conscription. It is generally agreed that Swedish defense would be significantly improved by increasing the Army's level of preparedness in peacetime. Defense is now critically dependent upon receiving at least three days of warning time for mobilization. And the decision to mobilize may be a painful step to take for political leaders who will not want to be seen as moving toward war. Despite this problem, the idea of a standing army as an alternative to a militia-based force posture is unlikely to make much headway in Sweden, where the concept of conscription and a citizen-army is almost universally accepted. Any improvement in peacetime preparedness of the Army will have to be made within the general context of conscription.

During the 1970s and 1980s, when major changes were made in the force structure of the Air Force and Navy, the Army remained about the same size. It did so by scrimping on hardware. Some Army units, particularly the Norrland brigades, are well equipped and trained, but others have serious deficiencies in firepower, mobility, and protective measures, and are poorly trained to boot. A large army is costly and tends to squeeze out resources needed for other missions and other branches of service.

During the late 1970s, Sweden devoted about three percent of its GNP to defense, about the same as the average of European member-states of NATO and significantly higher than that of the other European neutrals. The 1980s saw a slow and steady decline in defense spending, which was finally arrested with the parliamentary defense decision of 1987 approving a small increase in spending for the next five-year period.

The Total Defense Concept

Another legacy of Sweden's experience in World War II is the concept of total defense, the idea that all elements of society should be prepared for war, and that resistance should continue through all phases of a war. Total defense includes, in addition to military efforts, economic, civil, and psychological defense. It means making adjustments in all peacetime activities to assure that society can continue to operate during war and support the military defense effort.

Economic defense means the country's ability to survive as an autarky with a cohesive and supportive population. It requires the ability to sustain the domestic population, to maintain access to international commerce if possible, and to feed and clothe the population without recourse to foreign trade. It means the ability to survive an economic blockade. This is an increasingly difficult problem in an age of inter-dependence, and Sweden has struggled to reconcile the requirements of total defense with the need to be an active participant in the world economy.

Even if Sweden were to manage to stay out of a nuclear war, it would undoubtedly suffer collateral effects from nuclear exchanges. For this reason physical protection for the population plays a significant role in total defense planning, although Sweden's highly publicized civil defense shelter program receives less emphasis now than it did in earlier times.

Another dimension of total defense to which the Swedes pay special attention is psychological defense, the need to prepare the people for the stress of enduring military conflict and economic deprivation. One means of gauging the psychological state of the population is through public opinion polls, and for over two decades the Swedish government has regularly surveyed popular attitudes and beliefs about defense and foreign policy issues. The 1986 poll revealed some interesting results. While ninety-three percent of the population supports Sweden's policy of neutrality, only nineteen percent believe that Sweden will be able to stay out of conflict if war comes to Europe. Whatever the virtues of neutrality, the public obviously does not believe it reduces the risk of Swedish involvement in war. Even more surprising is the finding that less than a quarter of Swedes believe that their country could successfully defend herself if drawn into a war. When asked to consider Sweden's security environment five to ten years hence, about half the population saw the situation as remaining about the same, but of those who thought it would change, four times as many thought it would be more rather than less threatening. On the question of defense spending, more than

twice as many people supported an increase as opposed to those favoring
a reduction in funding.[21]

The Making and Implementation of Defense Policy

Given the Swedish fondness for studies, commissions, inquiries, and
planning in general, it is not surprising that defense policy is made
through an elaborate and systematic bureaucratic process involving perspective planning, program planning, system planning and budgeting.

During the 1960s, Sweden was much impressed with the systems
analysis innovations in defense planning made by the American Secretary
of Defense Robert McNamara. A new system of planning, programming,
and budgeting was introduced with a long-term planning cycle of five
years. Some of this work is done by the Secretariat for National Security
Policy and Long-Range Planning, the Ministry of Defense (MOD) office
with primary responsibility for "perspective planning," a look fifteen to
twenty years into the future at possible threats and appropriate program
planning. The aim of this reform was to rationalize and make more
efficient the process of defense planning, but it also strengthened political
control, particularly parliamentary control, over the military services.[22]

Also worth noting in the Swedish security bureaucracy is the role of
FOA, the national defense research institute.[23] FOA is the think tank
for the Ministry of Defense, and it conducts research in a wide range
of fields from basic research and weapons evaluation to defense policy.
The vast majority of FOA researchers are physical scientists, but the
institute also employs defense researchers and policy analysts. FOA is
an important national resource. Many senior officials in the security
community began their careers or have tours at the institute. FOA is
the largest research organization in all of Scandinavia, and its influence
is felt far beyond the limits of Swedish defense planning.[24]

One unusual aspect of Sweden's military organization is the fact that
the military services themselves fall under the command of a military
officer who is appointed supreme commander and is directly responsible
to the government. The supreme commander has his own staff independent
of the individual services, and military chain of command goes directly
from the supreme commander to the various regional commanders. The
chiefs of the various services are not in the operational chain of command.

The Domestic Arms Industry

As noted earlier, the Swedish arms industry began to revive during
the rearmament of the mid-1930s. During World War II, weapons
production came into its own as an important component of Swedish

industrial strength. By the mid-1950s Sweden had one of the most sophisticated arms industries in the world. While a wide variety of armaments were produced, including submarines and tanks, combat aircraft were the heart of the industry, as they continued to be into the late 1980s as Swedish Air Force began to take delivery of the JAS 39 Gripen.

Maintaining a successful arms industry has been good for Swedish economic growth and good for neutrality as well. Domestic arms production allowed Sweden to reduce dependence on foreign sources of weapons and to avoid the potential danger of having to rely on outside suppliers during times of war or crisis. This independence added great credibility to neutrality. In the 1980s Sweden supplied about 70 percent of its defense requirements through domestic sources. The increasing cost of modern weapons has created a more difficult environment for Swedish arms producers, and has forced Sweden, along with other arms producers, to consider two avenues for reducing costs: co-production or other cooperative ventures with other countries, and the sale abroad of domestically produced weaponry.

The Swedish arms industry faces two serious potential problems in exploring each of these two avenues. As a small country, Sweden has always been forced to include foreign technology in its advanced weapon systems. This requirement poses a potential conflict with the posture of neutrality, but in practice Sweden has managed to work out cooperative arrangements with the United States and many European members of NATO. Every Swedish jet aircraft has used foreign engines, avionics, and weapons systems produced under license or purchased abroad. The fighter version of the JA 37 Viggen contained twenty percent foreign components, two-thirds of which were American (Dörfer, 1982:276).

This arrangement allowed Sweden to have the best of both worlds. It could be non-aligned yet secure access to state of-the-art military technology as though it were an ex officio member of the Western alliance. Sweden does pay an indirect price for striking such a bargain. The government has informally assured the United States that it will observe and enforce all U.S. restrictions on the transfer of technology to third countries. Such acquiescence makes Sweden an implicit agent of U.S. technology transfer policy, and could be seen as a compromise of neutrality policy.

The second problem is selling arms abroad. Using foreign technology through co-production or licensing agreements obliges the user to give a veto over potential foreign sales to the originating country, as the United States did when Sweden attempted to sell the Viggen fighter to India in the 1970s.[25] Another part of the arms export problem is self-imposed. Swedish law prohibits the export of arms to countries at war or located in "zones of conflict," a broad category that has generally been understood to include the entire Middle East. The traditional Swedish policy on arms exports can be summed up as prohibiting the sale of weapons to any country that might conceivably be tempted to use them. Such restrictions on arms sales have tempted Swedish companies such as Bofors to circumvent such rules by dealing with middlemen in third countries in order to sell arms to countries on the government blacklist. In other cases, the Swedish government has determined that companies have paid millions of dollars in "commissions" in order to secure large arms contracts.[26]

The arms scandals of the late 1980s began a serious debate within Sweden and forced many people to rethink their attitude toward foreign arms sales and the indirect relationship between such sales and the successful maintenance of armed neutrality. For Sweden to remain neutral it must have an indigenous arms industry capable of producing its own weapons. To maintain its arms industry it must sell arms abroad—or impose an additional burden on Swedish taxpayers already burdened by some of the world's heaviest tax rates.

How Much Defense Is Enough?

In theory the level of a nation's defense spending ought to be determined by the external threat, and not by the vicissitudes of domestic politics. But in Sweden as much as in any other country, defense spending is the hostage of very powerful domestic political forces. Defense competes with numerous entrenched and popular claims on the public purse.

In the 1950s and early 1960s Sweden spent about five percent of its GNP on defense. In the era of detente the figure began dropping to around three percent. During the 1970s and 1980s (the external threat to Sweden—its strategic value to possible aggressors—increased), Sweden's investment in defense declined. In most years defense spending rose slightly in absolute terms, but the increase did not keep pace with inflation, rising manpower costs, and the higher cost of high-technology weapon systems. Even with a militia system a high percentage of Swedish defense expenditure is devoted to personnel (over seventy percent), thus making military spending particularly susceptible to adverse economic conditions in an advanced industrialized welfare state.

With the rising unit cost of new military equipment and the continuing commitment to conscription, Swedish defense is facing a budget squeeze perhaps more serious than that of many other Western nations. In the 1970s and 1980s Sweden deferred the acquisition of new equipment, reducing the quantities it purchased, but manpower continued to absorb most of the savings. Like other states, Sweden in the late 1980s is facing a "force–strategy mismatch." The country faces a difficult choice between greater resources to perform the assigned missions or reducing the missions to match the available resources. In Sweden as elsewhere, political authorities have been reluctant to decide between these painful choices, preferring the "middle way" of muddling through.

Among Swedish defense experts the consensus on the 1987 defense plan was that it stopped the gradual long-term decline in Swedish defense capability, but did little to improve capabilities. When Sweden devoted five percent of its GNP to defense, it could manage to maintain a wartime organization of twenty-nine army brigades, one of the most impressive air forces in Europe, and a navy with noteworthy antisubmarine and anti-invasion capabilities.

The continuing budget squeeze will force increasingly hard decisions about force posture. Almost certainly the Army will have to be restructured and reduced in total size, perhaps by moving to a "two-tier" system of well-trained and equipped first-line militia forces backed by a less capable and ready support force.

Sweden is a very successful advanced industrialized country with one of the world's highest standards of living. It is also a welfare state, with one of the world's highest rates of taxation. Over four decades of virtually uninterrupted rule by Social Democrats have given Sweden a pragmatic socialism, a government that delivers. In the late 1980s Sweden's economy was hailed as one of Europe's industrial powerhouses,[27] but even optimistic projections of growth in GNP seemed unlikely to keep pace with social spending.

The costs of administering the welfare state have risen dramatically. The percentage of gross domestic product expended in the public sector rose from forty-four percent in 1970 to approximately seventy percent in the mid-1980s, the largest share in any Western nation.[28] During the late 1980s the Swedish government came under growing pressure for tax reduction, based on the pragmatic grounds that high taxation was driving out profitable industries. At the same time there is a high level of national consensus on maintaining the welfare state. State services are popular, and have a powerful political constituency. The future thus poses a disturbing set of demographic and political trends that have a security implication: an aging population that will require increased social and medical services, a societal structure with powerful interest groups committed to preserving such services, and a decline in tax revenue. Defense spending will have a hard time holding its own.

Another aspect of Swedish domestic life exerting a dispiriting influence on defense policy is the popular tendency to treat military service as mere nine-to-five employment, subject to all of the rights and privileges accorded to workers in any other job in the welfare state. This is not a problem unique to Sweden, but its effect seem more apparent here than elsewhere. The Swedish military is one of the few in the world that is entirely unionized. This may not be surprising in a society in which almost everyone belongs to a union, but it does present special problems for the performance of military missions.

One defense analyst joked that the real problem in catching intruding submarines was not so much a question of technology or political will as a personnel problem. At the end of eight hours Swedish anti-submarine warfare (ASW) helicopter pilots in hot pursuit of a submarine would call off the hunt and quit for the day. In the summer of 1987 there were repeated sightings of suspected submarines in the far northern Baltic near the Boden military base, but these reports could not be verified because the local anti-submarine force was on vacation. In past years entire air bases have been closed down for summer holidays, thus diminishing, if not fatally compromising, air defense readiness. Perhaps war will not come during the summer holidays. And perhaps the mobilization system on which Swedish defense so critically depends will work flawlessly. Conceivably the defense forces who fight so enthusiastically in peacetime for the workers rights will set aside personal inconvenience and fight with equal fervor for their country. All of these things could happen, but they would require a considerable reversal of habits that have developed over decades.

Conclusion

The goals of any nation's foreign policy are to make the best of given circumstances, and to do what is possible to change the circumstances in a more favorable way. One might expect a small country like Sweden to expend more effort on adaptation and less on change, but Sweden has for decades played a major role in encouraging disarmament and fostering international cooperation. There is great idealism in the Swedish national character, and skepticism about the utility of defense spending. There is also a desire to lead by example in international politics, a reluctance to consider the value of military forces as a possible tool of crisis management in time of tension. Sweden has been a champion of tension reduction, as evidenced by support for detente and arms control, but not very interested in tension management.

States can be characterized by the relative emphasis they accord defense and foreign policy, the two components of security policy. Some neutrals stress foreign policy over defense: Austria is a good example. Others, such as Switzerland, give greater priority to defense policy (Vetschera, 1985:51-64). Sweden in the 1950s gave roughly equal emphasis to the two dimensions, if anything stressing defense over foreign policy. Under

Olof Palme, Sweden emphasized foreign policy over defense preparedness, and attempts to change the system over efforts to make the best of the given situation.

The flowering of detente made more of an impression in Sweden than perhaps anywhere else in the world. There was a real sense—encouraged by government—of a fundamental change in the nature of international relations, the ushering in of a new era of greater cooperation and diminished conflict. In particular, the Social Democrats wanted very much to believe this. After all, this was the confirmation and vindication of the wisdom of their foreign policy line. In this new era, high levels of defense spending might not only be wasteful; they might even be counterproductive as well.

"We have had 170 years with no war, a high standard of living, a quiet country with a welfare state. That tends to make you much less suspicious than you should be," said Anders Björck, a Conservative member of Parliament.[29] He might have added that it makes the credibility of defense an even greater problem since there is no reputation for wartime prowess on which to build.

The second half of the 1980s has not been kind to Sweden's self-image. A series of national scandals raised questions about the Swedes' vaunted sense of propriety and superiority. The unsolved assassination of Prime Minister Olof Palme, the corporate collapse of Fermenta, the resignations under pressure of national ombudsman Per-Erik Nilsson and Minister of Justice Anna-Greta Leijon, the escape of convicted spy Stig Bergling, and the Bofors and FFV arms scandals all contributed to a loss of national self-confidence. But something positive may emerge from this series of collective embarassments.

A new realism about Sweden and its external environment may allow for a forthright reexamination of issues that were formerly considered too sacrosanct for open public debate. There has always been an elliptical quality to security discussions in terms of morality rather than *realpolitik*. In the late 1980s, there was a healthy debate about arms trade policy. So, too, must the basic dictates of Swedish defense policy be reexamined in a vigorous and open public debate.

Sweden still gives high priority to improving the international climate, but by the late 1980s there was a reluctant consensus that the grand vision of detente has not been realized. There were some promising signs of an improvement in U.S.–Soviet relations, but Sweden's security environment seemed more dangerous than it had in earlier times. The parliamentary decision of 1987 mandated a modest increase in defense appropriations over the next five years, but even with additional funding Swedish security policy faces difficult challenges in the years ahead.[30]

Sweden faces a growing gap between the external threat and its own defense preparations. Again, this is not a problem unique to Sweden, but it poses special difficulties in its case. A neutral must face this problem unilaterally; there is no turning to allies for support. Credibility is everything for a neutral state, and the gap between threat perceptions and defense spending will raise questions in the East and West about the extent of the Swedish commitment to defense by military means. The declaratory policy is in place; the material support for the policy is lacking.

Sweden will have to respond to the peacetime threat posed by foreign submarines venturing into its territorial waters, while at the same time being mindful of the increased wartime threat brought about by the growing strategic importance of the High North. It will have to determine the means by which to maintain a high-technology defense industry. It will also have to come up with the money to pay for a defense establishment when demographic pressures, public opinion, and the cost of social services are likely to work against defense spending. This is a difficult set of challenges, but meeting them is critical to the continued success of Sweden's armed neutrality.

Notes

1. Sweden was at war for 154 years, and at peace for 139 years. The sign goes on to detail the particular adversaries and conflicts. The breakdown by country: Denmark-Norway, 12 wars lasting a total of 50 war-years; England, 2 wars and 10 war-years; France, 2 wars and 9 war-years; Holland, 2 wars and 9 war-years; Austria-Hungary, 4 wars and 28 war-years; Poland, 7 wars and 66 war-years; Russia, 9 wars and 64 war-years; German states, 10 wars and 75 war-years.

2. See Wahlbäck (1986). Bernadotte, who took the name Karl Johan, was not formally crowned king until 1818, but he effectively reigned from the moment of his arrival in 1810.

3. See the chapter by John Logue in this volume.

4. By 1930 the Swedish Air Force had 60 aircraft in its inventory. During the period 1936-1945 Sweden produced almost 1,000 combat aircraft and acquired several hundred more from other countries. See Böhme (1984:119–34).

5. See Hugemark (1986). See also Böhme and Hugemark (1982).

6. This concept too had a precedent in World War II. After the fall of Norway and Denmark, Swedish defense strategy was based on the assumption that the Allies would assist Sweden in defending against a German attack.

7. The definitive work on this subject is by Wilhelm Agrell (1985). See also Kristian Gerner (1986).

8. Some Social Democrats, Olof Palme among them, wanted to keep open the nuclear option for its value as an inducement for the superpowers to conclude

nonproliferation and limited test ban treaties, but this was a hollow threat, backed by no genuine interest in pursuing the nuclear option.

9. See SOU (1985:57f).

10. See Ingemar Dörfer (1985).

11. For a good overview see Erling Bjøl (1983). See also Jervell and Nyblom (1986).

12. The official rationale for contemporary Swedish defense policy is available in English as *Sweden's Security Policy: Entering the 90s, Report by the 1984 Defence Committee,* SOU 1985:23 (unofficial translation).

13. For a further elaboration of this "air scenario," see Jervas (1986) and Jervas (1987).

14. The official report of the Submarine Defense Commission has been published in English as *Countering the Submarine Threat,* (Stockholm: Ministry of Defense, 1983), Swedish Official Reports Series 1983:13. The best unofficial work in Swedish is Wilhelm Agrell (1986). For English language sources, see McCormick (1988), Leitenberg (1987), Agrell (1983), and Agrell (1986:197–217). See also Ingemar Oldberg (1985:51–60).

15. The precise rules of engagement under which the Swedish Navy operated have never been made clear. The Report of the Submarine Defense Commission acknowledges that "rumours circulated in the mass media to the effect that certain bans on the use of fire in force during the Hårsfjärden operation were attributable to a decision by the Government and/or Defence Command to let the submarine or submarines escape, out of consideration for Sweden's relations with the foreign power responsible." *Countering the Submarine Threat,* pp. 56–57. The debate was renewed in 1987 when Brigadier (Retd.) Lars Hansson accused former Vice Admiral Bror Stefenson, former Chief of the Defense Staff, of having issued a fire ban in the crucial moment of the hunt and of having declared that no blood of a Russian seaman should be shed.

16. Wilhelm Agrell, Kjell Goldmann, and Nordal Åkerman may be offered as examples.

17. *Dagens Nyheter,* (1987:6).

18. See Ries (1984:695–6).

19. In an article that attracted great interest within Sweden, Steven Canby (1981:116–23) drew a slightly different distinction, dividing Swedish defense capability into "extrovert" and "introvert" forces.

20. One might also consider as projection forces submarines and surface ships armed with long-range anti-ship missiles.

21. "Opinion 86," *Psykologist försvar,* Report No. 136. Data reported here is taken from Tables 7,9,12, and 20.

22. For more detail on the bureaucratic structure and processes of the Swedish defense establishment, see Ingemar Dörfer (1973). See also William J. Taylor, Jr. (1982). See also *Long-Range Planning of the Swedish Defence,* (Stockholm: FOA, 1980).

23. The Swedish acronym for *Försvarets Forskningsanstalt.*

24. See *FOA in a nutshell,* (Stockholm: National Defence Research Institute, 1986).

25. The Viggen engine was produced under license from the United States.
26. Kenneth R. Timmerman, "Arms Trade Scandal Shatters Image of Clean Dealings," *International Herald Tribune,* June 3, 1987. See also "Arms and Iran: the secret deals," *Times* (London), June 17, 1987. The most significant of these may have been the sale of a $2.8 billion Swedish artillery system to India.
27. "How Sweden Became Europe's Industrial Powerhouse," *Business Week,* August 4, 1986.
28. "Sweden, Time for a Call," *The Economist,* October 6, 1984, p. 17.
29. "No Longer Untarnished, Swedes Find," by William Tuohy, *Los Angeles Times,* November 11, 1987, p. 1.
30. See "Sweden's defence budget: expanding into the 1990s," by Nick Cook, *Jane's Defence Weekly,* May 23, 1987, p. 101ff.

References

Agrell, Wilhelm (1983) "Soviet Baltic Strategy and the Swedish Submarine Crisis," *Cooperation and Conflict,* Vol. XVIII, No. 4, pp. 269–281.

Agrell, Wilhelm (1985) *Alliansfrihet och atombomber, Kontinuitet och förändring i den svenska försvarsdoktrinen 1945-1982.* Stockholm: Liber.

Agrell, Wilhelm (1986) *Bakom ubåtskrisen–militärverksamhet, krigsplanläggning och diplomati i Ostersjoomrdet.* Stockholm: Liber.

Agrell, Wilhelm (1986) "Behind the Submarine Crisis: Evolution of the Swedish Defence Doctrine and Soviet War Planning," *Cooperation and Conflict,* Vol. XXI, No. 4, pp. 197-217.

Alford, Jonathan (1985) "The Northern Flank as Part of Europe—Some Thoughts on Nordic Security," *Värderingar av vår säkerhetspolitik.* Stockholm: Royal Academy of War Sciences, pp. 73-81.

Bjøl, Erling (1983) *Nordic Security.* Adelphi Paper No. 181, London: International Institute for Strategic Studies.

Böhme, Klaus-Richard (1984) "The Principal Features of Swedish Defence Policy 1925-1945," *Neutrality and Defense: The Swedish Experience.* Stockholm: Swedish Commission on Military History.

Böhme, Klaus-Richard and Bo Hugemark (1982) "Tradition and Modernization: Sweden as a Military Power in a Strategically Important Area, 1600-1982," Unpublished Paper.

Canby, Stephen (1981) "Swedish Defense," *Survival,* May/June, pp. 116–123.

Danspeckgruber, Wolfgang (1986) "Armed Neutrality: Its Application and Future," in S. Flanagan and F. Hampson, eds. *Securing Europe's Future.* London: Croom Helm.

Dörfer, Ingemar (1973) *System 37 Viggen.* Oslo: Scandinavian University Books.

Dörfer, Ingemar (1982) "Nordic Security Today: Sweden," *Cooperation and Conflict,* Vol. XVII, No. 4, pp. 273–285.

Dörfer, Ingemar (1985) "Swedish Security Policy Facing the Future," *Tio debattinlägg om svensk säkerhetspolitik.* Kalmar: Folk & Försvar.

Gerner, Kristian (1986) "The Swedish Defense Doctrine in the Postwar Era: Changes and Implications," *Scandia,* Vol. 52, No. 2, pp. 307-325.

Heginbotham, Stanley J. (1985) "The Forward Maritime Strategy and Nordic Europe," *Naval War College Review,* November-December.

Hugemark, Bo (1986) "Försvar för neutralitet: Några perspektiv på utvecklingen sedan 1945," in Hugemark, ed. *Neutralitet och försvar.* Stockholm: Militärhistoriska Förlaget.

Jervas, Gunnar (1986) *Sweden Between the Power Blocs: A New Strategic Position?* Stockholm: The Swedish Institute.

Jervas, Gunnar (1987) "Sweden in a Less Benign Environment," in Bengt Sundelius, ed. *The Neutral Democracies and the New Cold War.* Boulder, Colo: Westview.

McCormick, Gordon (1988) *Stranger Than Fiction: Soviet Submarine Operations in Swedish Internal Waters.* Santa Monica, Calif.: Rand Corporation.

Leitenberg, Milton (1987) *Soviet Submarine Operations in Swedish Waters, 1980-1986.* New York: Praeger.

Oldberg, Ingmar (1985) "Peace Propaganda and Submarines: Soviet Policy toward Sweden and Northern Europe," *Annals of the American Academy,* Vol. 481, September, pp. 51-60.

Ries, Tomas (1984) "Soviet Submarines in Sweden:psychological warfare in the Nordic region?" *International Defense Review,* Vol. 17, No. 6, pp. 695-6.

Sweden's Security Policy Entering the 1990s Commission Report published by the Ministry of Defense, *SOU,* 1985, No. 23. Stockholm.

Taylor, Jr., William J. (1982) "The Defense Policy of Sweden," in Douglas Murray and Paul Viotti, eds. *The Defense Policies of Nations.* Baltimore: The Johns Hopkins University Press.

Thunborg, Anders (1984) "National Security and Nuclear Weapons," *Bulletin of Peace Proposals,* Vol. 15, No. 4., p. 2.

Vetschera, Heinz (1985) "Neutrality and Defense: Legal Theory and Military Practice in the European Neutrals' Defense Policies," *Defense Analysis,* Vol. 1, No. 1, pp. 51-64.

"Västeuropa litar på Gorbatjovs fredsvilja," *Dagens Nyheter,* June 7, 1987, p. 6.

Wahlbäck, Krister (1986) *The Roots of Swedish Neutrality.* Stockholm: The Swedish Institute.

5

Sweden: Interdependence
and Economic Security

Ebba Dohlman

Sweden's small open economy has enjoyed considerable international respect for its foreign trade policies. With the exception of two sectors— textiles and agriculture—Sweden has remained consistently open to imports and has maintained tariffs that are among the lowest of the industrialized world. This openness, however, is not altogether surprising given Sweden's considerable dependence upon foreign trade that is typical of a small industrialized economy. In the current protectionist environment of the 1980s, the trade policies of the smaller nations tend to be overshadowed by the policies of such economic giants as the United States, the European Community (EC), and Japan. The challenges faced by the free trade orientation of the smaller states thus become minimized or even ignored.

The first part of this study will briefly review Sweden's foreign trade relations to include its overall posture toward international economic co-operation, and will provide some of the background to its free trade position. The next section will examine how Sweden's uncompromising support for international economic co-operation and liberalization has adjusted to demands imposed by the pursuit of a policy of neutrality and the subsequent perceived need for economic security. The traditional assumption that neutrality and trade policies were essentially unrelated was severely tested during the recessionary periods which followed the aftermath of the 1973-74 oil crisis. Interdependence was now regarded as a potential threat to governmental sovereignty and state security, rather than as a purely positive consequence of trade.

The conflict between trade liberalization and economic security has been confronted—to some degree—by nearly all industrialized states within the agricultural sector. Sweden, however, has developed a unique policy that is termed "economic defense." This policy finds its origins during the 1930s when a series of trade-restricting contingency plans for wartime were developed in order to safeguard neutrality. Gradually, Swedish authorities have extended the applicability of these measures to peacetime. The measures are concerned not only with such strategic sectors as agriculture and energy, but extend also to such traditional targets of multilateral trade liberalization as manufactures and semi-manufactures. Sweden's extension of the economic security argument to the textile and clothing sectors has indeed been unique.

The Foundations of
Sweden's Foreign Trade Policy

The development of Sweden's free-trade orientation coincided with industrialization. Prior to World War I, trade was relatively insignificant compared to the agriculture, forestry, and mining sectors which employed the vast majority of the population and were geared primarily for domestic consumption. The interwar period, however, witnessed numerous structural changes within the economy that spurred its rapid internationalization and sparked the increased interest in international trade.

Sweden's industrialization actually began through the export of increasing quantities of raw materials—primarily forestry products and iron ore—that could not be absorbed by domestic industries. The expanding export surplus permitted greater imports of capital goods which led to the development of even more sophisticated and specialized manufacturing. Industries that were previously protected gradually developed a reliance upon foreign imports and, therefore, began to recognize that the country would profit from more liberal trade if trade barriers were lowered. At the same time, it was expected that an active free trade policy would increase the export value of Sweden's own natural resources.

Sweden's free trade orientation, once established, survived even the protectionist trends that developed during the 1920s. Sweden joined other northern European countries to form what became known as the Oslo Convention of 1930—the so-called "low tariff club"—in order to counteract the trend toward autarky that was developing at the time (Ohlin, 1959).

In addition, Sweden experienced a number of internal changes that favored the policy of free trade. During the worldwide repercussions of the Great Depression, Sweden voted into power a labor party whose ideological roots could be traced to nineteenth century socialism. However, the Swedish Social Democrats (unlike most of the political parties which grew out of Western European socialist movements) accommodated themselves to parliamentary reformist politics. Their priorities were

Table 1. Impact of World War II on Per Capita Product

Country, Type of Product, and Prewar Base Year	*1945*	*1950*
United Kingdom		
National Income 1937		
(a) Total	111	103
(b) Excluding public authority spending	70	98
France		
National Income 1937	57	108
West Germany		
Net domestic product 1936	78	94
Switzerland		
Net national product 1938	90	114
Sweden		
Gross domestic product 1939	114	150

Source: Simon Kuznets, *Postwar Economic Change*, Four Lectures, (Cambridge, Mass.: Harvard University Press, 1964), p. 91.

security of employment, economic stability through the expansion of the public sector, growth through specialization and free trade, and a resistance to social and economic inequalities (Martin, 1979).

Complementing the rise of the Social Democratic Party, the Swedish trade union movement developed considerable strength and vitality. In contrast to developments within many other European countries, the Swedish trade unions (as well as the Social Democratic Party) were cognizant of the critical importance of free trade to the nation's welfare. Indeed, these groups have remained firm adherents to the principle of comparative advantage and support the view that global and domestic welfare could be maximized if every country specialized in sectors of greatest competitive strength. (See Table 1.)

From the interwar period onward the major exception to Sweden's free trade policy was agriculture. Like other industrialized countries in which the agricultural interests represent a stable conservative element in society, agricultural protectionism in Sweden reflected the salience of agricultural employment within the economy and the strength of the farm lobbies. The Swedish argument for agricultural protectionism, however, contained an important additional dimension—that of economic defense preparation. Because of the food scarcities Sweden endured during World War I, the policy of agricultural self-sufficiency became a major priority. The policy also had, of course, one additional justification— the policy of neutrality.

With this one exception, Sweden's adherence to the principle of comparative advantage was already affirmed by the outbreak of World War II. Although the war threw Europe into a turmoil, Sweden—on the other hand—had stockpiled considerable resources and its production machinery was virtually intact. Therefore, Sweden was (relatively speaking) better off than its neighbors and was able to resume both production and exports upon the conclusion of the war. Nevertheless, these facts should not undermine the very real threats that Sweden faced throughout the war (Ohlin, 1959; Fox, 1959). The war years represented perhaps the most serious challenge to Sweden's neutrality to date. It is interesting to note that after the war ended Sweden elected to pursue a strategy designed to *increase* interdependence. One may argue that it was precisely this sort of economic interdependence that forced Sweden's wartime compromises in its neutrality policies in the first place.

Postwar International Cooperation

During the aftermath of the Great Depression and the concomitant collapse of the liberal trading order, the United States made concerted efforts to prevent a recurrence. There was a strong conviction that there existed an imperative to reconstruct the international trading order based upon a solid institutional framework. The objective of the Americans was to create a framework for rules of conduct in trade relations that would lead not only to greater reliability in international transactions, but to the freedom of access of markets and the sustained growth of international trade, as well. The American government seemed convinced that these conditions were essential in order to maintain peaceful conditions (Brown, 1950).

Against this backdrop, negotiations were initiated to create an International Trade Organization (ITO). Despite the fact that the United States never ratified the ITO, a significant part of the proposal—known as the "General Agreement"—came into force in 1947. The General Agreement on Tariffs and Trade (GATT), in fact, became an international contractual agreement and institution. It was an off-shoot of a much broader plan to cover all aspects of commercial, financial, and monetary cooperation. Instead, the GATT dealt mainly with the reduction of tariffs in the trade of manufactured and semi-manufactured goods.

One of the important goals of this multilateral trading system was to divorce politics from commerce through the establishment of a set of rules limiting government intervention in trade matters. Another objective was to prevent a return to the inefficient and preferential bilateral agreements through a reduction of tariff barriers to trade on the basis of reciprocity and unconditional most-favored-nation status (Dam, 1970).

GATT's creation after World War II was accompanied by a series of other attempts to further international or regional cooperation, particularly in Europe. The Marshall Plan began as a U.S. proposal in 1947 to reconstruct Europe through the provision of extensive grants and credit. To administer the assistance, the Organization for European Economic Cooperation (OEEC)—later to become the Organization for Economic Cooperation and Development (OECD)—was formed. Other regional initiatives included the formation of the European Coal and Steel Community (ECSC) and, finally, the European Economic Community (EEC) in 1957. Although the general movement toward trade liberalization was warmly received by Sweden, various aspects of these developments were to provide serious challenges to Sweden's continued pursuit of a policy of neutrality.

Neutrality and International Solidarity

The concept of neutrality dates from the nineteenth century and presupposes a state of war between other countries. From the viewpoint of the neutral country, the idea of defense referred primarily to military preparations. Economic considerations applied only insofar as they related to military strength. However, an expansion of the concept of war, the increased complexity of international relations, and broadened requirements for the maintenance and security of neutrality have contributed to a blurring of traditional definitional lines. The focus of neutrality after World War II shifted from a system based on wartime to one based on *peacetime*. Given this new emphasis, neutral states did not renounce their neutrality, but shifted their orientation to one of striving for peace instead.

Sweden's neutrality policy—which was never granted international *de jure* recognition—adapted easily to this framework. Sweden's official policy was defined as *freedom from alliances in peacetime aiming at neutrality in the event of war*. Although Sweden maintains no *official* obligations in peacetime, it nevertheless follows certain principles and takes certain measures to insure that it can fulfill its obligations as a neutral country in wartime. One important principle is that of a "credible neutrality" through which Sweden seeks both to inspire and to maintain the world's confidence in Sweden's determination to remain neutral in wartime. This principle implies Sweden's need to maintain a strong military defense, necessary economic resources, and general freedom of action in international arenas.

Therefore, Sweden's participation in "peaceful" international organizations was ultimately reconcilable with its neutrality policy. Sweden's membership in the League of Nations, however, only was accomplished after lengthy internal discussions concerning the implications of League membership for the policy of neutrality. In fact, Sweden's decision to join the League of Nations was considered to be a departure from the neutrality policy which was confirmed during World War I, because the League's charter envisioned a system of collective security that included sanctions. Although League membership was not tantamount to joining an alliance, it would, nevertheless, require the sacrifice of certain sovereign rights in the event of sanctions imposed by the League. Those who supported neutral state participation, however, argued that military sanctions could not be obligatory, because they were unlikely to be enforced effectively. Moreover, enforcement required unanimity and the League was far from unanimous. In any event, both Sweden and Switzerland decided to join the League under special conditions that permitted them to retain a considerable degree of discretion in crisis situations, particularly with regard to sanctions.

The collapse of the League of Nations and the onslaught of World War II represented a watershed for neutrality and, consequently, for international cooperation. With the advent of ever more sophisticated weapons and technologies, the idea that a single state could rely on its armed forces for defense against aggression became questionable. Against this background, new questions emerged with respect to international cooperation. Sweden's U.N. membership debate was divided in much the same way as that of the League—between those who took a legalistic interpretation and those who perceived the limits of the U.N. security system. In the end, the latter group, led by Christian Günther, prevailed. Günther maintained that Sweden should demonstrate its international solidarity through active U.N. participation. However, the Swedish government also made explicit clear—both domestically and internationally—its own interpretation of the rights, responsibilities, and obligations of membership (Karre, 1956:3–4; Andrén, 1965).

Sweden's U.N. membership facilitated the development of a new and more active foreign policy—the so-called "policy of solidarity." Although such a policy—strictly speaking—contradicts the policy of neutrality, it reflected the official Swedish view that the credibility of neutral policies would be judged primarily by how they contributed to the construction of a new system for the peaceful resolution of international conflicts.

After the GATT was formed, Sweden's decision to join was marked by no such debates concerning neutrality. This may have resulted from Sweden's new, more active policy of the promotion of international peace and of support to those organizations with peaceful aims. More importantly, Sweden's GATT membership—which was designed to promote international economic cooperation—was not perceived as conflicting with neutrality, because it was not viewed as leading to divisions along political or ideological lines. Although GATT membership may imply a certain loss of autonomy in trade relations, Sweden regarded its commercial relations as being in line with GATT's own philosophy and as separate from political considerations. Therefore, there was no reason *not* to engage in trade liberalization or interdependence with the rest of the world irrespective of political alliances (Kock, 1969).

Although economic strength was indirectly important in providing the backbone of military strength, the issue did not surface as a primary consideration at the time. Even after Sweden's post-World War II trade relations tilted sharply toward the West, this trade dependence was never seriously viewed as compromizing the maintenance of a credible neutrality in peacetime. Thus, Sweden promoted liberalized world trade and established closer economic ties with Europe after the war.

The international trading order established by the GATT also made no particular exceptions for the neutral states. Although not explicitly stated, this was consistent with the philosophy of the GATT which regards neutrality as a purely political issue that has few—if any—economic implications and, therefore, is not necessarily in conflict with international cooperation. Liberal international trade was viewed as perfectly reconcilable with and, indeed, even beneficial to, a state's neutral policies. Indeed, trade—in keeping with the liberal tradition—was expected to enhance economic strength (considered an important prerequisite for neutrality) and to promote more peaceful economic conditions for *all* states.

Although the GATT made no special provisions for the neutral states, the agreement does contain at least nine different safeguard clauses which cover such exceptional circumstances as balance of payment difficulties, security or health considerations, the protection of infant industries (in the developing countries, for example), and the protection of domestic producers who are threatened with serious injury by imports.[1] The GATT, then, is designed to deal solely with trade problems and attempts to safeguard the sovereign rights of a government to fulfill responsibilities in those areas that transcend pure trade.

The two safeguard clauses that are perhaps of greatest relevance to Sweden include Articles XXI and XIX which pertain to security exceptions and serious injury from imports, respectively. Article XXI states that nothing in this Agreement shall be construed . . . to prevent any contracting party from taking any action which it considers necessary for the protection of its essential security interests (such as) . . . traffic in arms . . . (or generally) in international relations.

This clause—especially because it dispenses with reporting requirements—is the most far-reaching and sensitive exception in the GATT. Furthermore, the few cases that have been made public indicate that broad interpretations that have been applied to the concept of essential security interests. Indeed, a curious extension of this provision to include Sweden's trade in footwear will be highlighted in a later section of this chapter.

Article XIX of the GATT states that contracting parties have the right to take emergency action in case imports reach "such increased quantities under such conditions as to cause or threaten serious injury to domestic producers in that territory of like or directly competitive products." This clause may also, at the limit, be viewed as embracing "economic security" concerns. Indeed, this article has been subject to increasing evasion for a variety of reasons to include the absence of precise definitions of "serious injury," "threat," and "emergency situation" (Tumlir, 1974).

Economic Defense

Although all of the European states possessed a defense policy *per se* upon the outbreak of World War II, few had plans designed specifically for *economic security*. Switzerland had made certain preparations in the *Kommission für Kriegswirtschaft* (the Commission for Wartime Economics) which aimed to maintain stocks of important raw materials and to prepare a system of rationing. Norway also created a department to deal with the problems of economic defense and rationalized its creation with the claim that economic survival was the most important aspect of neutrality. From the beginning, however, Sweden's policies were the most developed in this respect (Mansson, 1976).

In Sweden, World War I resulted in a serious exhaustion of food and other vital stocks that was mainly caused by poor planning and organization. After the war, a serious debate ensued concerning the issue of economic defense and the question of how to provide for military and civilian needs during wartime. In 1928, a commission was appointed for "economic defense preparations"—the *Riks-Kommissionen för Ekonomisk Försvarsberedskap* (the RKE). The RKE's task was to "devote itself to the execution of necessary preparations so that during war, imminent war, or other extraordinary conditions, the armed forces'needs will be satisfied, national food supply secured, and the growth of the economy guaranteed as far as possible." The establishment of this commission reflected the increasing priority given to defense and to the acknowledgement of the reality of total war.

The RKE involved all interested sectors of the economy and included military defense, agriculture, commerce, welfare, and industry. The Commission drew up the necessary plans for all industrial activities to include the management of vital raw materials during a crisis or blockade. The RKE also prepared a series of regulations for trade and transport in wartime. With regard to subsequent developments for economic defense policy, the RKE—despite a generally positive regard for both increased domestic production levels and an international division of labor—anticipated that the complexity of increasing specialization within certain sectors might lead to problems for future defense capabilities. Economic defense planning has passed through several stages since then and, after World War II, became the responsibility of the *Överstyrelsen för Ekonomisk Försvar* (the ÖEF).

Postwar Challenges to Neutrality

The assumption that neutrality was a purely political concept permitted Sweden to cooperate in the postwar effort to de-politicize trade. In practice, however, Sweden—as well as the other neutrals—were confronted with a series of challenges resulting from the attempt to pursue liberal trade policies independent of the policy of neutrality.

During the period of postwar peace, Sweden managed to pursue—for a time—its various economic and trade objectives independent of its policy of neutrality. The first economic challenge to Sweden's neutrality concerned East-West relations. Despite the attempts by the United States to persuade Sweden to join the trade embargo against the Soviet Union, Sweden managed to maintain its independence up to a point.

The formation of the European Economic Community (EEC) threatened the construction of a common tariff wall to Swedish exports. The implicit political aims of the Treaty of Rome, however, could not be reconciled with Swedish neutrality. Sweden's dilemma was resolved, somewhat, with the creation of the European Free Trade Area.

A more diffuse challenge arose in the 1970s. It is perhaps reasonable to expect that a neutral country would seek to balance the nature of its interdependence—in particular through increased trade with the Eastern bloc, as well as the developing countries—in order to mitigate potential conflicts. A balanced or "diffused" interdependence, however, was never an explicit objective of the Swedish government. To the contrary, the benefits of interdependence were acquired mainly through increased trade with the "old" economic order—that is to say the Western countries—

Table 2. Sweden's Most Important Trading Partners, 1985

Exports to	Share of Swedish Exports	Imports from	Share of Swedish Imports
United States	11.6	West Germany	17.9
West Germany	11.5	Great Britain	14.1
Norway	10.5	United States	8.4
Great Britain	9.9	Denmark	6.8
Denmark	8.3	Finland	6.5
Finland	5.6	Norway	6.0
France	4.8	Japan	4.9
Netherlands	4.4	France	4.6
Belgium/Luxemburg	4.0	Netherlands	3.9
Italy	3.3	Italy	3.3
Switzerland	1.8	Belgium/Luxemburg	2.7
Canada	1.6	Soviet Union	2.3
Australia	1.4	Switzerland	1.9
Japan	1.3	East Germany	1.3
Spain	1.2	Austria	1.2
Austria	1.1	Spain	1.2
Soviet Union	1.0	Brazil	0.9
Saudi Arabia	0.9	Nigeria	0.8
China	0.7	Portugal	0.8
Iran	0.6	Hong Kong	0.8

Source: Sjöstedt, Gunnar, *Sweden's Foreign Trade Policy: Balancing Economic Growth and Security* (Stockholm: The Swedish Institute, 1987), Table 5, p. 15.

with little consideration of the possible negative consequences for such a one-sided dependency. Sweden's trade with the East developed slowly and—with the exception of the 1946 credit agreement—has remained somewhat restricted. With respect to the developing countries, relations evolved within a different and more open context, but still remained limited. (See Table 2.) It was this trade, however, that paradoxically presented the new challenge. We will now examine each of these three challenges in turn.

U.S. Export Controls to the East

Sweden's willingness to be an active participant in the postwar reconstruction of Europe represented an important first element in the development of its European trade policy. Sweden's efforts to assist the war-ravaged European states began as an independent policy of unilateral credits to various governments toward the purchase—from Sweden—of urgently needed goods. Sweden's subsequent participation in the Marshall Plan was a natural extension of its own efforts toward European reconstruction. The primary objective of Marshall Plan assistance was to help the participating European countries bridge the period of severely diminished productive capacity and disturbed international payments. The Organization for European Economic Cooperation (OEEC) was formed to serve as the administrative instrument for the reconstruction and was expected to deal with all aspects of economic policy.

At the close of the war, Sweden was in a good position to offer assistance to its neighbors. However, Sweden eventually found itself in the situation of having to request outside help in order to balance its *own* dollar payments. This form of "conditional assistance," however, provided the United States with direct leverage over Sweden, despite the fact that the latter was not a member of the Western Alliance. This developed into a significant challenge to Sweden within the context of U.S. policies during the Cold War.

In 1947, rising East-West tensions were punctuated by the U.S. decision to initiate a trade embargo toward Eastern Europe and the Soviet Union. Thereafter, a series of events prompted the United States to generalize the embargo by making it a condition for Marshall Plan aid. The most important of the events was the Berlin blockade in 1948 which was interpreted by the U.S. as a major Soviet thrust westward. In response to this action, the United States passed a series of laws controlling exports to the East. One important provision directed the administrator of the Marshall Plan aid to halt delivery to recipient countries those commodities "which go into the production of any commodity for delivery to any non-participating European country" (Hoover, 1956:620; Adler-Karlsson, 1968).

As measures for the embargo were stepped up, the "Coordinating Committee" (COCOM) was established to harmonize the trade policies of the North Atlantic Treaty Organization (NATO) countries. After the embargo was actually implemented, the neutral states proved to be unwilling to *openly* compromise their neutrality policies by engaging in a form of economic warfare.

The neutral states endured considerable pressure from the United States to join the embargo. Because Sweden and Switzerland were both industrialized states and potential suppliers of strategic goods to the East, their participation was considered to be crucial to the overall success of the embargo. The United States, however, could not apply the same leverage against the neutral states as against the others. The U.S., nevertheless, attempted to apply sanctions against these economies as a whole and private business interests in particular, as well as to engage in direct negotiations.

This example clearly illustrates the vulnerability of Swedish neutrality to pressures channeled through an economic dependence upon the West. Despite Sweden's considerable resistance to U.S. insistence, some compromises were inevitable. For instance, Sweden—within the context of bilateral agreements with Eastern European countries—agreed to a declaration of intent concerning the rules which would apply to both the export and trans-shipment of COCOM-listed goods (Hoover, 1956:620; Adler-Karlsson, 1968).

Primarily because of the different trading systems, Sweden's postwar trade with the East has generally hovered around four to five percent of Sweden's total trade. However, certain factions within the Swedish government—notably those led by the former Minister of Commerce, Gunnar Myrdal—did try to encourage trade with the East through the negotiation of an extensive credit agreement with the Soviet Union in 1946. This agreement sparked considerable domestic controversy in Sweden and prompted concern in the United States. In fact, the agreement likely provided additional motivation for the U.S. to step up its pressure on Sweden.

The argument that the Soviet trade agreement was made to promote credibility with the East was never directly advanced in Sweden. Negotiations for the credit had actually begun before the entry of the USSR into World War II and, hence, well before the onset of the Cold War. Yet, the agreement was clearly an attempt by Sweden to maintain good economic relations with all sides and to reconcile its neutrality with "depoliticized" trade. After Myrdal concluded his service as Minister of Commerce, he became Chairman of the United Nations Economic Commission for Europe, the central aim of which was to increase the possibilities of trade between East and West. Although the initiatives within the commission may also have represented a means for Sweden to circumvent the embargo's consequences, it never resulted in the expansion of trading ties to the East to the degree expected.

Even today, Sweden remains subject to pressures to limit its exports of certain technologically sophisticated goods to the East. It should be noted that whereas the nature of the pressures have changed, so has the Swedish response. Throughout the postwar period, Sweden has remained on a U.S. list of countries whose exports must be carefully monitored. Every Swedish firm that uses American components covered by export controls must abide by U.S. export regulations. These regulations seek to control the

1. export of goods and technology from the U.S.,
2. re-export of American goods from one country to another,
3. export and re-export from one country to another of non-American goods containing American components, and
4. export and re-export of non-American goods which are manufactured with the help of U.S. technology or know-how.

Firms that do not comply with these regulations may be sanctioned or even blacklisted, such as in the cases of the Japanese Toshiba and the Norwegian Kongsberg companies. Although Sweden has always faced such threats, the risks today are undoubtedly greater. One reason for this apparent vulnerability is that Sweden's technologically advanced and differentiated economy is so heavily dependent upon U.S. sources of high technology. For example, Sweden's electronics industry is almost completely dependent upon outside sources (primarily U.S.) for the supply of components. The nearly impossible task of stockpiling such goods clearly illustrates Sweden's difficulties in maintaining an economic defense and in protecting its neutrality policies from outside economic pressures.

In 1986, Sweden finally formalized an export control agreement that would provide for an uninterrupted supply of necessary technology from the U.S. Although most of the large Swedish firms would contend that the agreement is compatible with the neutrality policy, it appears that Sweden's neutrality—along with the other European neutrals that have signed agreements—has indeed been compromised.

Integration in Western Europe

The second major challenge to Sweden's neutrality resulted from stresses caused by an increased economic interdependence with Europe and the pressures for European integration. Already by the end of the 1940s, there was significant movement toward regional integration in Europe. This was prompted by several factors. First, the disastrous economic policies of the 1930s, which were based upon nationalism and protectionism, were thought to have been an important factor leading to World War II. Second, the European countries which emerged after the war were devastated both economically and politically. Third, the breakup of the colonial empires had already occurred or was well underway. Finally, there existed an almost unanimous conviction among the European states that war among themselves could no longer be tolerated because of its recently demonstrated disastrous consequences at nearly all levels. As a result of these considerations, considerable European effort was marshalled to achieve political reconciliation and to prevent a repetition of the hostilities. The means to achieve this goal—it was thought—was through economic co-operation and integration.

In 1950, negotiations were initiated for the creation of the European Coal and Steel Community (ECSC). The ECSC's objective was to secure a sustained and expanded development for the basic coal and steel industries. It was hoped that this would eventually lead to a form of supranational control over the production of armaments and that this, in turn, would pave the way for the ultimate unification of Europe. The ECSC was established when the Treaty of Paris—signed by Belgium, France, Italy, Luxembourg, the Netherlands, and West Germany—came into effect in 1952. Further efforts by the same six countries to achieve greater economic integration began in 1955. In 1957, they established the European Economic Community (EEC).

During this time, the Scandinavian governments were exploring the possibility of instituting a customs union in order to reduce Scandinavian trade barriers. From 1947 until 1959, negotiations were initiated several times, but the proposed Nordic Customs Union never materialized. Some argue that Sweden's primary concern was not the formation of a customs union, but the strengthening of its own position (with the help of its Nordic neighbors) in the then forthcoming discussions concerning a pan-European free trade area. Within Sweden, it was thought that free access to markets in Europe—not Scandinavia—would facilitate the process of economic specialization and the development of competitive goods. Being a small state, Sweden was certainly dependent upon international trade and, alone, lacked the negotiating strength of some of the larger European countries. During this time, few anticipated the negative consequences to a growing economic interdependence. Because Sweden's economy and the standard of living were steadily improving, there seemed to be no need to question the benefits of international trade.

Although many of the goals of the Treaty of Rome were similar to those of the OEEC, the EEC was much more ambitious, both in its methods and its objectives. The EEC's plans for a common commercial policy alarmed some of the non-EEC European states with the prospect of a relatively high EEC common tariff. Sweden and Britain—among others—reacted by presenting counter-proposals within the OEEC forum. However, the negotiations of 1957 and 1958 failed to create a free-trade area encompassing all seventeen OEEC states.

A potential EEC membership for Sweden, then, soon became a hotly-contested political issue. Sweden's decision to remain outside the EEC in the beginning was not so difficult, because Great Britain—one of Sweden's most important trading partners at the time—was also a non-member. Moreover, Sweden had discovered a different forum through which to resolve its conflicting desires for both a policy of neutrality *and* trade liberalization—EFTA.

The European Free Trade Association (EFTA) was created during the Stockholm Conference of 1960. EFTA then consisted of seven states—Austria, Denmark, Great Britain, Norway, Portugal, Switzerland, and Sweden. The objective of EFTA was to provide a free trade area within the industrial goods sector *without* aiming for either political union or the creation of a customs union. After the dismantlement of industrial tariffs within EFTA, it was hoped that a general liberalization of trade throughout Europe would occur.

EFTA, in fact, did serve two useful—although more modest—purposes. First, it provided a means for the European neutrals to participate in European integration without a renunciation of tariff sovereignty or political privileges. Second, it strengthened the bargaining position of the EFTA members vis-à-vis the EEC.

During the 1960s, the Swedish government twice considered whether Sweden should seek an EEC membership either as a full member or in some form of association. On both occasions, a number of political and economic factors were weighed. Several arguments, largely based upon trade and commercial reasons, were offered to support an application for full EEC membership.

According to one line of reasoning, trade barriers erected by the customs union would create an obstacle to growth and would lead to the loss of comparative advantage and the benefits from an increased division of labor. However, there were political reasons as well. Had not Sweden participated fully in European cooperation after the war and did not the continuation of this co-operation seem natural and beneficial? Neutrality had not, so far, prevented Sweden from co-operation in solely European matters. In addition, the lack of clear parameters for neutrality—even after World War II—and the desire of the Swedish government to maintain its general influence in Europe also contributed to the debate concerning a possible EEC application.

Although there were certainly other reasons which contributed to Sweden's decision not to apply for EEC membership, the most important *official* argument was that of neutrality. Although the Treaty of Rome is ambiguous with regard to foreign or security policy commitments, the Treaty has been interpreted as an instrument for securing greater political cooperation among member states. For Sweden, the first sensitive elements were the community's goals—as set out in Article III—to formulate a common commercial policy and to empower the EEC to conclude commerical agreements with non-member states.

Although Sweden's membership in the OEEC and the GATT had already moved its trade policies along similar lines as the EEC, these obligations did not extend to Eastern Europe nor did they apply—for a long time—to the developing countries. Because of the East's suspicions regarding the EEC, Sweden's membership was jeopardized even further. With respect to the developing countries, the question for Sweden was not so much one of a surrender of neutrality, but rather a surrender of its freedom of action. Through the Yaoundé and Lomé Conventions, the EEC had already harmonized somewhat its policies toward the the Third World. Despite these actions, however, the Swedish government had developed a reputation as a "progressive" in its relations with developing countries that it understandably wished to maintain.

Another concern was the effect of an EEC membership upon Sweden's policy of economic defense and the related issue of access to necessary supplies during a crisis. Although Article 223 of the Treaty of Rome acknowledges that certain measures may be taken in consideration of a state's security interests, the Treaty states that this may be done only so long as the measures have no detrimental effect upon normal competitive conditions within the community. This provision applies to products that are not destined for direct military end-use and precludes the subsidized production of non-military products in peace-time regardless of whether stockpiling is appropriate or not. This section also precluded the possibility of implementing measures during less serious economic situations or in anticipation of a crisis.

Before 1970, the problem of maintaining production for economic defense needs—apart from stockpiling—was viewed primarily within the context of agricultural policy and the production of military goods. Sweden's economic defense requirements, however, would eventually transcend these two concerns. In any event, the contention that Sweden's economic defense plans would have conflicted with EEC regulations seems very reasonable.

Finally, the ambiguity in the definitions of "war" and "crisis situation" was also a potential obstacle to Sweden's EEC membership. Sweden's 1954 law on economic defense covered three different situations—war, risk of war, and extraordinary crises in which there is a shortage or a risk of shortage of goods necessary for economic defense. In the last case, it would have been most difficult to justify independent action to the community if the "extraordinary crisis" did not, in fact, lead to war. Article 224 of the treaty states that consultations should continue during crisis periods in order to develop common measures that would prevent one state from disturbing the normal operations of the Common Market. Although there were no provisions to prevent a state from implementing independent measures *after* the consultations, the Swedish government, nevertheless, foresaw possible conflicts with respect to neutrality.

The EEC has, however, changed radically since its formation and has, again, called into question the future of relations between Sweden and the EEC. Membership has doubled to twelve from the original six and, with the passage of the Single European Act of 1985, the EEC has targeted 1992 for the achievement of an "internal market" in which all barriers to the movement of goods, people, services, and capital are removed. Clearly, the decisions now being made in the Community have potentially far-reaching consequences for the development of Europe, such as the joint research programs in high technology. Sweden, along with the other EFTA countries, must be careful that they are not left watching from the sidelines.

Trade between Sweden and the Community is massive. In 1985, more than half of Sweden's exports were destined for EEC countries (Holmström, 1985). To complete the trade cycle, nearly half of all Swedish imports originated in the EEC. This trade dependency has prompted a number of Swedish businessmen to observe that it will be nearly impossible for Sweden to remain outside the organization. As recently as May 1988, however, the Swedish Prime Minister, during a whirlwind tour of major European capitals, reaffirmed the view—unchanged from 1971—that membership within the EEC was incompatible with Sweden's neutrality policy.

Sweden and the Developing Countries

With few exceptions, Sweden's trade with the Third World evolved within the context of its aid policies. During the 1950s, Sweden's concern for developing countries grew as the number of impoverished newly independent Third World states increased and as the Swedish public became more aware of and sensitive to the needs of its own underprivileged. As Susan Holmberg argues in chapter five, Sweden's development policies were seen as a logical extension of its own domestic security program and were based upon the idea of solidarity with the poorer people of the world.

In spite of attempts during the late 1970s to alter the direction and focus of aid policy, the basic principles of assistance—firmly rooted in social democratic tradition—seem to be unchanged. The onset of world recession, however, increased the pressures both to reduce assistance, as well as to insure that greater amounts yield reciprocal benefits. Some of the suggestions for altering development assistance policy include an increase in the access to export markets and, overall, more of an emphasis upon the trade dimensions of the assistance relationship. This change in focus may also have been a response to a change of emphasis by the developing countries, themselves, who place increased priority upon export promotion and in gaining greater access to the markets of the developed world.

Sweden has good economic reasons to develop good relationships with the countries of the Third World. Sweden—as a small vulnerable country—is acutely aware of its economic interdependence with the rest of the world. As a major manufacturer and exporter, Sweden is also dependent upon reliable markets and a steady inflow of raw materials and other imports. Not least, Sweden's non-aligned posture and its traditional identification with small states—two basic principles of Sweden's foreign policy—have also influenced the development of Sweden's relationship with the Third World.

Although Sweden's identification with non-alignment and with other small states had been couched primarily in political terms, the Third World demands for the creation of a New International Economic Order (NIEO) prompted the Swedish government to consider the neutrality policy more specifically in economic terms. This resulted from the fact that, on the one hand, the NIEO demands originated with the mostly non-aligned developing countries with whom Sweden had tried to cultivate a special relationship and, on the other, because they were targeted at the industrial countries of which Sweden was most certainly a member. As a beneficiary of the "old" economic order, Sweden was not in a position—despite its progressive Third World policy—to align itself completely with the NIEO program.

Apart from the possible economic contradictions, Sweden also feared the unpredictable effects upon its neutrality policy from a potential North-South cleavage in which it would be forced openly into an ideological camp. It was within this context that Olof Palme began to modify his "small state doctrine." Whereas many of his early speeches during the 1960s referred to Sweden's identification with "small states " (the emphasis then being the need to protect the sovereign rights of the small in a world divided by the Superpowers), he began to emphasize Sweden's ideological solidarity with "democratic socialist" states in an attempt to distance Sweden both politically, as well as economically, from both the Eastern bloc, as well as the Western "capitalist" powers (Barnes, 1980). This reflected his conviction that Swedish autonomy could only be preserved through the bridging of the gap between the industrialized West and the developing countries. In Palme's view, this required a new formula which could be distinguished from both traditional neutrality and Third World non-alignment. This effort, however, has not been totally successful.

In effect, Sweden was attempting to balance its traditional commitment to liberal trade, as well as its extensive ties with the West, to its courtship of the Third World. During the period of rapid growth, these various policy aims were never seriously questioned. During the financially constrained 1970s, however, many Swedes began to question whether the liberalization process had indeed gone too far and had left the country excessively dependent upon imports and vulnerable to a wide variety of external demands which were unacceptable to a neutral country. In the beginning, this import dependence was most notable in the energy sector and many felt that their worst fears had been confirmed during the 1973–1974 oil shock.

This argument, however, was not confined to the energy sector, but was extended to cover trade in manufactures, as well. Thus, Swedish authorities began to call for selective protection (aiming at self-sufficiency) for those industries that were declining most rapidly. It was feared that as imports grow, the greater Sweden's vulnerability would be to embargoes and to external trade demands. In effect, Sweden (like many other industrialized countries) began to question the rationale behind a further liberalization of trade and, as a result, revived one of the traditional arguments concerning the benefits of industrial self-sufficiency in those sectors essential for defense. The Swedish case, however, was complicated by additional arguments derived from the country's status as a neutral state. Although Sweden did step up its economic defense preparations in general, the only manufacturing sectors to which Sweden applied "economic defense" import restrictions were in textiles, clothing, and footwear. For this reason, these sectors have been selected for further analysis.

Traditionally, Sweden has regarded international economic cooperation as being fully compatible with neutrality. Within the Swedish government, a new mood became evident as early as 1979.

> We rely upon a close and extensive economic cooperation across borders even for the future. But measures may become necessary to prevent Sweden from becoming too dependent on other states for supplies of important goods and services. An all too heavy dependence could be taken advantage of in order to demand political and economic favors (SOU, 1979:42).

There appears, then, to be an emerging contradiction between Sweden's commitment to lower international trade barriers and its recent policy of restricting imports of textiles, clothing, and footwear from developing countries based upon the justification of economic defense.

Sweden's Textile Policy and Economic Defense

The decline of Sweden's textile and clothing production, coupled with increasing imports, led to an increasingly protectionist trade policy within the framework of the Multi-Fibre Arrangement (MFA). Although the arrangement in certain respects contradicts the basic principle of the liberal trade system (*i.e.,* most-favored-nation treatment), the MFA was negotiated under the auspices of the GATT. The background of the MFA, in fact, can be traced to the establishment of the GATT in 1947. Pressure was then applied by the textile and clothing manufacturers in the major industrial countries to achieve selective protection from imports. Beginning with the United States, this pressure led eventually to the signing in 1962 of a special international agreement on cotton textile trade, the "Short Term Arrangement." This agreement was renewed a year later as the "Long Term Arrangement." Eventually, it became the MFA, which now has a history of over 25 years.

The essential feature of the MFA was a set of rules to govern the negotiation of bilateral agreements to fix quotas for the textile trade. Originally, this special framework was designed to allow the textile industries of the major industrialized countries some time in which to adjust to new competition from the developing world, particularly from Asia. It soon became the firm conviction of producer groups within the industrialized countries that the export oriented policies of some developing countries—together with their allies among policy-makers—had led to a "flood" of low-cost goods into their markets. According to the manufacturers, the resultant market disruptions had led to increasing unemployment at home and had created the political necessity for countervailing action.

In Sweden, the initial demands for protection were based (as elsewhere in the industrialized world) upon rising unemployment levels within the textile sector. When the MFA was negotiated in 1973, however, an argument for a "minimum viable production" (MVP), based upon security reasons, was added.

The MVP clause, which provided an exception to the 6 percent growth rate stipulated in the MFA, was included to meet the interests of the Nordic countries as a whole. The clause provides for additional restraint (lower growth rates) in order to avoid damage to the "minimum viable production" of countries which have "small markets," an "exceptionally high level of imports," and a "correspondingly low level of production." (See Table 3.)

Given these factors, it was believed that the absorption capacity might be affected if imports were allowed to grow at 6 percent. Instead, import growth should be regulated to keep pace with product and market growth. The primary concern of the Nordic countries—Finland, Norway, and Sweden—was that the domestic production of textiles had reached a level below which, for political, social, and, particularly in the case of Sweden, perceived strategic or security reasons, it should not be allowed

Table 3. Imports of Yarn, Textiles, etc. *(except clothing)*

Ranking			1985 figures	
1980	1985	Imports from	in Skr (millions)	Share %
1	1	West Germany	1059	16.8
2	2	Great Britain	523	8.3
5	3	France	442	7.0
7	4	Italy	426	6.7
6	5	Belgium/Luxemburg	390	6.2
3	6	Finland	362	5.7

Source: *Utrikeshandel och handelspolitik 1986* [Foreign Trade and Trade Politics], (Stockholm: National Board of Trade, 1986) p. 166.

to fall. This minimum production has also been described as "vital for the basic needs of the population."

Sweden also applied the economic security argument to the footwear sector in 1975. However, because footwear was not included in the MFA, Sweden was obliged instead to consider invoking one of the two safeguard measures within the GATT. At a GATT meeting in October 1975, Sweden's representative informed the council of Sweden's intention to introduce a global import quota system for leather shoes, plastic shoes, and rubber boots, because of the sustained downward trend of Swedish shoe production and the rising number of imports. Because these developments were viewed as a "threat to the planning of Sweden's economic defense," the Swedish government decided that the import quotas would have to be applied "in conformity with the spirit of Article XXI" (GATT, 1975). The initiative sparked such serious objections, however, that Sweden reversed itself and decided in the end not to invoke Article XXI. Instead, Sweden sought other avenues through which to protect its footwear industry.

The application of the "MVP" to the Swedish clothing industry was not seriously contested until after 1977. Then, bilateral agreements between Sweden and the developing countries increased both in number and in scope.

After the world recession of the mid-1970s deepened, Sweden began to broadly interpret the MVP clause and extended its application well beyond the growth provisions. Sweden soon became recognized as one of the most restrictive of all industrialized countries in the textile and clothing sectors. It has only recently begun to liberalize this trade.

From the viewpoint of political necessity, it is not difficult to understand why the Swedes and, for that matter, most of the importing countries, imposed these restrictive measures. First, the countries had the legal means to do so. Second, they faced compelling domestic pressures. In Sweden, however, the protectionist inclinations likely sprang from at least two other sources—that of the perceived need for security based upon the principles of social welfare and that of the unique requirements of an independent security policy.

Welfare

For most of its postwar history, Sweden has been governed by the Social Democratic Party. One of the priorities in Sweden's economic policy, therefore, has been the maintenance of high levels of employment together with a wage policy of "solidarity" which was designed to equalize wages. The trade union movement has been exceptionally robust and well organized. These facts have contributed to the pressures on the government to intervene in the maintenance of an active labor market and to provide strong regional policies. Although the original trade union policy supported free trade, the worsening situation in the textile and clothing industries of the 1970s, as well as the apparent inadequacy of government subsidies to relieve unemployment, led to strong pressures to protect these industries through trade restrictive measures (Weidung, 1987).

Moreover, the government's wage policy of solidarity actually led to a levelling out of wages in the total labor force. Therefore, wages for the traditionally lower-paid textile and clothing workers increased and led to higher prices, as well as reduced competitiveness, for domestically manufactured clothing and textiles. Indeed, Sweden's labor costs within these sectors are among the highest in the world. Despite support for the wage policy, the Swedish government believes that the cost discrepancy between Swedish-produced goods and those produced in the developing countries is so great that it may be impossible to compete, solely on a price basis. This is one of the main justifications for the quotas imposed on the developing countries as opposed to the industrialized world.

National Security

Whether or not Sweden's trade policy has effectively prevented the extinction of the Swedish clothing industry is an open question. What is clear is that some major weaknesses have surfaced in the security argument for protectionism.

The decline of Swedish self-sufficiency in the textile and clothing industries is virtually indisputable. At the beginning of World War II, Sweden was about eighty percent self-sufficient in clothing. Today, the

Table 4. Imports of Clothing

Ranking			1985 figures	
1980	1985	Imports from	in Skr (millions)	Share %
1	1	Finland	1155	12.0
2	2	Hong Kong	1129	11.7
4	3	Denmark	1113	11.6
6	4	Italy	972	10.1
3	5	Great Britain	934	9.7
5	6	Portugal	910	9.4

Source: *Utrikeshandel och handelspolitik 1986* [Foreign Trade and Trade Politics], (Stockholm: National Board of Trade, 1986) p. 167.

situation is the reverse. Nearly eighty percent of Sweden's total consumption of clothing is provided by imports. There is a very legitimate concern that Swedish clothing industry may disappear altogether unless some drastic steps are taken.

The importance of clothing is undeniable. Clothing has always been considered a basic need, along with food and shelter. The risk of wartime shortages, then, particularly for a neutral country without allied sources, would seem to be a very valid consideration.

Given that Sweden's preoccupation with security is legitimate (it clearly is), there are at least three considerations which weaken the credibility of the security argument for trade restrictions. First, trade restrictions on clothing imposed under the MVP clause of the MFA are directed against *low-priced* imports. These restrictions, however, do not prevent the importation of higher priced goods from the other EFTA countries or from North America. Although more expensive than the foreign goods of the developing world, these products may *still be somewhat cheaper than Swedish goods*. The reduction of trade barriers in Europe, which Sweden fought so hard to obtain, is not negotiable. In the case of other industrialized countries, imports are not restricted because of the ever-present risk of retaliation. In fact, imports from the industrialized countries now make up the vast majority of Swedish clothing imports, as much as *seventy* percent.

Viewed from this perspective, then, Swedish production may decline anyway and Sweden's self-sufficiency in textiles and imports may be no more "secure" than if the restrictions had not been imposed in the first place. To the contrary, restrictions on lower-cost goods may trigger a shift by the developing countries to those categories of higher-priced goods that Sweden produces and, thereby, increasing the already tight competition. Sweden's security problem, then, primarily arises within the context of its free trade agreements with the industrialized countries, rather than its trade policies toward the developing world.

Second, a policy should, above all, ensure the provision of basic materials. However, no restrictions are placed on the imports of such materials as cotton, wool, synthetic fibers, or fabrics. It seems, then, that during a blockade or other crisis, Swedish authorities expect continuous inflows of raw textile materials, *but not of finished clothing!* While it is true that stocks of raw materials are maintained, the considerable costs limit their size. During World War II, Sweden's economic defense policy concentrated not only on stockpiling, but on increasing the availability of such raw materials as linen, wool, and cellulose fibers, as well. The reverse seems to be the policy today, even though import dependence upon such raw materials has not decreased.

Although this policy may seem paradoxical from the standpoint of national security, there is one plausible political explanation to support the inconsistency of the argument. Textile firms were among the first to go through a labor reduction or "rationalization" process. However, it was not until the clothing firms began their steep decline that the government began its intervention process. This may stem from the fact that clothing firms were much more labor-intensive than textile firms and could, therefore, generate more union support.

It is also evident from a number of surveys that the amount of clothing already owned by most citizens far exceeds the minimum basic needs for a three-year war. It is also clear that a number of home furnishings could quite easily be used to make clothing if the supply sank to dangerously low levels. Furthermore, clothing production is not dependent upon the continuous operation of machinery, but can be set-up and dismantled more easily than many types of production—certainly more easily than the technologically sophisticated textile machinery.

Finally, the economic defense provided by clothing must be weighed against that of other sectors of the economy. Sweden, as a small country, is dependent upon a wide variety of imports for its well-being, especially petrochemicals and certain components of high technology. Yet, it is impossible to guarantee a three-year supply (the goal for clothing) for oil or for many other vital goods.

Technological developments, although blamed by many economists for reduced employment, have greatly improved production possibilities both in the variety of goods produced and the flexibility with which it can be done. This should contribute positively to the enhancement of economic security.

Economic Security and
the Contemporary Trading Order

Sweden has been confronted with the recurring tensions between the commitment, on the one hand, to promote the liberalization of trade and to support the international obligations of the GATT and, on the other, to face the increasing demands for economic security, not only for traditional defense purposes, but also for the social welfare of the nation as a whole. Although the conflict between these policy goals has earlier origins, it only became apparent as a result of a series of economic shocks during the 1970s.

For a long time, Sweden was able to sustain the belief that there was no fundamental conflict between a liberal trade policy and economic security. So long as the GATT system functioned well, there was no need to question the foundations of the liberal trading order nor its domestic counterpart. Growth and prosperity vindicated the theoretical division between politics and commerce. For Sweden, in particular, the success of the system also contributed to the official belief, on the one hand, that the political stance of neutrality was not in conflict with the commercial system and, on the other, that security was not an issue of relevance to trade.

Despite the fact that GATT was dominated by Western capitalist states, the commercial world was never expected to have permanent ideological divisions, nor was it to be divided according to levels of development. Therefore, no conflict was envisaged between neutrality, aid to developing countries, and liberal trade obligations. In fact, a policy of liberal trade was positively required in order maintain the economic prosperity and strength necessary for upholding a credible policy of non-alliance as well as for maintaining a generous assistance policy. However, general economic prosperity for a long time masked the contradiction between principles of the universal market and those of what was, in effect, a preferential system of Western security and European integration.

To a certain point, Sweden was a beneficiary of its economic interdependence with the West. In fact, along with other small market economies, Sweden is exceptionally dependent upon international trade and exports more than forty percent of its industrial production. If one looks at specific sectors within Sweden's economy, this fact becomes even more pronounced. These exports are concentrated in certain sectors and companies. Moreover, much of this export depends on a regular flow of imported components and raw materials, including oil.

During the 1960s and 1970s, Sweden's trade in goods increased tremendously. As a percentage of GNP, Swedish exports came to nineteen percent in 1960 and increased to twenty-five percent by 1980. Corresponding figures for imports are twenty-two and twenty-seven percent, respectively (Radetzki, 1981). Discounting the large percentage of service trade in the GNP, these figures are even higher.

Swedish companies are becoming increasingly multinational. The twenty largest Swedish multinationals account for at least forty percent of Sweden's industrial exports and for at least sixty percent of private investment in research and development. Similarly, foreign ownership in Sweden is on the rise (Agrell, 1984). Sweden's efforts to broaden and facilitate relations with Europe resulted in an interdependence which has ultimately proved to be much more damaging to Sweden's economic security than the apparent threat of Third World imports.

In fact, Sweden's response to interdependence has been complicated by its special relationship with the developing countries. This relationship is not dictated by strategic or even economic motives, although there is a convenient symmetry between Swedish neutrality and Third World non-alignment. Both economic and, in a broad sense, strategic benefits may, therefore, accrue from it. For this reason and because of the generous aid and development programs run by the Swedes, it has gained respect in the Third World. The extension of Sweden's economic defense policies to include protectionist measures may, however, seriously affect the export possibilities of the developing countries and, therefore, undermine the special relationship.

This tension between Sweden's deliberate courting of the Third World countries and an economic defense policy in which Third World countries are the main target of Swedish protection, is central. The contradictory nature of the Swedish position has been brought to the fore as it became evident that economic security arguments have been used precisely against those countries with which interdependence is most tenuous rather than against those countries with whom interdependence is the actual problem. Thus, the "solution" to the challenge of the EEC, namely the establishment of the European Free Trade Area, was an ironic one. One reason why, of course, Third World countries are singled out for protection is that the harder it became for the original member states of the GATT to impose trade restrictions on one another, the greater was the temptation to seek a target from the outside world. But if the attempt to resolve the problem of overall security in the case of textiles under the MFA failed, it is not clear how this issue can best be handled within the existing trading system in this sector or, indeed, in any other.

Notes

1. The safeguard articles in the GATT include: XI(2c), XII, XVIII(2), XIX, XX, XXI, XXV, XXVI, XXVII, and XXVIII.

References

Adler-Karlsson, G. (1968) *Western Economic Warfare.* Stockholm: Almquist & Wiksell.

Agrell, Wilhelm (1984) *Sveriges civila säkrhet.* Stockholm: Liber.

Andersson, Sten (1987) "Speech to the Uppsala Students' Union," *The Economist.* 21 November.

Andrén, Nils and Åke Landquist (1965) *Svensk Utrikespolitik efter 1945.* Stockholm: Almquist & Wiksell.

Barnes, Ian (1980) "The Changing Nature of the Swedish Aid Relationship during the Social Democratic Period of Government," *Cooperation and Conflict.* Vol. XV, No. 3, pp. 140–150.

Brown, Jr., William Adam (1950) *The United States and the Restoration of World Trade.* Washington, D.C.: The Brookings Institution.

Dam, Kenneth (1970) *The GATT: Law and International Economic Organization.* Chicago, IL: University of Chicago Press.

Fox, Annette Baker (1959) *The Power of Small States.* Chicago, IL: University of Chicago Press.

GATT (1975) *Document C/M/109.* 10 November.

Holmström, Mikael and Tom von Sivers (1985) *USA's exportkontroll-tekniken som vapen.* Stockholm: Ingenjörsförlaget AB.

Hoover, John (1956) "East-West Trade," in *Department of State Bulletin.* 9 April, p. 620.

Kärre, Bo (1956) "International Organizations in the Economic Field," in Swedish Institute of International Affairs, eds. *Sweden and the United Nations.* New York: Manhattan Publishing Company.

Kock, Karin (1969) *International Trade Policy and the GATT 1947–67.* Stockholm: Almquist & Wiksell.

Martin, Andrew (1979) "The Dynamics of Change in a Keynesian Political Economy: The Swedish Case and Its Implications." in Colin Crouch, ed. *State and Economy in Contemporary Capitalism.* London: Croom Helm.

Månsson, Olle (1976) *Industriell beredskap och ekonomisk försvarsberedskap inför andra världskriget.* Stockholm: Liberförlag.

Ohlin, Bertil (1959) *Utrikeshandel och handelspolitik.* Stockholm: Natur och Kultur.

Radetzki, Marian (1981) *Sverige avskärmat.* Stockholm: Studieförbundet Näringsliv och Samhälle.

SOU 1979:42.

The Economist. 7 April 1956.

Tumlir, Jan (1974) "Emergency Action Against Sharp Increases in Imports," in Hugh Corbet and Robert Jackson, eds. *In Search of a New World Economic Order.* London: Croom Helm.

Weidung, Anders (1987) *Frihandelns dilemma.* Ph.D. Dissertation, Uppsala, Sweden: Department of Government, University of Uppsala.

6

Welfare Abroad:
Swedish Development Assistance

Susan L. Holmberg

And then there are the Swedes,
the darlings of the Third World,
Whose good works are matched only by
their glutinous smugness.

— Maurice Keens-Soper

Sweden's extensive program of development assistance to the Third World is both broad-based and far-reaching. Indeed, Sweden has ranked among the top three donor nations in the world since the early 1970s. In sharp contrast, the United States ranks last among Organization for Economic Cooperation and Development (OECD) countries.

The strong commitment to development assistance almost seems paradoxical considering that Sweden has had little, if any, historical interaction with the Third World. For example, Sweden is not a former colonial power and has not engaged in trade with the Third World to any significant extent. From a political standpoint, Sweden's security and foreign policy interest have traditionally focused upon offsetting dominant forces to its east and west.

After World War II, Sweden has been largely preoccupied with its key strategic role as the armed pillar of the high north. Economically and culturally, Sweden continues its extensive ties to the West. The political and economic factors would seem to indicate little, if any, strategic military, political, or economic interest in the developing world. The question that is inevitably begged, then, is—*Why such an extensive Swedish commitment to foreign assistance?*

Part of the explanation may lie in the importance of the United Nations to Sweden. Following World War II, the U.N. quickly became a prominent platform for Sweden's foreign policy and occupied a central—

if not pivotal—role for the active expression of Sweden's policy of non-alignment. As former colonies obtained independence during this period, the global "balance" in the U.N. General Assembly began to shift. In fact, the newly independent states had become a majority in the U.N. by 1960. Given this development, the basis existed for a Swedish Third World policy that would harmonize with its independent status in East-West relations.

Indeed, the only Swedish precedent for bilateral Third World assistance had been mission work which had a rather long history of involvement in selected African countries. Both the State Lutheran Church and the "free church" missions had engaged in development-related activity through their overall evangelical operations, but much of this involvement was indirect.

Direct economic relations with the Third World were extremely limited. In 1960, only four percent of Sweden's foreign investment assets were located in Africa and Asia combined, whereas the vast majority—some eighty-seven percent—was concentrated among the industrialized countries. Swedish Third World investment was directed to the more industrialized states in Latin America—such as Brazil—and in Africa and Asia to such countries as South Africa and Taiwan (Hermele, 1981:16).

Trade flows reflected a similar bias. As late as 1970, Sweden's exports to lesser developed countries amounted to only 11.6 percent of its yearly total, whereas the OECD average was 20.9 percent. Imports from the developing countries were even lower, with Sweden purchasing just 2.7 percent of its total imports from these countries that same year (Radetzki, 1981:76).

Thus, in the absence of significant economic and political experience, Sweden's emerging Third World aid policy was based upon charitable mission work and the framework of the United Nations and the World Bank for technical and financial assistance, respectively. Although these channels were of limited scope, they superceded direct political and economic experience and allowed plenty of room for indulgence in broad idealistic imperatives.

Reflecting early Swedish aspirations for development, Swedish economist Gunnar Myrdal called for increased integration of the global economy and for the eradication of nationalistic protectionist thinking. He argued that this shift would contribute to the economic growth of underdeveloped countries relative to wealthier ones, and that a "substantial increase in the bargaining power of the poor countries is necessary for attaining a new situation of world stability" (Myrdal, 1960:236). Accepting stability as a central objective, Myrdal contends that "in the longer range . . . our hope of world stability is dependent upon the underdeveloped countries using all the means at their disposal to increase their strength and power" (1960:238). This theme was echoed by Myrdal's influential contemporary, Dag Hammarskjöld, who was Secretary General of the United Nations during much of the 1950s. Hammarskjöld also promoted the national strength of the small and newly independent states for the cause of world peace and stability. Like Myrdal, Hammarskjöld believed that the appropriate means to this end entailed a more evenly distributed balance of global power.[1]

Without a history tarnished by colonialist exploitation, Sweden was in an unusual position to initiate fresh, positive relations with these countries. The mutual benefits of such relations are apparent from several perspectives. From a political standpoint, increased relations might help to offset superpower influence and thereby promote the goals of non-alignment and solidarity. From an economic standpoint, the extension of assistance would help the developing countries' economies which would, in turn, stimulate growth in the global economy. Reflecting a "Marshall Plan" mentality, the foundation of the Swedish assistance program—Government Bill 1962, No. 100—states that through the promotion of economic growth, these countries might eventually be able to participate in fruitful trade and investment relations in the future.

As more new states emerged, Sweden reacted by adopting a Third World policy motivated by impulses of humanitarian concern and solidarity. The goal was a more equitable distribution of global political and economic resources.

> Injustice in the distribution of the world's resources gives rise to tensions and conflicts within and between nations. An important task for Swedish foreign policy is to contribute to equality and greater understanding between peoples, and through this to promote international solidarity and a peaceful development in the world. Our active support to the United Nations is one aspect of this policy. (SOU, 1968:128)

The relatively high generosity of Sweden's foreign aid—both rhetorical and real—has led to Sweden's characterization as a "darling of the Third World." Any "smugness" that Sweden may exhibit most likely stems from the widely-maintained Swedish view that not only is its aid program *justly* motivated, but its goals are more democratic and humane than those of most other donor countries, as well.

This essay will examine Swedish development assistance within the context of its domestic foundations—*the principles of welfare in Sweden*. The goals and structure of foreign assistance will then be assessed and will be related to the various domestic, multilateral, and bilateral arenas in which they function.

The Principles of Swedish Welfare
at Home and Abroad

Although the development of foreign aid policy was directly linked to mission work, to multilateral cooperation, and to the nature of commercial and political relations, each of these conditions was filtered through the prism of Sweden's welfare state experience. Foreign aid, in effect, became an extension of Sweden's domestic welfare policy. One parliamentarian observed that "foreign aid is a mark of universal humanity" and further noted that Sweden could not "conduct a welfare policy without an international dimension."[2]

The parallels and distinctions between Sweden's domestic and "international" welfare systems become much clearer when examined against the backdrop of Sweden's welfare principles. To facilitate the analysis, the welfare ambition is divided into two dimensions—growth and distribution.

Growth and distribution refer to the acquisition and allocation of wealth, respectively. Although "pure" welfare is, in a sense, associated with the distributive aspect, it is also apparent that this component would not be possible without a strong economic base. In order for the system as a whole to work properly, *both* components must be present and functioning.

Samuelson (1975:335) lists six primary values that are associated with the distributive aspects of Swedish welfare. These values are

1. humanitarianism or mercy,
2. resocialization or rehabilitation,
3. integration,
4. solidarity,
5. equality and justice, and
6. social security.

Although these themes overlap in many policy areas, they also follow to an extent the evolution of Sweden's welfare system. These themes are generally self-explanatory, although solidarity and equality have acquired a distinctive "Swedish" flavor.

Solidarity implies a common responsibility for all citizens and to all citizens—a brotherhood of humanity. Solidarity suggests a vertical transfer of resources from rich to poor, and manifests itself, in the imagery of Samuelson, as a "gigantic insurance company for all citizens" (1975:346). Equality implies a decrease in the inequities of economic, social, and cultural conditions and the ultimate attainment of equal opportunity, wealth, and power. It should be noted that equalization within the

Swedish context tends to focus upon equality *among,* not within, groups. Some examples of this may be the equality that exists between the rich and the poor, men and women, employees and employers, or the young and the old.

According to Danish professor Bent Rold Andersen, these themes are oriented toward "dignifying the common man so that he feels on an equal footing with the rich and the famous" (1984:111). Some of the concrete policy implications include the availability of social insurance based upon residency rather than income or occupation, a more equal distribution of wealth through progressive income taxation, and the equal allocation of education, health care, and social services that have been described as "more extensive than in any non-socialist society" (Andersen, 1984:109). The objective of Swedish welfare, then, is the reduction and elimination of social, economic, and political disparities. Such ideals as democracy, individual rights, and the responsibility of community (government) to the individual are integral concepts within Sweden's welfare system.

To provide these services reliably on a national scale requires a substantial economic base. Thus, the growth dimension of the welfare system encourages private capital gain. In this regard, the Swedish policies for economic growth are ultimately pragmatic and rationalistic. Economic activities are geared to market conditions and to competitive industries. Sweden's system may be characterized as that of a "mixed economy" in which private capital fuels economic growth and pays for a welfare distribution policy that, in turn, counters the inequalities generated by growth (Lewin, 1975:335).

The International Mirror
of Swedish Domestic Policy

The international "mirror image" of Sweden's domestic welfare system is reflected within the dimensions of distribution and of growth. International trade and investment represent growth, whereas development assistance represents distribution. As in the domestic arena, the distributive policy of development assistance requires a healthy economy. Because Sweden is so dependent upon external markets for its own economic growth, the premise that foreign aid is based upon international capital accumulation is logical.

Sweden's international resource flow tends to support the "mirror" argument. Regarding capital accumulation, it should again be noted that Sweden's commercial relations are heavily biased in favor of industrialized countries. Indeed, most of the Third World transactions are concentrated among the newly-industrialized countries (NIC's). The lack of idealistic motives in matters of growth is illustrated by a distinct policy bias against poor countries through protectionist trade barriers. These barriers have not been reduced despite the increased visibility of Swedish development assistance and the progressive-sounding, altruistic rhetoric (Dahlgren, 1976:7–15). In fact, Sweden joins other industrialized countries in opposing Third World demands for an indexation of export items and contributes to the closing of agricultural export markets to the Third World through the sale of agricultural surplus through aid channels (Dahlgren, 1976:12).

In financial markets, a certain bias—albeit less intentional—also exists. During the mid-1970s, Sweden's temporary requirements for borrowed capital may have contributed to the crowding out of poorer nations from the financial markets, because of Sweden's competitive edge as a better credit risk.

One aid official characterizes the nature of Sweden's Third World policy in terms of "Dr. Jekyll and Mr. Hyde." He questions how such a policy can be conducted without a dissenting voice from the so-called "aid opinion" in Sweden (Goppers, 1984:107–18). One might also question why such a "schizophrenic" characterization was suggested in the first place. After all, isn't this the mirror image of Sweden's domestic welfare policy? In reality, this may well be the case, but in the minds of many Swedes, the international welfare "system" should have only *one* component—distribution.

Because of its presumed altruistic character, foreign assistance has a much higher idealistic profile than either trade or investment policy. Certainly, broader constituencies are involved in the support of the aid budget. Aid is the component of the mirror image that seemingly penetrates the public eye, and its image is primarily that of a distributive welfare expenditure based upon the welfare principles of solidarity, humanitarianism, and equity.

In contrast to the rationalistic growth motives of trade and of investment policy, the government bill of 1962 that established the official aid program states that the underlying motive for assistance is based upon a moral imperative "to raise the living standards of the poor." In effect, this provides the mandate for the Swedish state to act as a welfare distributor abroad. Indeed, the idea to "help those in acute need" formed an integral part of this proposal. A strong element of mission-inspired humanitarianism was combined with the more secular spirit of solidarity. Another welfare theme that has also gained prominence is the principle of equality as it relates to the distribution of power and of wealth.

In applying its welfare principles internationally, the Swedish government has acted to expand its welfare community to include recipient countries. For instance, these countries are often portrayed as extensions of Sweden's political culture during debates on the aid budget.[3] The extension of the welfare community, however, actually goes deeper than this. The poor countries should not only receive welfare inputs from Sweden, but should—as much as possible—*reproduce the Swedish welfare system within their borders.* This extension provides an external legitimation for Sweden's domestic welfare system.

In principle, the Swedish "aid model" of the early 1970s represented an ideal for assistance programs. Sweden, as a donor country, needed only to plant the seeds of welfare and let them grow.[4] Throughout the years, however, this ideal has been severely tested by numerous complexities, both in Sweden as well as in the recipient countries. The distribution *principles,* however, have not been abandoned. The discussions have instead centered upon the adjustment of the means to meet the desired ends. In order to reach the poor and to improve welfare delivery, Swedish aid has become more project oriented. More direct Swedish intervention and oversight have also been applied. Because of Sweden's own economic needs, the benefits that foreign assistance can provide to Swedish industry has also received greater emphasis. The boundary separating aid from commercial gain has been transcended with the result that a "crisis" of identity, of principle, of purpose, and, particularly, of means within Swedish assistance has developed.[5]

Boundaries Cognitive and Real

Sweden's development assistance can be conceptualized as one component of the international extension of its domestic welfare system. Within this context, it seems reasonable that the gaps between rhetoric and reality should reflect the conflicts in the perceptions of political, economic, and social boundaries among the actors that constitute the "aid community."[6]

Figure 1 presents a conceptualization of the cognitive boundaries of growth and distribution at different levels of welfare system operation. Although this chart is a simplified representation, it does convey some essential distinctions.

The third welfare category—the "ideal global"—represents the long-term, ultimate achievement of assistance objectives. This concept, in fact, is manifested at different levels of Swedish political thought.[7] The dream of the "global village" that includes a universal allocative body (*e.g.,* a strengthened United Nations), as well as a global progressive taxation, is a powerful driving metaphor for ideal global welfare. It represents the achievement of total solidarity and equity. Capital is accumulated from profitable sources and is distributed justly and evenly among the world's population. This model assumes free trade and, in some respects, is

Figure 1. Cognitive Boundaries of Growth/Distribution at Different Levels of Welfare System Operation

	Capital (Growth)		Welfare (Distribution)	
Level of Operation	*for*	*from*	*for*	*from*
Domestic Welfare	Swedes	Anyone	Swedes	Swedes
Development Welfare	Swedes	Anyone	LDCs	Swedes
Ideal Global Welfare	Everyone	Everyone	Everyone	Everyone

Source: Susan L. Holmberg

reminiscent of Myrdal's ideas regarding integrated economic planning. The global welfare ideal is also comprehensive in that it represents just distribution both *within* and *between* countries.

Many of the difficulties for Swedish development assistance stem from from the incongruities between the horizontal and the vertical boundaries. Within the Swedish domestic welfare system, interests are relatively clear and justifiable. The same could also be said for the global ideal model, because the communities are theoretically united. However, certain conflicts of interest appear at the development welfare level. Here, capital is accumulated for the Swedish economy (to provide the economic base for a foreign aid program), yet distributed to an external recipient group. If Swedish foreign aid was not guided by such strong welfare principles (and if the global welfare ideal was not included in the repertoire of Swedish thought), this incongruity would not be problematic. Foreign assistance would simply be a minor expenditure—a minor political issue— and its budget would swing according to the health of the domestic economy and the demands for welfare services by the domestic population.

Figure 1 illustrates the incongruities of Swedish aid. On the one hand, the inconsistencies result from the "loss" of capital from Sweden to recipient countries, and, on the other, from the fact that capital must be acquired from the outside world to fuel the Swedish economy. This may generate confusion in terms of both goals and identity. If the aid budget is sustained during a decline in the domestic economy, this can only be justified through an expansion of the cognitive welfare community which recognizes recipient countries as "rightful" beneficiaries of aid and emphasizes the "responsibility" of Sweden to these countries. In other words, the welfare bond between the state and its "clients" abroad must be strengthened.

In fact, this is largely how the argument proceeds in Sweden. Because the recipient countries are not an integral part of the Swedish economy, it is maintained that they should not have to bear the burden of Sweden's economic difficulties through a reduction of their aid allocations. However, this argument reveals the weakness of the one-sided projection of Swedish welfare principles into the global arena. Because these countries are viewed as unequal and helpless, they are not expected to contribute to Sweden's development. This formulation is somewhat hypocritical, at least with regard to the ideas of solidarity and equity among countries. By excluding the poor countries from the growth dimension of the welfare system, Swedish welfare idealists or "purists" believe that they are somehow contributing to a proper form of development.

This one-sided approach to Third World relations may have resulted from Sweden's own experience with economic and political development. Swedish policy-makers assumed that what happened in Sweden would happen in recipient countries. It was assumed that the educated leaders in recipient countries would act "rationally" and would, therefore, be able to distribute aid resources "properly" (*i.e.* equitably by prioritizing the most needy). In other words, they were expected to act as Swedish political leaders and bureaucrats would act. Aid policy also assumed greater level of cultural homogeneity and social harmony than existed within the recipient countries. A somewhat naive belief was held that the colonial masters were the only truly divisive element within society and that the indigenous people were as culturally unified as Sweden. Other assumptions concerned the degree of institutional and infrastructural development within the countries. In Sweden, industrialization occurred during a time when most of the people could already read and the entire country had already been "bureaucratized" by a legitimate and respected government. These were crucial preconditions for welfare in Sweden, and they could not be reproduced in any of the developing countries of the 1960s or 1970s.

Despite these realizations, however, Sweden has retained the distributive welfare ideal in its assistance policies. Sweden has also taken steps to ensure that these ideals have a better chance of success in the Third World. This has involved a shift away from the recipient *governments* to that of recipient *groups* as the primary target for assistance. In several ways, then, the encroachment of the growth component of welfare has been countered with a stepped-up effort on the part of the Swedish government to play a more direct role in the distribution of aid to the populations of foreign (and sovereign) states.

The Global Setting
of Swedish Foreign Assistance

The connection between the global economy and Sweden's capacity to maintain an extensive aid commitment is an obvious point, but is sometimes taken for granted. Nearly twenty-five percent of Sweden's GNP results from exports. Therefore, Sweden's economy is highly susceptible to changes within world market conditions. During favorable economic circumstances, Sweden can afford to generously disburse foreign assistance. This was the case during the economic growth of the 1960s when Sweden's official foreign assistance program was taking shape.

It was during this period that the one percent goal for development assistance was adopted. By the time the Swedish aid budget finally approached this target (the mid-1970s), the Swedish economy had begun to feel the effects of the energy crisis and international recession. For the first time in decades, the Swedish government was forced to borrow internationally. The increasing constraints on the Swedish economic resources generated by the global recession, together with the consequent drops in Swedish exports, prompted new debates about the effectiveness of the greatly expanded foreign aid resources.

Prior to the domestic economic crunch, the foreign assistance debates tended to be highly ideological in tone and largely emphasized Swedish welfare principles. The "loss" of Swedish resources through aid was not considered to be a key factor. In 1972, a report by the Industrial Aid Commission succinctly outlined the idealistic distinction between aid and trade.

> Private investment in developing countries are in the first place a commercial matter, as is trade with these countries. Seller, investors, as well as buyers make transactions for the main purpose of making a profit. The purpose of development assistance on the contrary is only to support the development of the recipient country. (SOU 1972:90)

This statement predates the Third World call for a New International Economic Order (NIEO) which aspired to create more equitable relations between the rich and poor countries. Certainly, NIEO's objectives seemed to fit in well with the Swedish notions of equality and solidarity. The economic realities of the mid-1970s, however, did not. Yet even during the 1976/77 parliamentary session, the Foreign Affairs Committee of Parliament argued that it was "still necessary to make the distinction between public aid and commercial transactions with developing countries" (UU, 1976/77:17).

Although the "true" relationship between economic conditions and foreign aid policy is difficult to ascertain, it is apparent that in Sweden's case a dramatically increased budget, coupled with a serious domestic economic downturn, contributed to a reassessment not only of Sweden's development assistance policy, but its role in the Third World as well.

The Multilateral Arena

Given the ideal of a global welfare community, it seems reasonable that Sweden would shift its aid resources into the multilateral arena during situations of international recession. Would not this channel be the best choice to effect the "mass transfer of resources" from the rich countries to the poor? In theory, this may be correct, but in reality this is not the case. It is in the arena of multilateral cooperation that one can detect the Swedish disappointment in and frustration with the global welfare ideal. In this case, the Swedish "smugness" alluded to at the outset of this essay shows through.

During recent years, member state contributions to the World Bank's International Development Assistance (IDA) division have dropped off considerably in real terms. The Swedish government soundly criticized the industrialized countries for their lack of support for the World Bank.

It is indefensible that the international financial system is weakened in this way when the critical conditions in developing countries necessitate increased inputs in the transactions between donor and recipient countries (Prop. 1984/85:47).

This criticism stems from the fact Sweden, unlike other donor countries, has maintained its general level of support to multilateral agencies even in times of recession. SIDA head Carl Tham, a former Minister of Development Assistance, made the following, rather pointed, observation:

It is a strange situation if Scandinavian countries and the Netherlands are to answer for the major part of contributions to the U.N. agencies. It is unreasonable that Sweden should be the third largest contributor to several agencies (Jellenik, 1984:374).

In fact, the four Scandinavian countries together provide nearly twenty-five percent of the funds for the United Nations Development Program (UNDP). Other agencies that receive disproportionally large Scandinavian contributions are the Food and Agricultural Organization (FAO), the World Health Organization (WHO). and the United Nations Children's Fund (UNICEF). It seems that only Sweden and a few other small countries are living up to the "global welfare" responsibility.

Sweden, however, still regards multilateral organizations with a certain ambivalence. On the one hand, this assistance channel provides a forum for the smaller states to promote international ccoperation and the development of international norms. This is particularly important to the small neutral states whose arenas for joint action are more circumscribed. On the other hand, multilateral agencies are often criticized as being highly inefficient bureaucracies whose appropriateness as vehicles for "proper" Swedish assistance is highly doubtful.

The Swedish response to the contributions of international donor agencies depends on the degree to which multilateral assistance harmonizes with the policy goals of Swedish aid. One example of a multilateral influence that has met this criteria is the concept of the "forgotten forty percent," *i.e.,* the percentage of the world's population estimated to be living in absolute poverty. This group was quickly targeted by Swedish aid officials for development assistance. This orientation was in keeping with the objectives of equality and democratic social development.

In addition, the "basic needs" and "program countries" strategies also supported the Swedish assistance goals of political and economic independence for the recipient in that they implied less control over the aid resources by the donor. The basic needs approach was first articulated by the World Bank during the 1970s and focused primarily upon the provision of food, shelter, basic health care, and education to mostly rural populations. Sweden embraced the basic needs idea—at least in part—because of its earlier emphasis upon bilateral projects in education and health care. The basic needs approach fits in with the desire to reach the "forgotten forty percent" and supports the social and equity goals of Swedish assistance.

On the other hand, Sweden did not approve of the World Bank's refusal to support Chile's Allende government, nor of its sudden change of heart after the military coup in 1973. The Swedish government detached itself somewhat from the World Bank at this time and asserted that the Bank's policies were counter to the Swedish assistance goals of equity and democratic social development. In the Swedish view, the Allende government was an equity-oriented and popular regime, whereas the military regime that followed was not considered legitimate or desirable.

Assisting the Third World Countries

It has been argued that the Swedish welfare experience has greatly influenced both the goals and the content of Swedish foreign assistance policy. Domestic ideals and experiences are reflected in the policy's international targets and objectives. This section will examine some of the major objectives of the foreign aid program and will attempt to outline the sometimes serpentine process of turning these goals into reality.

The Basic Features
of Swedish Bilateral Assistance

When the official aid program was established in 1962, its budget amounted to a mere one tenth of one percent of GNP. By 1976, it had increased to one percent of gross national income (GNI).[8] This commitment placed Sweden squarely in the highest echelons of all donor countries. Influenced by the U.N. discussion, the 1962 parliamentary bill which established Sweden's official aid program expressed the determination (without setting a target date) to attain a one percent of GNP assistance goal. By 1968, however, the government decided that this level should be achieved by the 1974/75 fiscal year. From 1968 to 1975, the aid budget was increased dramatically until the one percent goal was achieved in 1976. This target percentage is a concrete example of Sweden's commitment to transfer a relatively large portion of its wealth to poorer countries. This level of assistance (which since has become almost sacred) is tantamount to a form of self-imposed global taxation. It has been sustained on many occasions despite downturns in the Swedish economy.

In addition to moral imperatives, the parliamentary bill of 1962 also included several substantive goals. Besides raising the living standards of the poor and helping those most in need, there was an assumption that economic growth would lead to democracy, equity, and progress. World peace and stability would naturally follow. By the late 1960s, the goals of Swedish aid were listed as

1. economic growth,
2. economic and social equity,
3. economic and political independence, and
4. development of democracy in society (Frühling, 1986:315).

By this time, the discussion had focused on what was considered the "natural" results of independence, namely equity and democracy. The main emphasis of the policy was to support the "efforts conducted in the developing countries" to increase "the living standards of the poor" with the ultimate aim of achieving a "just distribution of the world's resources." The Swedish world view, then, considers proper development to include both improved economic and political conditions, as well as increased economic and political equity. In fact, this may be regarded as a reformulation of the Swedish emphasis upon balanced welfare.

A fifth objective—the so-called "environmental goal"—has recently been passed by the Swedish parliament. According to this objective, each transfer or project must be evaluated with regard to its possible environmental impact. The articulation of a new goal after a relatively long period of time is particularly interesting and is subject to a variety of interpretations.

On the one hand, the environmental goal may be a genuine response to the spead of deforestation, floods, famine, and environmental contamination. On the other, it could be a further reflection of the domestic setting in which a recently prominent "green" party has challenged the establishment on environmental issues. This activity, as well as the traditional efforts of the Center party, have raised the profile of environmental issues both within Sweden and within the foreign aid program.

With the inclusion of an environmental goal, solidarity between Sweden and recipient governments may be jeopardized. In some cases, the objective may lead to direct confrontation with recipient governments that do not wish to elevate environmental concerns over industrialization or rapid growth. Thus, clashes of interest would seem to be inevitable once the environmental objective is implemented. It does, however, reflect Sweden's strong inclination to export its principles.

An indicator of the increased salience of foreign assistance within overall foreign policy is the expansion—both in number and in size—of the foreign aid administrative bureaucracy. In 1962, the *Nämnden för Internationellt Bistånd* (NIB) was established. Bureaucratic and political difficulties, however, led to its replacement by the Swedish International Development Authority (SIDA) in 1965. It is not insignificant that Ernst Michanek, the first successful head of the bilateral program, was appointed by virtue of his administrative experience in *domestic* welfare programs.

From these humble beginnings, Sweden's development assistance program has grown. Within the Ministry of Foreign Affairs, the sizeable Department for International Development Cooperation is responsible for multilateral assistance programs. SIDA's extensive responsibilities include bilateral relations with program countries, the administration of emergency aid and humanitarian assistance, and cooperation with voluntary associations active in the assistance area. Indeed, SIDA has been the primary arm of Swedish foreign aid from the early 1970s. It administered, on average, approximately sixty-four percent of net annual aid disbursements between 1980–1984.

In the early 1980s, a number of new administrative agencies were formed after a heated political debate. Opponents to these new entities argued that they did not represent the true interests of development, but were, instead, motivated by potential commercial gain. For this reason, it was argued that their operations should not be included in the yearly aid budget.

In any event, after nearly five years of debate, the government established the Swedish Commission for Technical Cooperation (BITS), the Special Fund for Industrial Cooperation with Developing Countries (SWED-FUND), and the Import Promotion Office for Products from Developing Countries (IMPOD). BITS administers technical cooperation and concessionary credits for Swedish exports. SWEDFUND initiates joint ventures and promotes investment cooperation. IMPOD provides support to the export promotion efforts of the developing countries. These entities are clearly more commercial in nature and tend to involve countries that are wealthier than those typically associated with SIDA's activities.[9]

Together, these activities received less than three percent of the total assistance budget outlays in 1984. Their budgets, however, have been significantly increased over the last few years. The BITS budget, in particular, has been growing at a rapid rate. In 1986/87, the BITS budget alone absorbed nearly 8.6 percent of the total assistance appropriation. In comparison, SWEDFUND accounted for only 0.6 percent.

Another agency, the Swedish Agency for Research Cooperation with Developing Countries (SAREC), was established in 1975. The purpose of SAREC is to promote research cooperation in science, technology, and development issues. Thus, SAREC's funds are distributed both within Sweden as well as internationally.

With the exception of the multilateral division located within the Ministry of Foreign Affairs, all of these agencies are—in the administrative tradition of Sweden—semi-autonomous. They are granted considerable latitude to set priorities and to allocate funds. Their budget proposals, however, must be submitted to and approved by the parliament through the Ministry of Foreign Affairs.

Foreign aid operations account for over eighty percent of the total budget of the Ministry of Foreign Affairs. Figure 2 presents the financial breakdown of the assistance program. Bilateral activities absorb the bulk of aid expenditures, even though SIDA's budget has been diminished, somewhat, by the addition of the three "commercially-oriented" assistance agencies. Multilateral expenditures, which account for less than one third of the total, have remained steady since the early 1970s. The prominence of bilateral over multilateral assistance clearly indicates the priority placed upon direct Swedish input into the international development process.

Figure 3 provides a breakdown of Swedish bilateral assistance. The major portion is absorbed by the various development agreements with the seventeen "program countries." Sweden selects these countries and negotiates renewable three-year term assistance agreements. The program country component of the assistance program is the clearest manifestation of the "Swedish model" that evolved during the late 1960s and the early 1970s. This model, referred to as "recipient-oriented" assistance, was

Figure 2. Aggregate Appropriations 1985/86

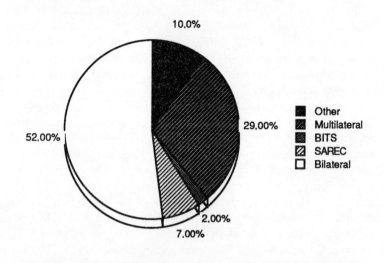

Source: Johan Åshuvud, "Statistical Review of Swedish Development Aid," in
Pierre Frühling, ed., *Swedish Development Aid in Perspective.* (Stockholm:
Almqvist and Wiksell, 1986), p. 290.

based upon sizeable financial commitments to governments on very liberal
terms and involved little project involvement and oversight. The most
important decision with respect to recipient-oriented assistance was the
selection of the program country itself. It was assumed that the correct
choice would yield results that would support the Swedish assistance
goals.

The remainder of the bilateral programs is divided fairly evenly among
the categories of humanitarian aid (mainly to southern Africa), disaster
relief, nongovernmental activities, and "other." Considerable support is
provided to areas outside the seventeen program countries. For example,
Sweden is a major source of funding for the "front-line" states and
liberation movements in southern Africa.

The prominence of import support reveals the unintended conflict
within aid transfers. Unrestricted funding for imports (extended in part
as a "recipient-oriented" gesture of solidarity to recipient governments)
rarely has the desired direct or positive impact for the poorest people
within the countries. Thus, to counter the unexpected or negative effects
of excessive and uncontrolled import support, efforts have been made
to curb large-scale industrial projects. Instead, the focus has shifted to
smaller-scale development in the rural sector that will provide basic needs

Figure 3. Bilateral Appropriations 1985/86

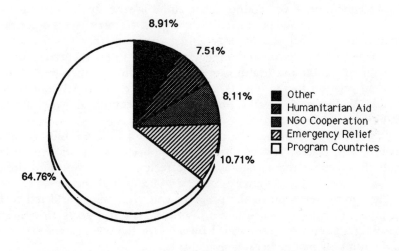

8.91%

7.51%

8.11%

■ Other
▨ Humanitarian Aid
▨ NGO Cooperation
▨ Emergency Relief
□ Program Countries

10.71%

64.76%

Source: *Prop. 1984/85, No. 100, Bilaga* [Appendix], Ministry of Foreign Affairs, p. 85.

more effectively to the poorest segments of society. In fact, a freeze on new large-scale industrial projects has been in effect during the past few years. The significant increases in humanitarian and disaster relief assistance, together with increased support of the activities of the grassroots organizations, reflect the recent trend toward prioritizing direct inputs to the most needy.

Government-Oriented Assistance

In the earliest years of aid, before the policy goals were formalized, much of its content represented an extension of the non-governmental Central Committee (CK) whose primary emphasis was on education and family planning.[10] In Sweden, education is seen as a vital part of stable democratic development. The scarcity and uneven distribution of education and training within the developing countries seemed like a crucial gap that Sweden was well-equipped to fill. Sweden had already acquired a good deal of experience with education and it was decided that through teacher training and instruction in health care and family planning, Sweden could provide relevant, as well as useful, expertise. In addition, these projects were not heavily capital-intensive and, given the limited aid budgets of the 1960s, this approach suited the program quite well.

As the aid budget increased and the policy directions became more clearly delineated, Sweden began to provide cash and industrial capital. The "recipient-oriented" country programming strategy that was adopted during the early 1970s permitted the recipient countries to allocate their aid resources as they saw fit. More often than not, they opted for pulp and paper mills, dams, and other large-scale infrastructural projects. Though education and health care projects continued, they were diminished in relation to the import support and the industrial components of aid. As Figure 4 reveals, this pattern has continued since the late 1970s.

Country programming, the strategy adopted to carry out recipient-oriented aid, places great emphasis upon political, economic, and social goals. Respect for the autonomy of the recipient government to decide the allocation of the resource transfers was a central theme.

The careful selection of the program countries was considered to be the most effective means of attaining Swedish assistance goals. In addition, the program country idea meshed nicely with the one percent target, as larger sums of money became available.

Certainly, the selection of the program countries is the most *political,* as well as critical, decision in the implementation of the recipient-oriented policy. Once selected, the relationship becomes long-term and involves large resource allocations. Because of its extended nature, this relationship represents an unusual degree of confidence by the donor toward the recipient.

The process of country selection was guided by the degree to which the recipient country pursued an "equity-oriented" development plan. Because of this conceptualization, most of Sweden's new program countries were socialist in orientation, and many of them had just emerged from liberation struggles. Cuba, Tanzania, Mozambique, Angola, Vietnam, and Nicaragua are prime examples of this category. India, Pakistan, Tunisia, Ethiopia, and Kenya, on the other hand, were awarded program country status largely as an extension of prior aid relations with Sweden. Because of their relative wealth, Pakistan and Tunisia were dropped during the mid-1970s upon the completion of their assistance agreements. Cuba was dropped for both economic and political reasons in 1976.

The war in Vietnam served as a catalyst for the politicization of Swedish foreign aid policy. Before the war ended, Sweden entered into aid negotiations with the North Vietnamese government. Because North Vietnam was viewed as a struggling, war-torn country that was trying to unify, it fit the Swedish assistance goals of economic and political independence. Its government was regarded as popular and Sweden believed that the north had both the capacity, as well as the desire, to develop a system of democracy and equity in the country as a whole.

Figure 4. SIDA Aid by Sector

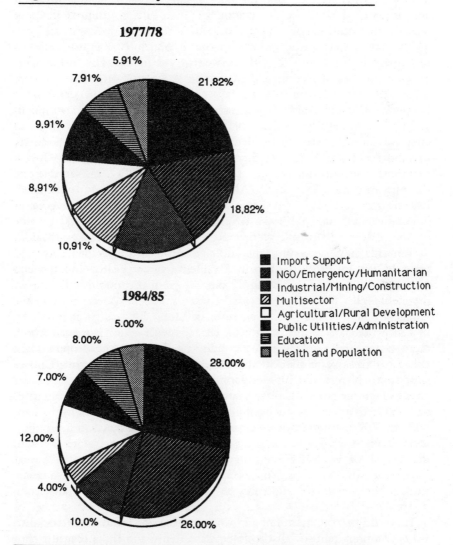

1977/78

5.91%
7,91%
9.91%
8.91%
10.91%
21.82%
18,82%

■ Import Support
▨ NGO/Emergency/Humanitarian
▨ Industrial/Mining/Construction
▨ Multisector
□ Agricultural/Rural Development
■ Public Utilities/Administration
▤ Education
▧ Health and Population

1984/85

5.00%
8.00%
7,00%
12,00%
4.00%
10,0%
28.00%
26.00%

Source: Johan Åshuvud, "Statistical Review of Swedish Development Aid," in Pierre Frühling, ed., *Swedish Development Aid in Perspective.* (Stockholm: Almqvist and Wiksell, 1986), p. 292.

The North Vietnamese government requested resources for a large-scale pulp and paper mill which would be used to reduce dependency on imports of paper for school materials such as notebooks. The Bai Bang pulp and paper mill became the big "solidarity" project and absorbed approximately twenty-five percent of Sweden's bilateral industrial sector outlays over nearly a twenty year period.

The "front-line states" which surround South Africa also retain a prominent political profile within Swedish aid policy. The former Portuguese colonies of Angola and Mozambique became program countries upon achieving independence. In these cases, political independence from Portugal and from neighboring South Africa were dominant themes. In addition, the socialist policies of these governments were seen as an effective channel for equity and democracy. Another expression of Sweden's anti-apartheid position is its financial support since the early 1970s of the South West African Peoples' Organization (SWAPO) in Namibia and the African National Congress (ANC) in South Africa. Because the latter two are not sovereign states, this assistance falls under the category of "humanitarian" aid and seeks to provide "support within and outside of South Africa to people who oppose and are victims of apartheid."

Tanzania has had a very special relationship with Sweden since the early 1970s. In 1969, Tanzanian President Nyrere visited Sweden and was roundly praised by Swedish officials and the public alike as he proclaimed his plans for Tanzania's development. Nyrere envisioned a village-oriented society in which rural development was paramount and in which the state would provide all citizens with education, health care, clean water, and sanitary living conditions. In short, he proposed the creation of a welfare state in the Third World. Sweden provided major support to Nyrere and his development program.

Although the emphasis placed upon the selection of reformist countries has declined somewhat during recent years, the recent relationship with Nicaragua is an important extension of this trait in Swedish aid policy. Here as elsewhere, political and economic independence, along with an impression of equity-oriented development by the government, were important considerations. Thus, Nicaraguan aid is motivated by a desire to help the "efforts to build up the country after civil war and natural disaster."

It should be noted that not all Swedish program countries are socialist. Primary among non-socialist recipients are Kenya and India. Because they have been independent states for a longer period of time, the independence goal of Swedish assistance is less applicable. Other non-socialist program countries include the front-line states of southern Africa whose poverty levels and proximity to South Africa elevate the political and economic independence goals to more basic considerations.

In each of these examples, the welfare principles are quite evident. *Solidarity* is embodied in the goals of political and economic independence and emphasizes the human and societal bonds between Sweden and the aid recipient. *Equity* is embodied in the goal of economic and social equality and emphasizes Swedish support of the *peoples* of the recipient countries. *Humanitarianism* is embodied within the ideas of equity and democratic social development, as the Swedish government expresses the hope for an improved standard of living for the poorest strata within recipient countries. Finally, *economic growth* is the foundation upon which the previous goals rest.

Early in this essay, it was noted that the basic assumption of Swedish foreign aid was that economic growth would lead automatically to the other goals. As the "recipient-oriented" strategy developed, however, Sweden acknowledged that this formula was not universal nor was it inevitable. The country selection criteria served as a safeguard to ensure that this formula would have the best chance of success, because the economic inputs would be optimally channelled into those countries that were pursuing equitable and democratic principles.

Throughout this period, a conceptual distinction was made between aid and commerce. Growth in the developing country was viewed as a phenomenon separate from the Swedish economy. This distinction tended to reinforce the recipient country's role as welfare recipient, rather than as partner in development. Through time, the recipient countries *themselves* began to cross the line separating trade from aid in an attempt to conduct business. The pursuit of development according to the Swedish model was only of secondary importance, if at all. Thereafter, the focus of Swedish assistance shifted drastically away from the recipient governments to the populations of these states—to the masses that had little, if any, voice in the government-directed development process.

From Recipient-Oriented Country Programs . . .

Although the intentions behind the selection of program countries largely concerned the promotion of independence, equity, and democratic development, the actual selections led to a concentration upon economic growth (mainly industrial) at the expense of other goals.

> We were a bit ignorant about conditions in the Third World. We over-estimated the impact of economic growth, thinking that import support and industrial aid would help the small farmer, but it didn't have that effect and this hurt the equity goal. Therefore, more and more we have to think of ways to reach the poor (Edgren, 1984).

As Gösta Edgren observes, most of the Swedish aid was used for industrial projects with long-term development objectives in mind. These projects often entailed such unforeseen difficulties as cost overruns, inefficient administration, occasional corruption, and completion delays. The training of skilled operators and maintenance personnel often proved to be extremely difficult. In addition, the supply of spare parts—most of which were imported—was a constant problem. In short, the projects often took longer to complete and consumed more resources than expected.

From the political level, recipient governments conducted policies that favored the wealthier urban populations at the expense of the rural and agricultural segments. Continued or increased dependence upon agricultural and industrial imports exacerbated the already crippling economic conditions in many countries. The sufferings of the poorest increased as income and power gaps widened, thereby counteracting the primary goals of Swedish assistance: namely, equity and democracy.

Although the pattern of industrialization and import dependence was not exclusively associated with socialist regimes, the fact that it occurred in these countries at all prompted an awareness of the complexities of development. Swedish policy-makers were forced to confront their own idealism in the ability of such of regimes to administer Swedish assistance. Even in Tanzania, where much of the Swedish assistance was in the form of basic needs and rural development, the results were largely disappointing from a political development and mobilization standpoint.

Particularly disturbing were the problems encountered in Vietnam with the Bai Bang pulp and paper mill. According to SIDA's Vietnam country officer, Cecilia Molander (1984):

> If we knew then what we know now, we never would have begun those projects. . . . They can administer a war perfectly well, but they can't seem to administer a peaceful development.

This observation is consistent with large-scale industrial projects elsewhere. The Mufundi paper mill in Tanzania, as well as the Kotmale dam project in Sri Lanka, have both required much more time and resources than were originally estimated. Political and social struggles have plagued these and other projects. Some of the more prominent examples that affect Swedish assistance are the allegations concerning the use of forced labor to supply wood at Bai Bang, the civil war which threatens the stability of the Kotmale facility in Sri Lanka, and the recent scrutiny directed at Kenya for possible human rights violations.

Ms. Molander's observation also points indirectly to an additional problem with recipient-oriented strategy. Although a regime may be socialist, this is no guarantee that it will necessarily be peaceful or stable. The increased militarization of and aggression by certain program countries have made it particularly difficult for Sweden to justify the continuation of assistance in some cases. For example, the aid programs to both Cuba and Vietnam have been the subject of heated debate during the 1970s and 1980s. Nicaragua has also become more controversial in this regard.

The long-term nature of the program country relationship makes it particularly susceptible to damaging economic or military activities by the aid recipient. Such realities, whether due to Swedish input or not, can call the accomplishment of the Swedish aid goals into question. Not only may the goals seem distant, in some cases it may appear as if the aid has had a directly damaging effect upon the sort of development envisioned by Sweden. Indeed, a 1980 SIDA report stated that, in measurable terms, none of the goals were being met in any significant fashion in any recipient country (*Landöversyn,* 1980).

In fact, one of the true beneficiaries of Sweden's recipient-oriented aid strategy has been Swedish industry (despite the fact that this was intentionally *not* an assistance goal). Large-scale industrial projects tended to be conditional upon the purchase of Swedish goods (often as much as fifty percent of total outlays). In addition, voluntary purchases of Swedish goods often accompanied these transactions. In this regard, Vietnam is exemplary. Although only fifty percent of Bai Bang resources were tied, an additional twenty-five to thirty percent was recycled to Sweden in the form of voluntary purchases. The case of aid to Angola also reveals a similar pattern of unidirectional trade-following-aid. Ironically, it is the most socialist of countries that are often the best customers for Swedish industry. Because these countries are often isolated from the rest of the Western markets, Sweden becomes much more competitive. Sweden's aid purists, however, still consider such tied aid and total return flows to be undesirable and contrary to the objectives of aid. This, despite the willingness of recipient governments to participate in such transactions.

. . . to Donor Country–Oriented Assistance

After gaining valuable and somewhat disappointing experience with excessive recipient autonomy, Sweden began to search for possible alternatives. Although such welfare-oriented sectors as education, health, basic needs, and agriculture were still held as overall policy priorities, this reality did not reflect the increased salience of import support and industrial sector projects. During the latter half of the 1970s, a general policy diversification occurred. In the midst of an intense domestic debate, two directions—*broader cooperation* and *concerned participation*—

emerged as a modification of the more open-ended recipient-oriented approach.

Some of the demand came from the program countries themselves. In 1978, a Tanzanian official asked Sweden to assume greater responsibility in the direction of Tanzania's aid flows. Within Sweden, there was also a strong push for greater accountability. It was also during this time that the shift in emphasis to democracy and equity became evident. These "end product" goals were treated more directly than they had been previously. Possibly the Swedish government needed more "results" in order to maintain a favorable public opinion for foreign assistance.

One of the primary mechanisms to facilitate these two goals is the "concerned participation" approach, which entails a greater degree of conditionality. In order for Sweden to grant funding, goods, or services to a particular project or development program, the recipient government is required to follow more restrictive rules concerning the use of resources. Thus, Sweden can more effectively guide its aid flows in directions that are more attuned to its goals. "Concerned participation" is also inherently more project oriented and, therefore, donor controlled.

Within this new orientation, greater attention is paid to basic needs and rural development in an attempt to support the agricultural population. New emphasis has been placed upon the development of cottage industries. An important component of this overall approach is the increased use of voluntary associations in development activities. Such organizations tend to bypass recipient government channels and reach the poor more directly. The effect of this strategy in combination with stricter aid conditionality has been a decrease of recipient government autonomy in the administration of assistance. The solidarity partner has shifted from the recipient government to the recipient population.

Together with the push toward democracy in development, a definite business influence has made its mark on the policy. The euphemistic name for this trend is "broader cooperation." Its activities concern a wider range of wealthier developing countries. Originally, "broader cooperation" reflected the desire to establish commercial relations with member states of the Organization of Petroleum Exporting Countries (OPEC) and such "newly-industrializing countries" (NICs) as Taiwan, South Korea, and Singapore. These objectives were pursued largely through the activities of BITS and SWEDFUND and were spurred, at least in part, by a slump in the Swedish economy during the 1970s. Subsequently, Sweden sought to adopt measures that would tighten relations with the oil exporting countries and would form the foundation for increased technical cooperation and joint ventures. Though still reflecting only a minor portion of Sweden's total aid budget, these agencies—particularly BITS—have received considerable budget increases.

Another aspect of "broader cooperation" that is not associated with the commercialization trend is the general expansion of relations beyond the horizon of the program countries that has occurred after 1980. Sweden has engaged in increased activities with non-program countries, particularly on political and humanitarian grounds. This activity has been necessitated by numerous Third World natural and political disasters. Humanitarian and disaster relief operations, often conducted by non-governmental organizations, have been expanded to provide immediate assistance to the victims of flood, famine, and civil war. In a sense, the urgent needs of these people have superceded the longer-term goals of Swedish development assistance and may have preempted the normal decision-making process. In other ways, however, the Swedish goal of democratic development is being upheld. The geographic expansion of humanitarian or "regional" aid is yet another expression of solidarity with the poor as opposed to their governments.

In the space of just a few years, the idea of "aid on the recipient's own terms" seems to have passed. Without shirking its responsiblities to the program countries, Sweden has taken steps to reduce the decision-making autonomy of central authorities in recipient countries. In its dealings with these countries, "concerned participation" has had the effect of tightening the rules and stipulation. This has resulted in a shift from the more flexible program approach to the more circumscribed project approach. The result of this shift has been to place more decision-making into the hands of the donor country, Sweden.

The Domestic Arena
of Swedish Foreign Assistance

The domestic context of foreign aid policy-making is a crucial component of this analysis. In a 1986 study, Goldmann, et. al., employ a "tripartite" model of democratic participation (bureaucracy, parliament, and interest organizations) to test the degree of democratic procedure in the formulation of Swedish foreign policy. They postulate that a reasonable balance among these institutions constitutes an ideal model of democratic participation. On the other hand, a prominent influence by the bureaucracy constitutes a bureaucratic model which, although perhaps more rational, is also less democratic.

For the purposes of this essay, the most interesting observation by the Goldmann team is that the formulation of foreign aid policy bears a closer resemblance to *domestic* policy-making than it does to the more general foreign policy-making model in terms of tripartite participation. Besides being less dominant, the bureaucracy also possesses certain "pluralistic" elements (*e.g.,* SIDA, SAREC, and BITS) that do not have parallels in other facets of foreign policy such as the defense or security policy dimensions. In addition, interest organizations perform a larger role and their access to information is more open and reciprocal than in other areas of foreign policy.

According to the Goldmann study, the only area in which foreign aid does not reflect a democratic model parallel to the domestic sphere is in the area of representation. In this instance, party lines are not as distinct. The influence of activists, parliamentarians, and general public opinion serve to reduce the distinction between parties and results in more heated debates within parties than among them. In general, these findings tend to support the idea that foreign aid is an international extension of the domestic system.

Part of this democratic character may result from the manifold increase in the number of groups in Swedish society that play a role in the formulation and implementation of the foreign aid policy. This expanded mobilization of the Swedish population has catapulted foreign aid to a prominence in the public policy arena that far outweighs the relative position of U.S. foreign aid in the American debate.

In the earliest years, the "aid community" consisted of a handful of charity-oriented private organizations and the Foreign Ministry (including SIDA). During the late 1960s and the early 1970s, the community expanded to include political parties, a greater variety of activist groups, and, consequently, a radicalized and mobilized public opinion. From the mid to later-1970s to the present, these actors have been supplemented by Swedish industry and an expanded role for SIDA in the process of public information and opinion building. Because many more groups and individuals now claim a "stake" in foreign aid, the policy largely reflects a mix of these interests. The separation of authority among multilateral, bilateral, research, and commercial agencies provides a more pluralistic policy-making context for the formulation of aid than for other dimensions of foreign policy.

The Aid Bureaucracy

The nuts and bolts of foreign assistance are worked out by SIDA. Within this agency resides unparalleled national expertise in foreign aid matters. From its inception in 1965, SIDA was staffed with individuals who had been working with development projects sponsored by such organizations as the mission, the Red Cross, and Save the Children, as well as other humanitarian and religious groups. This heritage from the cultural and religious groups represents one of SIDA's most important distinctions from the other Swedish agencies involved in development assistance.

Over the years, SIDA's organizational structure has expanded to include a global network of program country offices and such home-based functional divisions as industry and agriculture. Despite the bureaucratic expansion, SIDA retains its ideological character. Its sole interest remains the promotion of development and *not* the pursuit of commerce or trade. Based on interviews conducted during 1984, the widely-shared sentiment within SIDA is that any commercial endeavors on its part would threaten the credibility of the aid program. The persistent emphasis on solidarity, equity, and humanitarianism is enhanced by the fact that "the missions and other idealistic organizations have influenced SIDA's operations to the highest degree . . . most employees here are either currently or formerly active in the organizations."

SIDA's links to its Swedish constituency is formalized by a laymen's Board of Directors which consists of representatives from the five political parties, the major trade union organizations, the cooperative movement, and the missions. Further, the political party representatives also serve as members of Parliament and may sit on the Foreign Affairs Committee. In this fashion, they act as a direct channel between the Parliament, SIDA, and the concerned public. Absent from the board are representatives from Sweden's capital interests. The spokesmen for trade, finance, and industry serve instead on the boards of BITS and SWEDFUND. Thus, the two types of voices remain distinct and, in particular, SIDA remains more clearly associated with non-profit interests.

The grassroot movements are an important part of SIDA's internal organization as well. A separate subdivision, the Independent Organization Section, concerns itself exclusively with the overseas development activities of official Swedish organizations such as the trade unions or relief agencies. The Information Office is staffed by officers who are responsible for funding the public education and information projects of these opinion-transmitting organizations. This incorporation of more widely based groups with SIDA's administrative structure is a strong indication of the powerful links that exist between SIDA and the popular movements. Neither the Ministry of Foreign Affairs nor any of the other semi-autonomous aid agencies maintain such connections with the society at large.

SIDA's extensive network of relations with Swedish interest groups provides it with a more domestic orientation than is common for most agencies dealing with foreign relations. SIDA is more attuned to public opinion and press relations than other agencies and, perhaps, in this respect it is a little more "democratic," as well as "domestic," in character. Speaking in purely impressionistic terms, SIDA seems to have a far greater sense of internal identity and of mission than that of other agencies. SIDA's effort to keep commercial interests out of its institutional structure is an important expression of that ideological identity.

The most vivid reflection of SIDA's idealistic welfare orientation is the adamant stance it has taken on all aspects of aid commercialization. In general, SIDA held firmly to the "purist" position during the foreign aid debates around 1980. SIDA strongly opposed the overt use of tied aid to increase the return flow of aid and to sustain the one percent budget. SIDA also stood firm against the inclusion of any profit-oriented funds (such as export credits) within the aid budget. In short, SIDA opposed the establishment of any commercial operations within its realm. The division between foreign assistance and commercial interests was implemented literally as well as figuratively. The newly created "commercial" agencies—BITS, SWEDFUND, and IMPOD—not only were separate from SIDA from an administrative standpoint, they were located in buildings separate (and distant) from SIDA headquarters. In contrast, SAREC (the independent development research agency) shares administrative links and is housed within SIDA. Although the government has recently sought to expand cooperation between SIDA and Swedish industry, its efforts have met with only limited success.

The Political Parties

The distinctions between the various aid orientations of the assistance agencies are perhaps more easily identifiable than those among Sweden's political parties. According to the Goldmann thesis, the greater the similarity on policy between the parties, the more "typical" the pattern for the foreign relations arena. Conversely, the greater the disparities, the more "domestic" the pattern. Swedish political parties, however, are difficult to place on this spectrum. Despite varying degrees of polarization and shifting party alignments, the political parties have generally maintained an admirably harmonious front on development assistance throughout the years.[11]

The relative party consensus of the earlier period may possibly be explained by the fact that foreign aid was not viewed as involving essential or strategic economic resources. Swedish party support is primarily based upon divisions among economic classes rather than upon ideology. Although their overall goals are relatively harmonious, their preferred economic strategies differ substantially. Thus, aid defined as an ideological issue could draw upon considerable political consensus for several years. After aid became an economic issue, however, a certain polarization occurred. This polarization was exacerbated by simultaneous changes in the party composition of government. In 1976, the bourgeois coalition ended four decades of uninterrupted Social Democratic rule. Within an environment of economic crisis, political change, and greatly expanded assistance budgets, each party's position on aid tended to crystallize.

Because of their preponderant political influence, the Social Democrats have greatly influenced the development of aid policy throughout the years. Within the Social Democratic party, there have been considerable differences of opinion concerning assistance policy almost from the beginning of the official aid program. Endorsing the humanitarian and moral imperatives of the early 1960s, Ulla Lindström (the new aid minister) fought for a greatly expanded budget until she resigned in frustration in 1966. Her nemesis was a fellow Social Democrat, Finance Minister Gunnar Sträng. Sträng argued that the existing level of public support for foreign aid could not justify an increased budget.

The welfare idealist spirit, however, gradually gained momentum within the party (spurred particularly by youth, women's, and religious organizations) and helped to mobilize the party's position on foreign aid by the end of the decade. A number of other factors (the Vietnam War, the political rise of Olof Palme, and an unprecedented economic prosperity) also contributed to the growing support for foreign aid within the Social Democratic Party. Within a very short time the basic tenets of the aid policy—the one percent target, the four goals, and country programming—were adopted by the Social Democrats and passed by the Riksdag.

The basic position of the Social Democratic Party on the aid issue is best understood in terms of the economic goals of growth and distribution. The goals of solidarity and equity may only be prioritized if the budget permits. Thus, during the growth period of the early 1970s, the party became radicalized and stressed the independence and equity issues in the choice of recipient countries. Tanzania, Vietnam, Angola, Cuba, and Allende's Chile were party favorites not only for reasons of poverty, but of politics, as well. These countries were believed to be either in need of support for their political independence or better suited to promote the value of equity in their development.

Pragmatism, possibly as a function of its traditional role as the governing party, soon surfaced within the party. As the Swedish economy faced increasing constraints, the Social Democrats became less idealistic in aid matters. Even during the opposition years of 1976–82, the Social Democrats did not unite against the government in favor of aid "purity." Rather, the party seemed to split largely along the lines of growth and distribution.

Upon their return to government in 1982, the Social Democrats proposed an overt reduction of the one percent goal. Although the party itself formally established the goal in 1968 and nurtured it to realization over the following eight years, the Social Democrats deliberately reneged on this goal in 1983, presumably for pragmatic reasons.

On the basis of budgetary conditions, the government has found it necessary to include the international development cooperation within the realm of spending cutbacks (UU, 1983/84:7).

A compromise with the advocates of aid "purity," however, was achieved through the government's decision not to include export credits within the aid budget. This was recommended by a special commission appointed to study the matter (DsUD, 1983:2). Such an inclusion would have maintained the assistance level at one percent, but part of that amount would have been commercial. According to the Social Democrats, the "inclusion of the entire credit amount within the aid budget would not lead to increased aid, but would (instead) reduce the faith in Swedish aid" (UU, 1983/84:7). Clearly, the Social Democrats are interested in protecting the Swedish economy first and seek aid measures that support that goal.

The Social Democrats are also very interested in the strategy of "broader cooperation." This strategy promotes expanded commercial and technical relations with the wealthier Third World countries (Hellström, 1981:22). In a 1981 party report, the Social Democrats actually proposed the establishment of a new central agency for investment and trade that would parallel SIDA and would include BITS, SWEDFUND, and IMPOD (Hellström, 1981:22).

It is indeed ironic that the only other political party to support the Social Democratic budget reduction proposal was the Moderate (conservative) party. The Moderate party also supported increased returns to Swedish industry. The Liberal, Center, and Communist parties were, in contrast, adamantly opposed to both of these measures.

The Center party has recently emerged as a principal proponent for environmental concerns in aid matters. This position represents an international extention of the party's domestic environmental protection agenda and is rooted in the party's primarily rural and farming orientation. The Center party also prioritizes rural development over industrial growth. This is particularly the case with regard to the benefits that private organizations can provide in smaller-scale project implementation.

Because of its historic links with "popular movements," perhaps the Liberal party places the aid issue higher on its agenda than the other parties. In terms of humanitarian and moral imperatives, Liberal rhetoric on foreign assistance is perhaps the most idealistic of all. More often than not, the Center party aligns itself with the Liberals on aid issues. To be sure, both the Liberal and the Center parties place an almost sacred value on the one percent target. According to Rune Angström (Liberal representative on the Foreign Affairs Committee and the SIDA board), the party actually began to discuss the one percent level during the 1950s and, in fact, consider it to be merely a step toward even higher levels of commitment (1984).

Differences among the parties tend to be most clearly illustrated in the debate concerning program country selection. During the early to mid-1970s, the Liberals, Social Democrats, and Communists tended to favor socialist regimes and those countries just emerging from a liberation struggle. Today, however, the Communists—in a departure from the preferences of the other parties—favor resumed aid relations with Cuba, increased aid to Vietnam, and the withdrawal of Sweden from the multilateral Inter-American Development Bank (IDB) which extends concessional loans to military dictatorships in South America.

On the other hand, the bourgeois parties have moved closer together in their skepticism toward socialist regimes as reliable agents of democratic and equitable change. Generally speaking, the bourgeois parties promote countries characterized by non-socialist regimes that pursue capitalist policies and possess relatively stable political systems. Some of the countries favored by the Moderates include Kenya, Sudan, and pre-coup Ethiopia. The preferred countries of the Liberal and the Center parties, however, include Zambia, Botswana, Sri Lanka, Pakistan, and Tunisia.

Another indicator of increased bourgeois unity is a 1985 joint proposal for the abolition of the program country strategy altogether. In its place, an exclusively project-oriented approach would be employed. These parties also jointly criticize aid to Vietnam because of its invasion of Kampuchea in 1978.

There is a tacit agreement among all parties that the one percent target, as well as the goals of assistance, are based on consensus. Thus, these policy anchors are held in deep respect. Even when the Social Democrats proposed a budgetary reduction, the party characterized this as only a temporary measure. Differences of opinion, both within and among parties, are purely a matter of means, rather than ends. Despite occasional shifts of party positions, the overriding inter-party positions are marked by continuity and compromise. For example, even during the years of the bourgeois coalition governments (1976–1982), the policies developed during the Social Democratic years were largely maintained. The bourgeois parties upheld the one percent goal and continued the essential framework of the country programming strategy. In 1977, they went a step further and *cancelled* all Third World debts. Some claim, however, that the coalition government commercialized aid during its tenure through the establishment of BITS and SWEDFUND. It is interesting to note that upon their return to power in 1982, the Social

Democrats did not disband the commercial agencies. Instead, the Social Democrats increased their budgets.

Non-Governmental Organizations[12]

As the parties have become more mobilized around aid, so too have the interest groups, many of whom have close attachments to various political parties. The proliferation and importance of Swedish voluntary associations is a reflection of the deep belief that interest organizations are the pillars of democracy. Gunnar Heckscher characterized the structural expression of this belief.

> Sweden is exceedingly well organized; there is no important economic or idealistic interest which does not find expression in an organization. Such associations cover every social class and nearly all age groups. Young Swedes in their twenties usually belong to several societies and many of them hold offices in one or more (1958:133).

Sweden is a nation of members. Most people, in fact, belong to several organizations. It is not surprising, therefore, that the influence of these groups on Swedish citizens is great. The larger organizations conduct regular educational activities, often in the form of study circles (Michanek, 1977:3). They remain the crucial link between the mass public and the governing elites and represent a wide range of ideologies and interests. From the very beginning, their participation in foreign aid has been instrumental. Recently their influence has grown, both at home as well as abroad.

In matters of foreign aid, the nongovernmental organizations serve a dual function which, to an extent, reflects their dual domestic roles. First, as "pillars of democracy," they conduct their own development works abroad and act in support of the policy goals of democracy and equity. Second, as educators and cultivators, they spread information about aid and development to their members in Sweden. This serves to raise the public consciousness and to help maintain a public opinion that favors the maintenance of the expensive aid program.

Interest group influence in Swedish policy-making has a long precedent. Most administrative bodies, particularly those concerning domestic policy-making and implementation, are headed by laymen's boards of directors. Swedish foreign assistance policy-making is no exception. Laymen's boards head SIDA, BITS, SWEDFUND, IMPOD, and SAREC. Appointments to the boards are made by the government which effectively renders the selection of societal representation a political matter. Through these boards, interested groups can influence the foreign aid budget and policy process. SIDA's Board of Directors (as noted earlier) maintains, by far, the strongest corporatist links.

SIDA supports the overseas development activities of over one hundred Swedish voluntary associations. Certain broadly-based and central organizations receive a lump sum for such operations based upon a "frame agreement." This funding is untied to specific projects. Other groups apply for project support on an individual proposal basis. Generally, the grantee must provide twenty percent of the necessary funding with SIDA providing the remainder. Thus, SIDA channels a good deal of development work through these groups. In fact, allocations for this type of development activities has tripled between 1976 and 1986. The major recipient of SIDA support are the churches. They have traditionally received more than half of these funds. Such organizations as the Red Cross and Save the Children also receive significant amounts. In addition, the unions and cooperatives are receiving increased priority as SIDA seeks to promote the establishment of such groups overseas. The enhanced position of nongovernmental organizations in development assistance coincides with the shift in aid emphasis away from recipient governments to that of recipient peoples (Lewin, 1986:224). Thus, NGO's are a primary expression of the goals of democratic social development, as well as social and economic equity. In bypassing the recipient governments and maintaining closer contacts with the poorest target groups, the unofficial organizations are considered to be better equipped for certain types of development activities.

In addition to funding for overseas development projects, Swedish interest groups receive financial support from SIDA for domestic public information and educational projects. Indeed, about two thirds of SIDA's total information budget is channelled through these intermediaries. Generally known as opinion-building, SIDA recognizes the crucial role interest groups can play in sustaining popular support for the assistance budget during times of economic hardship. Most of the popular movement activities involves the arrangement of study groups, exhibits, publications, films, and trips or tours to developing countries for selected groups (such as journalists of trade magazines). Target groups for this information span the entire population from the pre-school level up to the adult education and study circle networks.

The funds to support domestic information activities parallel the allocations for international activities. The large grassroots organizations are believed to be better suited to inform the public and are provided block grants from SIDA for this purpose. Among these groups are the trade union federations and the large adult education organizations that work together with the unions, churches, political parties, and other interest groups. Such nondiscretionary funding constitutes nearly ninety percent of SIDA's information grants. The remainder is provided to other groups that submit proposals for individual information projects. From the late 1970s, SIDA's total information budget has increased nearly fifteen percent.

The public education function of the mass organizations is a critical factor in upholding a favorable public opinion for foreign aid. A core link in the information and opinion chain is study circle leaders of the local organization.

> If our money goes to the leaders, then we know it reaches the members. People work from nine to five, and their opinions can't be too well developed. Therefore, they depend on the leaders to think about things (Nilsson, 1984).

Mr. Nilsson's comments raise the interesting question concerning how "grassroot" and democratic these organizations truly are. How popular is an organization that depends largely upon the activism of its leaders? How democratic is an organization whose membership more or less passively absorbs beliefs transmitted by strategically placed and "properly informed" leaders. It is quite possible to view the representation of these organizations on SIDA's board and their incorporation into SIDA's operations as a cooptation of authority, rather than as a decentralizing or democratizing force. The involvement of the grassroots organizations in foreign aid reflects the nature of Swedish corporatist democracy at home and the effort to project this model abroad.

Public Opinion

Given the size of Swedish aid relative to the national budget, the wide support that foreign assistance has enjoyed is indeed remarkable, particularly in times of economic slump. Public opinion is an important factor in aid policy. Without a strongly favorable (or at least indifferent) opinion, the budget cannot be maintained or increased. Indeed, the government cannot set a legitimate example for democratic development in the Third World if its own policies are not supported by a majority at home. Because of various feedback mechanisms, public opinion can thus influence changes within the policy itself.

In the late 1970s, certain pitfalls in the assistance program received increased media coverage. Reports concerning the problems associated with the large industrial projects (particularly the pulp and paper mill at Bai Bang in Vietnam) appeared more frequently. A general deterioration of conditions for the people of the Third World was portrayed. Serious questions concerning the efficacy of aid were raised and numerous debates concerning nearly all aspects of aid ensued. The public discussions on aid policy resulted in even larger budget allocations for public information and education through SIDA and the grassroots organizations.

The primary motivating force behind the aid opinion or "aid will" (as it is called in Swedish) has been the missionary spirit of helping the poor. On a purely intuitive level, this makes perfect sense. Images of suffering evoke emotional response that are easily nurtured through information channels. This is particularly true with regard to geographically distant aid recipients. Whereas the relevance of day-to-day policy matters is easily recognizable, the assistance community is further removed. In order to "engage" the mass public in the pursuit of international welfare, it must be emotionally charged and the boundaries of community must be globalized. Thus, the primary thrust of public opinion on aid has been the yardstick of success in "reaching the poor." Lars-Erik Birgegard postulates that an "ideal" aid policy would be based upon "measures that immediately and directly reach the poorest people" (1984:37).

Research probing the extent and nature of public knowledge about foreign aid and development lends support to this characterization. Two lengthy studies discovered that the general public's level of knowledge about development and foreign aid is very low and that public opinion has not changed a great deal despite changes in the budget and the "psychological climate" of the debate. Lindholm's 1970 study concludes:

> Good-will and solidarity . . . seem to be based more upon humanitarian feelings than upon knowledge of, and analysis of, the situation. . . . One can therefore be somewhat skeptical about the durability of this solidarity in situations which demand actual sacrifices (238).

Lindholm also states that, despite a good deal of information through the mass media, people do not seem to be absorbing or receiving this information (1970:238). Lowe Hedman's 1978 study finds that people's opinions about the Third World do not correspond to the left-right ideological spectrum, and that the general level of support for foreign aid had been essentially stable during the period from 1962 to 1978 (207-10). According to Hedman, those shifts that did occur were a reflection of the "psychological climate." Thus, the increased support for foreign assistance during the late 1960s was attributable to the "climate" of radicalism. On the other hand, Hedman notes that a "general worsening of the economic situation" would tend to make people less "Third World oriented" (1978:210).

Public opinion statistics are available for various years during the period from 1961-1987 and are presented in Tables 1a and 1b. The

Table 1a. Public Opinion Polls on "Aid Will" (1961-76)

	1961	1968	1970	1974[a]	1976
Increase	24	33	26	32	26
About Right	67	57	60	58	59
Decrease	9	10	14	6	10
Eliminate	—	—	—	—	—

[a]Two polls were conducted in 1974 and 1976 (May and November). The figures
shown are from the November polls. All figures in percentages.
Source: *SOU*, 1977, No. 73, Table 3.2

Table 1b. Public Opinion Polls on "Aid Will" (1977-87)

	1979	1981	1983	1985	1987[b]
Increase	16	17	15	16	18
About Right	60	56	60	61	59
Decrease	19	17	18	18	18
Eliminate	5	9	7	5	5

[b]SIDA conducted yearly polls from 1977-87 with the exception of 1978. All figures
from selected years in percentages.
Source: SIDA Press Release, April 6, 1988.

figures reveal a pattern of relative consistency for the entire period with
some fifty to sixty percent of the respondents indicating satisfaction with
the existing levels of aid. The percentages basically illustrate the intensity
of aid support from an essentially passive and satisfied public. A possibly
distinct trend during the 1980s, however, is that *fewer* individuals support
an increase in aid. Indeed, those preferring a *decrease* actually outnumber
those preferring an increase in aid levels. This reversal of the past few
years raises questions about the relationship of assistance outlays to
periods of economic sacrifice. Certainly, 1983 was a better year for the
Swedish economy than 1976.

One possible explanation for the decline in support may be the timing
of the budget increases. The level of preference for budget increases is
fairly consistent up to the time of the achievement of the one percent
target. It seems, then, that until about 1976/77, people actually *expected*
the aid budget to grow. After the goal was reached, however, a sort of
"status quo" mentality may have taken over.

Swedish Industry

The moral imperative of aid calls for its separation from business.
Lars Rudebeck observes that Sweden, with its strong and diversified

export economy, has "held on the longest to the doctrine of separation," whereas Denmark—whose export economy consists mostly of agricultural products—never assumed the pretense of such separation and set up mechanisms for economic expansion into Third World markets long ago (1978:3). It appears that Sweden's economic security has permitted the luxury of development assistance untainted by commercialism for quite some time. The economic realities of the post-oil shock era, however, seem to have forced a merger between economic and idealistic interests.

The complexities of the debate concerning "pure" versus "commercialized" aid lie largely beyond the scope of this essay. Suffice it to say that various groups (both within and out of the Swedish government) have developed a strong interest in the maintenance of a morally righteous aid program. By allowing recipient-oriented aid to expand during the 1970s, the idealists inadvertently stimulated a new market interest for the Swedish export economy. Companies such as Skanska Cement, Alfa Laval, and ASEA have all benefitted from large orders for their industrial goods and services.

Swedish industry has not come rushing to aid sources, however. After the economy weakened during the post-oil shock and global recession of the mid-1970s, the recovery was believed to lie in Sweden's traditional global markets. The oil crisis itself brought immediate scrutiny to the economic potential of the OPEC countries after Sweden's oil imports nearly quadrupled in just three years from (1972–75) (OECD, 1984:64).

The Swedish aid agency, BITS, was designed originally to help secure economic relations with the oil-exporting countries and to create a more balanced interdependence through the exchange of technical expertise to these countries in return for guaranteed oil deliveries. It should be noted, however, that the idea of incorporating this activity into the assistance program was *not* the ideal of Swedish industry groups. Even today, these associations are not aggressively pursuing increased participation in foreign aid activities. After the release of the 1983 export credit report (which proposed the inclusion of the non-grant portion of Third World export credits in the aid budget), industry respondents opposed this idea and upheld the doctrine of separation (DsUD 1983:2).

Swedish trade and investment interests have generally not been interested in working with the recipient countries of Swedish aid (usually the poorest countries). After the government extended the range of recipient countries for credits and guarantees, private capital began to show interest (Rudebeck, 1983:5). The attempt to formally merge capital interests with development assistance was, therefore, made by the government and not by industry. The Social Democratic party report of 1981 cited earlier is but one example of the political concern for creation of longer-term outlets for the shrinking options of Sweden's export-led economy.

Viewed cynically, it might be argued that the private capital interests of Swedish industry does have an increasing stake in aid matters. Indeed, some may contend that it has already carved a small, but growing slice of the assistance pie, particularly through BITS and tied aid. It is estimated that of the fifteen or so percent of aid that is tied, some *forty* percent is actually recycled to the Swedish economy. The result—the greater stake of export interests in aid—may be obvious, but the cause is certainly less clear.

It should be noted that purchases through tied aid has been a contentious issue for several years. The resultant benefits of the purchases have the potential for creating stronger industrial lobbies for even greater amounts of tied aid. Purists, however, vehemently oppose such increases and argue, instead, that aid should not be tied under any circumstances. Such confrontations are potentially damaging, especially at a time when the government is shifting away from large-scale industrial projects. The present program still contains import support in which most of the tied aid and industrial allocations appear (see Figure 4). Thus, the Swedish industrial sector today is more actively involved in assistance projects than ever before. Likewise, it also appears that while the industrial interests may not be an aggressive lobbying force, they are, nevertheless, mobilizing to push for increases in tied aid.

Ironically, the recipient-oriented strategy of SIDA and the parallel establishment of BITS and of SWEDFUND may have helped to preserve the moral character of Swedish aid by delineating the "welfare" territory more precisely. Thus far, the Swedish industrial and aid communities have not been forced to work together to any appreciable degree. For the most part, the idealists have been free to pursue policy from the standpoint of relative purity. On the other hand, the capital growth interests have been free to expand wherever they choose. Even with the creation of new assistance programs, the separation of interests still exists because different countries are involved. For example, the limited efforts of the Swedish Export Council (jointly administered by government and industry) to act as broker and coordinator between SIDA and Swedish industry has met with limited success. The true convergence of growth and distribution has yet to occur.

Transcending Boundaries

The principal objective of this essay has been to present a view of Sweden's foreign aid policy as an international extension of its approach to domestic welfare. The accumulation of capital (the *growth* dimension) provides an economic base capable of supporting a policy of equitable *distribution*. In turn, this sharing is based on the principles of solidarity, humanitarianism, and equality. Its aim is to reduce the gaps of wealth and power. In Sweden's comprehensive approach to the Third World, the distributive component is represented by foreign aid policy and the growth dimension is represented by trade and investment policy. The geographic orientations of these elements diverge with clear distinctions between commercial markets and "welfare" or aid recipients.

Some of the difficulties associated with the formulation and implementation of Sweden's foreign aid policy stem from the inherent contradictions between growth and distribution as one shifts from the domestic to the international setting. Another problem results from Sweden's inability to recognize its own ethnocentricity as it designs policies that are heavily based upon Sweden's own unique development. Both of these difficulties may be viewed as a problem of boundary distinction.

At the level of "development welfare" or bilateral assistance, the target of distribution shifts to groups in distant lands that are living under conditions that are quite alien to Sweden. Sometimes, it is difficult for Swedes to feel a great sense of immediate involvement with, or even to see the relevance of, these societies. For such a substantial foreign aid budget to be supported, a global welfare obligation must be inspired. Somehow, this distant world must be brought closer to home. A short-term charity instinct works well in this setting, particularly if the donor country's economy is strong. A long-term, more complex development strategy, however, requires extra effort in order to build sustained domestic support.

The Swedish aid policy has been paralleled by a domestic campaign to educate and to mobilize the mass public. As much as possible, the efforts of the countless Swedish private organizations are included in the development process. The attempt is made to transcend the cognitive distinction between a Swedish resident with the right to welfare, and a citizen in a developing country who should also enjoy the same privileges. However, this is a difficult gap to bridge.

Part of the reason that the Swedish government continues to exert such efforts in mobilizing strong and consistent foreign aid support at home is the conviction that the promotion of a global welfare community is a righteous cause. Through its foreign aid principles, Sweden seeks to provide an example of global welfare behavior. The fact that the rest of the world may not be following the example has caused considerable frustration and disappointment in Sweden. In particular, the perceived failure of the multilateral sphere of foreign aid activities has further convinced many Swedes that their formulation of global responsibility and distribution is correct.

The aid principles are never really questioned. Objectives are not abandoned nor are they opposed in the heat of political debates. Only the strategies for goal attainment are subject to public scrutiny. There remains a strong faith and determination to continue to grapple with the problems of development until they are overcome. To question the activity on principle would be to attack fundamental notions about welfare, solidarity, and equity.

Underneath the preoccupation with means rather than ends lies the consumate irony. It seems that the more rigidly Sweden advocates global consciousness and responsibility, the more nationalistic it becomes. In trying to hurdle all of the distributive boundaries (performing simultaneously the roles of domestic, bilateral, and multilateral benefactor), Sweden has consistently sought the solutions to the problems of the outside world from within. Nearly all of the major policy directions have been premised on the historical and structural features of Swedish society.

During the early period of development assistance involvement, Sweden possessed the blind faith that economic growth would lead "automatically" to the development of democracy and equity. Certainly, many other Western purveyors of assistance shared similar views. As time passed, however, Sweden's policy began to reflect its own specific and unique characteristics. Even with regard to "recipient-oriented" assistance, an "automatic" pay off was again expected to result from the careful selection of countries chosen for their presumed desire to promote equity and democracy. When it was discovered that these states would not implement such policies, the focus shifted to new strategies that involved greater Swedish oversight and conditionality. The fundamental assumption now seems to be that smaller-scale projects, together with the participation of the grassroot organizations, will best contribute to the principles of equity and democracy.

The new emphasis upon private organizations in development activities, the passage of a new environmental goal, and the efforts to more directly reach the poorest elements of the recipient society more easily will bring Sweden into direct confrontations with the governments of the recipient countries. The boundaries of foreign aid are changing. The Swedish state is now assuming the role of *direct* provider to the populations of foreign countries. Solidarity toward the recipient *states* has been replaced by solidarity to recipient *peoples*.

It is also paradoxical that an emphasis upon distributive welfare principles has been accompanied by an promotion of the interests of growth. The blurring distinction between growth and distribution has led to a crisis of identity and purpose within the Swedish aid community. This distinction, however, may well be an artificial one. Swedish domestic welfare and the global welfare ideal contain *no* separation of growth and distribution. Only in the awkward limbo of bilateral aid does the boundary appear.

The ideal future for Swedish aid would consist of an increased mutual sensitivity by commercial and development assistance interests. On the one hand, the commercial elements must become more aware and supportive of development needs and humanitarian contributions. On the other, the development community must respect the benefits that appropriate industry, properly tailored to indigenous conditions, can provide. Within Sweden, these two components have been able to cooperate to the benefit of widespread prosperity. The challenge today is to get these interests to "transcend the boundary" and to work together abroad as well.

Notes

1. Interview, Professor Carl Hallencreutz, Theologian, Uppsala University, and member of SIDA Board of Directors, June 7, 1984.

2. Interview, Sture Korpås, Center Party MP, member of the Foreign Affairs Committee in the Riksdag (parliament), and member of the SIDA Board of Directors, May 8, 1984.

3. One example, describing the implicit injustice of "tied aid" (tied to the purchase of Swedish goods or services), used this Swedish metaphor: "how, for example, would Swedish parents or retired persons react if childrens' allowances and pensions were predicated upon the purchase of Swedish goods?" (Dahlgren, 1976:14) An illustration in a Swedish junior high textbook highlights the primary goals of the Swedish political economy. The images of economic growth, full employment, price control, environmental protection, and energy conservation appear together with a thin black child holding a tin dish and looking up, presumably for help. See Andres Kung and Lennart Frantzen, *Så Fungerar Sverige*, Helsingborg: Bokförlaget Bra Böcker, 1976, p. 12.

4. This model embodied the Swedish welfare principles of (1) *solidarity*, through the provision of aid on concessional (primarily grant) terms, and "on the conditions of the recipient" (essentially trusting allocative decisions to the recipient government) and (2) *equity*, through the selection of program (or long-term recipient) countries whose own development plans are in accordance with the Swedish aid goals (particularly emphasizing the equal distribution of wealth and power in the recipient country). This model was premised on humanitarian instincts, although its actual profile was more political in nature (see Odén, 1984:17–26).

5. See the essays in Andersson, et. al. (1984) for numerous examples of the identity crisis of Swedish aid during the 1980s.

6. The "aid community" refers to institutions and persons who participate in the articulation, formulation, and implementation of Swedish foreign assistance policy.

7. The "global welfare village" concept is a synthesis of the literature and personal interviews that I conducted in 1983–1984. More specific referrents include interviews with Gösta Edgren, State Secretary for Development Assistance, Foreign Ministry, June 7, 1984, and Thorsten Nilsson, INFO SIDA, June 6, 1984. See also Myrdal (1960).

8. The actual calculation was changed from one percent of Gross National Product (GNP) to a measurement using Gross National *Income* (GNI). The difference between the two is the inclusion of national debt in the GNI formula. By subtracting the debt owed on the balance of payments, the GNI figure is lower than GNP. This change was adopted during the mid-1970s at a time when the aid budget was rapidly expanding, whereas the economy was contracting. Thus, after 1976 (when the aid budget actually reached one percent of GNI), the percentage measured against GNP has been approximately 0.9 percent.

9. In Swedish, the titles of the agencies are (1) SWEDFUND (*Fonden för industriellt samarbete med u-länder*), (2) BITS (Beredningen för internationellt tekniskt samarbete), and (3) IMPOD (Importkontoret för u-landsprodukter).

10. The Central Committee (*Central Kommitté* or *CK*) was established in 1952 and consisted of forty-five non-governmental organizations (NGO's). It was the first centralized aid-related organization, but stood outside the government and was firmly rooted in the so-called popular movements. The activities of the *CK* involved small-scale vocational training projects, primarily in Ethiopia and Pakistan (Heppling, 1986:19-22).

11. The six political parties in the Riksdag (parliament)—moving along an ideological spectrum from left to right—are the Communist Party, the Social Democratic Party, the Environmental Party, the Center Party, the Liberal Party, and the Moderate Party (the conservatives). The latter three parties comprise an informal "bourgeois" coalition.

12. To avoid confusing terminology, the term non-governmental organization (NGO) is used in this section to represent *all* forms of non-governmental interest representation. Thus, such groups known as interest groups, voluntary associations, or idealistic organizations are covered under the NGO term as is done in SIDA information.

References

Andréen, Rolf (1986) "The International Commitment," in Pierre Früling, ed. *Swedish Development Aid in Perspective.* Stockholm: Almquist & Wiksell, pp. 129–46.

Andersen, Bent Rold (1984) "Rationality and Irrationality of the Nordic Welfare State," in *Daedulus.* Winter. pp. 109–40.

Andersson, Christian, Lars Heikensten, and Stefan de Vylder (1984) "Biståndet inför 90–talet—slutord," in Andersson, et. al., eds. *Bistånd i kris.* Stockholm: LiberFörlag, pp. 215–22.

Andersson, Christian (1986) "Breaking Through," in *Swedish Development Aid in Perspective.* Stockholm: Almquist & Wiksell, pp. 27–46.

Arnold, Steven H. (1982) *Implementing Development Assistance*. Boulder, Colo.: Westview Press.

Beckman, Björn (1979) "Aid and Investment: The Swedish Case," in *Cooperation and Conflict*. XIV, pp. 133–48.

Berger, Suzanne, ed. (1981) *Organizing Interests in Western Europe*. Cambridge, England: Cambridge University Press.

Birgegård, Lars-Erik (1984) "Vad styr biståndet," in *Bistånd i Kris*. Stockholm: LiberFörlag, pp. 27–38.

Dahl, Hans F. (1984) "Those Equal Folk," *Daedalus*. Winter, pp. 93–108.

Dahlgren, Göran (1976) "U-landspolitik och bistånd," in L. Wohlgemuth, ed. *Bistånd på mottagarens villkor*. Stockholm: SIDA.

DsUD, 1983:2 *U-krediter: en del av vårt u-landssamarbete*. Stockholm: Government Printing Office.

Från Riksdag & Departement. 1987:27, Stockholm: Government Printing Office.

Goldmann, Kjell, Sten Berglund, and Gunnar Sjöstedt (1986) *Democracy and Foreign Policy: The Case of Sweden*. Hants, England: Gower.

Goppers, Karlis (1984) "Bistånd och handel: Dr Jekyll och Mr Hyde i svensk u-landspolitik," in Christian Andersson, Lars Heikensten, and Stefan de Vylder, eds. *Bistånd i kris*. Stockholm: LiberFörlag, pp. 107–18.

Grettve, Anders (1986) "White Elephants and Little Sisters," in Pierre Früling, ed. *Swedish Development Aid in Perspective*. Stockholm: Almquist & Wiksell, pp. 147–56.

Heckscher, Gunnar (1958) "The Role of the Voluntary Organizaton in Swedish Democracy," in J. A. Lauwerys, ed. *Scandinavian Democracy*. Copenhagen: Universitets-Bogtrykkeri, pp. 126–39.

Hedman, Lowe (1978) *Svenskarna och u-hjälpen*. Stockholm: Almquist & Wiksell.

Heppling, Sixten (1986) "The Very First Years," in Pierre Früling, ed. *Swedish Development Aid in Perspective*. Stockholm: Almquist & Wiksell, pp. 13–26.

Hermele, Kenneth (1981) *Sweden and the Third World: Development Aid and Capital Involvement*. AKUT II. Uppsala, Sweden: Institute of Development Studies.

Jellenik, Sergio, Karl-Anders Larsson, and Christian Storey (1984) in Olav Stokke, ed. *European Development Assistance, Volume 1: Policies and Performance*. Tilburg, Netherlands: University of Tilburg Press.

Landöversyn 80. (198?) Stockholm: SIDA.

Lewin, Leif (1975) "The Debate on Economic Planning in Sweden," in Steven Koblik, ed. *Sweden's Development from Poverty to Affluence, 1750-1970*. Minneapolis, Minn.: University of Minnesota Press, pp. 282–302.

Lewin, Elisabeth (1986) "The Qualities of Smallness," in Pierre Früling, ed. *Swedish Development Aid in Perspective*. Stockholm: Almquist & Wiksell, pp. 221–32.

Lindholm, Stig (1970) *U-landsbilden: en undersökning av almänna opinionen*. Stockholm: Almquist & Wiksell.

Lindström, Ulla (1970) *Och regeringen satt kvar!* Stockholm: Tiden.

Michanek, Ernst (1977) *Role of Swedish Non-Governmental Organizations in International Development Cooperation*. Stockholm: SIDA.

Millwood, David and Helena Gazelius (1985) *Good Aid: A Study of Quality in Small Projects.* Stockholm: SIDA.

Myrdal, Gunnar (1960) *Beyond the Welfare State.* New Haven, Conn.: Yale University Press.

Odén, Bertil (1984) "Svenskt bistånd rättar in sig i OECD-ledet," in Christian Andersson, Lars Heikensten, and Stefan de Vylder, eds. *Bistånd i kris.* Stockholm: LiberFörlag, pp. 17-26.

OECD (1984) *OECD Economic Survey 1983-1984: Sweden.* Paris: OECD.

Parliamentary Records, Government Bill 1962:100, Stockholm: Government Printing Office.

Parliamentary Records, Government Bill 1968:101, Stockholm: Government Printing Office.

Parliamentary Records, Government Bill 1970:100, Bilaga 5, Stockholm: Government Printing Office.

Parliamentary Records, Government Bill 1984/85:100, Bilaga 5, Stockholm: Government Printing Office.

Parliamentary Records, Government Bill 1986/87:101, Bilaga 5, Stockholm: Government Printing Office.

Radetzki, Marian (1981) *Sverige och den Tredje Världen.* Stockholm: Studieförbundet Näringlsliv och Samhälle.

Rudebeck, Lars (1982) "Nordic Policies Toward the Third World," in Bengt Sundelius, ed. *Foreign Policies of Northern Europe.* Boulder, Colo.: Westview Press, pp. 143-76.

Rustow, Dankwart (1969) *The Politics of Compromise.* Westport, Conn.: Greenwood Press.

Samuelson, Kurt (1975) "The Philosophy of Swedish Welfare Polities," in Steven Koblik, ed. *Sweden's Development from Poverty to Affluence, 1750-1970.* Minneapolis, Minn.: University of Minnesota Press, pp. 335-53.

SOU, 1968:128.

SOU, 1972:90 *Industriutveckling och utvecklingssamarvbete.* Stockholm: Government Printing Office.

Stokke, Olav (1978) *Sveriges utvecklingsbistånd och biståndspolitik.* Uppsala, Sweden: Nordiska Afrikainstitutet.

Tingsten, Herbert (1973) *The Swedish Social Democrats.* (City: State): Bedminster Press.

UU, 1976/77:17, *Committee on Foreign Affairs Report,* Stockholm: Government Printing Office.

UU, 1983/84:15, *Committee on Foreign Affairs Report,* Stockholm: Government Printing Office.

Wahlström, Görel (1987) "Demokrati underifrån—orealistisk önskedröm," *Kvällsposten.* February 23.

Wohlgemuth, Lennart (1976) "Förord," in Wohlgemuth, ed. *Bistånd på mottagarens villkor.* Stockholm: SIDA.

7

Role Model or Power Pawn? The Changing Image of Swedish Foreign Policy, 1929–1987

Mikael S. Steene

This chapter will survey the changing image of Swedish foreign policy as reflected in the writings of prominent American scholars from the late 1920s until the present. The gradual shift in Sweden's foreign policy image from that of a vital and theoretically relevant model for small state emulation to that of a policy—specifically that of *neutrality*—that seems to work for Sweden alone will be illustrated. The shift in image is highlighted by recent American scholarship that portrays Sweden as a pawn within the context of superpower competition in the northern tier. Whereas the focus once may have been upon the moral virtues of neutrality, the interest today is concerned less with neutrality as concept and more with Sweden's actual ability to maintain neutrality within an environment punctuated by increased strains upon the Nordic strategic setting.

Beginning with Eric Bellquist (1929) and concluding with Paul Cole (1986), the image of Swedish foreign policy will be traced through the writings of several generations of American scholarship. The discussion is divided into the following periods which also demarcate important eras of Swedish foreign policy: *Joining the New World Order* (Swedish membership in the League of Nations); *Neutrality Under Pressure* (Sweden's dilemma during World War II); *Armed Neutral Promoting Peace* (maintenance of Swedish neutrality during the Cold War); *The Era of Internationalization* (Third World solidarity, anti-Vietnam War sentiment, and questions of increased interdependence); and *Eroding Boundaries* (the contemporary period marked by declining defense capability and increased superpower activity in the region).

Joining the New Order

Characterized by an unprecedented favorable strategic setting in the high north, the inter-war era began with the Swedish decision to join the League of Nations after an extensive parliamentary debate. Sweden became an active member of the League and decided to place its faith in collective security. The early 1920s also witnessed a dispute between Sweden and Finland over the Åland Islands. The affair was submitted to the League of Nations for adjudication and was finally settled in Finland's favor. Sweden—despite the adverse ruling—continued its policy of support toward the League until 1936 at which time Sweden joined the Nordic countries in a departure from the principles it represented. Sweden soon thereafter returned to a policy of armed neutrality.

The role of Sweden within the League of Nations was a topic of major interest to American commentators of the inter-war period. Eric Bellquist (1929) and Samuel Shepard Jones (1939) focused upon Sweden's relationship to the League. Hans Morgenthau (1939), however, concentrated upon Sweden's part in the reemergence of European neutrality in the wake of the collapse of the League of Nations.

In his 1929 monograph, Eric Bellquist characterized Sweden as a "proponent of peace" within the League of Nations and emphasized Sweden's acquiescence to the League's ruling on the Åland Islands. Through its compliance with the ruling of the Supreme Council, Sweden legitimized the League and placed the international order above national self-interest.

The second crucial policy point Bellquist described concerned Sweden's adherence to the disarmament doctrine of the League Covenant, in spite of the fact that such a policy ran counter to previous Swedish defense policy and resulted in serious domestic debate. The third important area of policy formation Bellquist discussed is that of Sweden's efforts as a "peace promoter" to secure Germany's admission into the League. To accomplish this, Sweden relinquished its preferred position as a permanent member of the League's governing council.

In a 1939 study, Samuel Shepard Jones widens the perspective somewhat by tracing the League from the time of its founding in 1919–20 to the exit of the Scandinavian states in 1936. Jones examines the common bond between the Scandinavian countries as a basis for an analysis of the policies toward pertinent League issues. Jones concludes that there never was an unreserved pan-Scandinavian approach to such matters and surmises that cooperation in the League was more a result of common war experiences which did not affect the internal differences that existed before World War I.

According to Jones, Scandinavian policy makers felt that the League's primary functions were to maintain peace and justice, and to promote cooperation in technical and economic areas. The crucial and uniting issue that remained for the Scandinavian countries, then, was the promotion of internationalism between the nations of the world without their loss of sovereignty. To Jones, Sweden and the other Scandinavian states played a crucial moral role in the international system and emerged as a "conscience to the Great Powers" (1939:274).

In a 1939 article, the point of departure for Hans Morgenthau is the joint declaration by the small European powers on July 1, 1936, which effectively cancelled their obligations to the League of Nations. Statements by Swedish foreign minister Rickard Sandler soon thereafter focused upon Sweden's right to maintain freedom of action and independent judgment that the political insecurity in Europe, as well as Sweden's own vital interests, necessitated. Morgenthau sympathetically argues that the great powers' lack of respect for the principles of international law had by then created a moral and political climate whereby the small states could no longer decide their own fates through traditional neutrality and political isolation.

Morgenthau's essay essentially views neutrality from the perspective of the international system. Morgenthau observes that commitments to an organization such as the League of Nations by any individual or bloc of small nations should be avoided, because they may lead to "risky obligations" (1939:486).

Morgenthau's work provides an early example of an analysis of Sweden's neutrality policy viewed from its relationship to the great powers. Sweden's policy itself is considered to be of little importance. Rather, it is Sweden's relationship with the overall balance of power that is worthy of scrutiny. The writings of Bellquist and Jones, however, provide early analyses which regard Swedish foreign policy as a contributor to the international system in its own right.

Neutrality Under Pressure

After the outbreak of World War II, Sweden—along with the other Scandinavian states—declared an adherence to the policy of neutrality. This commitment, however, was tested almost immediately after the Soviet Union attacked Finland during the Winter War of 1939–40. Despite strong domestic opinion, Sweden limited its assistance to Finland to humanitarian aid and the supply of volunteers. Sweden's emotional anguish over the question of assistance to Finland finally resulted in Sweden's self-declared "non-belligerent" status which represented a move away from a strict interpretation of neutrality. After the occupation of

Norway and Denmark by Germany, Sweden struggled to maintain independence in the face of increasing German pressures. Early in the war, Sweden permitted the transit of "holiday" troops through its territory and in the summer of 1941 authorized the passage of a full German division through northern Sweden to be employed on the new Russian front. During the latter stages of the war, Sweden again faced demands— this time from the Allies.

Two conflicting assessments of Swedish foreign policy during World War II—both focused upon the legal and moral implications of Sweden's neutral position—emerged in 1943. Although published in the same year, the articles arrive at distinctly different conclusions. Joesten (1943) is highly critical of Swedish policies, while Hedin (1943) manages to find the basis for a defense. These articles—with their contrasting assessments—illustrate the divergent opinions on the nature of Sweden's wartime policies held by many foreign observers at the time.

In *Stalwart Sweden,* Joachim Joesten (1943) links the Social Democratic Party's rise to power in 1932 to the fact that a strong Nazi party did not exist in Sweden at the time. Joesten asserts that not only the Social Democrats, but many of the other levels of the Swedish power establishment including the king, the police, and the major newspapers were under Nazi influence. According to Joesten, the primary reason for Sweden's pro-German stance—which allegedly included the supply of Hitler's Germany with both iron ore and poison gas—stemmed from a small group of Swedish business groups with heavy investments in Germany.

Joesten characterizes Sweden's wartime foreign policy as a form of "homespun isolationism based on egoism and fear" (1943:25). In Joesten's view, Sweden's flexible neutrality initially led to a clearly pro-German bias bordering on appeasement. However, when the tide of the war turned against Hitler in 1942, Sweden adapted its policies to better suit the Allies. Viewed in this light, the Swedish policy of neutrality is understandably given little merit by Joesten. The image of Sweden that emerges is, in his words, one of a "modern Jezebel" pursuing a "coolly selfish and even callous policy" (Joesten, 1943:204–5).

Naboth Hedin (1943), on the other hand, viewed Swedish neutrality as a viable political course and as a positive outgrowth of specific geographic, historic, and economic conditions. Hedin relates Swedish foreign policy both to the failure of the League of Nations and to the strong German presence in the Nordic area. According to this line of reasoning, Sweden—encircled by the Germans—had no recourse but to accept certain provisions.

Hedin, however, emphasizes the economic aspects of Sweden's neutrality policy. According to Hedin, the main Swedish objective was to maintain production in order to ensure employment (1943:60). After the invasion of Norway and of Denmark, Sweden had three possible foreign policy avenues, each of which were attempted at one time or another: 1) it could increase trade with Germany and the German-occupied nations, 2) it could improve its trade relations with the Soviet Union, or 3) it could attempt to trade with overseas countries with German consent. Sweden followed the first course during the initial invasion period. Hedin, in fact, asserts that Sweden needed the iron ore trade with Germany in order to avoid economic bankruptcy. Faced with an issue of national economic survival, Sweden had no alternative but to accede to German demands for the transit of troops through Sweden. In Hedin's view, any other course would have been suicidal (1943:54-6).

Hedin attributes the success of Sweden's neutrality to several factors— a domestic situation based upon cooperation between the main political parties, a strong military defense, a balanced economic system, and a favorable strategic circumstance that initially prevented a German invasion. In addition to emphasizing Sweden's domestic structure, Hedin also stresses the role of external events and forecasts that Sweden's expectations rests with the twin hopes for a new post-war world organization and for increased Nordic strategic cooperation.

While Joesten and Hedin both stress the enormous impact of economic factors upon Swedish foreign policy formulation, they arrive at largely different conclusions. In Joesten's estimation, Sweden acted in an opportunistic and timid fashion. To Hedin, Sweden successfully and pragmatically navigated a dangerous course based upon an assessment of the strategic environment. It is important, however, to remember that while Joesten's book was written soon after the Swedish concessions to Germany, Hedin's article appeared after the tide of the war had changed and Swedish foreign policy had begun a return to "normalcy."

The impact of timing should not be underestimated. In a subsequent article published in 1945, Joesten states that neutrality must ideally balance the relationship of neutral nations to various belligerents. In practice, however, this ideal is seldom achieved. Instead, neutrality becomes a policy of adjustment, tilting toward whichever side is currently winning. As Joesten writes in 1945, Sweden is not necessarily pro-German; rather, its policies are dictated by economic and strategic necessity and may be viewed as simply pro-Swedish. Clearly, the sympathetic tone of Joesten's 1945 article is a significant shift from his previous assessment published just two years earlier.

Armed Neutral Promoting Peace

Sweden joined the United Nations in 1946 and—although not a charter member—pursued a highly visible policy within the organization. During the initial post-war period, Sweden also pressed for a joint Scandinavian defense arrangement. However, largely as a result of divergent attitudes toward NATO, the negotiations broke down in 1949. After some domestic debate, Sweden opted to continue the traditional policy of neutrality, defining it as *non-alliance in peace aiming for neutrality in war.* This remains the official doctrine to this day.

The American scholarship of the immediate post-war period is largely retrospective in nature. Sweden's World War II role is assessed and different facets of the neutrality policy as a strategic doctrine are examined. Overall, the tone is generally positive. Bruce Hopper (1945) cites Sweden as a "test example" of the important role which small states can play within the international system. David Hinshaw (1949) praises Sweden's neutrality as a rational foreign policy, while Annette Baker Fox (1959) examines neutrality from the standpoint of a skillfully implemented diplomacy. Franklin Scott (1950) and Samuel Abrahamson (1957) trace the history of Swedish neutrality focusing primarily upon its adaptability to international events. William Zartman (1954) regards Sweden's foreign policy as being both anticipatory and active. More so than the others, Zartman stressed the relationship of neutrality to the Cold War.

The 1930's image of Sweden as a peace-loving nation, then, had returned to American scholarship by the end of World War II. Such analysts as Bruce Hopper and David Hinshaw emphasized Sweden's role within the international system as a "champion of peace." In a 1945 article, Hopper challenged the popular postwar sentiment that neutrality and small states have become mere "appendages" to the Great Powers. In Hopper's view, small states may to the contrary play a major role in international affairs.

According to Hopper, Sweden is unique because its neutrality is both relatively recent and recently tested during World War II. In Hopper's opinion, this sets Sweden apart as a successful European neutral under great stress. To substantiate his observations, Hopper lists specific periods during the course of World War II and compares Sweden's reactions to different power constellations. The periods of greatest stress for Sweden's neutral position were the Finno-Russian War and the invasions of Norway and of Denmark by Germany. When the balance of power was reestablished during the course of World War II, Sweden's policy of neutrality returned to normalcy. Hopper cites the refusal of the Swedish government to permit continued German troop movements, an increase in trade with the Soviet Union, and Sweden's prominent role in the peace agreement between Finland and the Soviet Union to illustrate this point.

Although Hopper concludes that neutrality is dependent upon the existence of a balance of power, he also asserts that the existence of small neutral states is essential to the overall system of nation-states and that little international collaboration can occur without them. Hopper argues that large powers have been restrained by small states that adhere to the values of decency and that small states often take on the role as conscience to the Great Powers. Without small states, the Great Powers themselves would have to "invent" such a moral code.

Hopper's article raises several issues that other American scholars of the period do not examine. First, Hopper makes the theoretical connection between the nature of neutrality and its relationship to the balance of power. To Hopper, the neutrality question cannot be answered only in terms of the particular strategic problem; rather, it must be viewed in terms of its existence within a larger global picture as well. Second, Hopper maintains that there is not "sufficient support for the thesis that small states are doomed, and along with them neutrality and the Balance of Power" (1945:449). The developments after the end of World War II which culminated in the establishment of today's balance of power in Europe also seems to fit into Hopper's typology.

David Hinshaw (1949) praises Sweden's successful avoidance of the war. Hinshaw connects Sweden's neutrality policy to a national mentality focused upon the promotion of a secure environment—not through force—but through logic.

According to Hinshaw, Sweden's policy of neutrality differed greatly during the two world wars. During World War I, Sweden's fear of Britain and fellowship with Germany dictated the nature of the neutrality policy. During World War II, however, Sweden's fear of Germany and sympathies for the Allies were of decisive importance. Hinshaw believes that in both cases the policy pursued by Sweden was one of pragmatic necessity (1949:88).

Hinshaw observes that Sweden's foreign policy took a decisive turn when the League of Nations began to deteriorate. Sweden moved from the collective security of the League to an policy of independent rearmament. Hinshaw asserts that this was done largely to insure that the Great Powers would not disregard the Swedish desire to remain neutral.

In tracing the development of this policy through World War II, Hinshaw illustrates the tenuous nature of the Swedish position. During the initial period of the war, Sweden's policy was based upon two assumptions—that the Allies would continue to believe in Sweden's intent to pursue neutrality and that Sweden could continue unbiased trade with both sides (Hinshaw, 1949:102). Thus, Sweden's wartime policy is viewed as being almost entirely dependent upon external conditions. The main challenge confronting Sweden, then, was the difficulty in reconciling economic and military problems with the maintenance of internal psychological and spiritual strength (Hinshaw, 1949:116).

According to Hinshaw, the need to balance these demands greatly influenced Sweden's foreign policy. Given these constraints, Sweden generally followed a rational approach to its situation. The concessions to Germany during the early part of World War II were based upon a sober assessment of the strategic situation, whereas the successful avoidance of the "hot" war was counterbalanced through the promotion of decency at humanitarian levels.

Hinshaw's discussion of the post-war situation focuses upon the general deterioration of Sweden's strategic position. Sweden no longer enjoys an isolated perch situated on Europe's northern tier, but now lies directly on the path between Washington and Moscow. Hinshaw regards this shift as creating new problems for Sweden's continued adherence to neutrality. He argues that the advent of nuclear weapons may render Swedish defensive efforts pointless and that—in light of the awesome destructiveness of modern weapons systems—the Swedish people may well feel that no victor will emerge from future conflicts (Hinshaw, 1949:274). Hinshaw continues by linking the external threat to an equally imminent domestic danger—*statism.*

Hinshaw asserts that the socialist reforms that were being implemented within Sweden during that time were threatening the resolve of the Swedish people (1949:192). Hinshaw argues that increasing statism will force Sweden to enter into agreements with the rest of the world because of economic necessity. This will result in a reduction of both national sovereignty and the capacity to pursue an independent foreign policy. If one accepts this line of reasoning, then Sweden's neutrality will not be shaped by domestic consensus but by external events. Within this framework, the role performed by democratic institutions and traditional diplomatic channels will be minimized.

In contrast to Hinshaw, Annette Baker Fox (1959) places great emphasis upon the relationship between Sweden's policy of neutrality and its skillfully implemented diplomacy that are coupled with "favorable circumstances." Fox regards Sweden's decision to remain non-aligned during World War II as neither the result of ideological considerations nor of a consciously determined foreign policy. Fox suggests that Swedish neutrality during that period was shaped by events and not dictated by policy makers. However, Fox does stress the fact that Sweden—in her view—has the capacity to exhibit a certain amount of policy-making capability when called upon. To support this idea, Fox cites Sweden's successful rearmament during World War II and the fairly balanced economy that was supported by a stockpiling of vital goods. To summarize, Fox views Sweden's foreign policy as being both *active* and *reactive,* the beneficiary of a fortuitous combination of political luck and economic skill.

Several other analysts, however, have characterized Sweden's neutrality policy as being either wavering or ambiguous. In a 1950 study, Franklin Scott likens Sweden's neutrality policy to a "weather vane," twisting and turning with the change in the political winds. Scott traces the origins of Sweden's neutrality to the quest for peace after the end of Sweden's great power status in the 18th century. On the whole, Scott describes Sweden's neutral role as largely successful. Like Bellquist, Scott praises Sweden's acquiescence to the League's decision concerning the Åland Islands. Scott also contends that Sweden and other small states acted as a "buffer" in conflicts between the large states and within the League itself.

Scott characterizes Sweden's position during World War II as one of occasional vocal opposition, but little action. Sweden's policy was largely one of adaptation to the changing conditions of the war. Scott contends that while Sweden's neutrality may have been the policy of the possible and was "frankly opportunistic," he also adds that no viable alternative policy existed. To keep trade routes open Sweden had to placate the dominant powers within the Baltic region. However, Scott also emphasizes that Sweden remained an outspoken critic of Nazism, never advocated the actions taken by Germany, and offered assistance to the occupied nations.

Scott also examines the issue of Nordic cooperation after World War II. He links the unsuccessful attempt to coordinate a common Scandinavian defense pact to war experiences and to the advent of a new strategic environment that included an increased Soviet presence. According to Scott, Sweden has acted to preserve the Nordic East-West balance through its policy of non-integration within the Western Alliance.

Scott's examination of post-war Scandinavian and Swedish foreign policies links the policies of the individual states to changes within the international power structure during the 20th century. In Scott's view, these developments have essentially served to take away the sovereignty of the Nordic states. Scott asserts that Sweden's policy of neutrality is largely symbolic and likens it to an act of "whistling in the dark." In an era of superpower tensions Sweden must reconcile independent values with external pressures.

Scott's point of view may have been affected by the tensions of the Cold War period. He expresses concern for the Soviet threat and for the role played by the United States. In a 1975 work, Scott's focus shifts to the major issue of the sixties and seventies—that of the possible impact of a potential European Community membership for Sweden upon its continued adherence to a policy of neutrality. To Scott, Sweden again displayed its adaptability and, thus, maintained an image as a northern "weather vane."

In a 1957 study, Samuel Abrahamson embraces a view of Sweden's neutrality policy similar to that of Franklin Scott. Abrahamson asserts that the oscillating nature of Sweden's neutrality policy was not seriously questioned because of Sweden's isolation from European "entanglements" (1957:11). However, in Abrahamson's view Sweden's neutrality from World War II to the present has not been a policy of pure neutrality, rather, a policy in which Sweden's own welfare comes first. Abrahamson asserts that Sweden began the World War I period with a clearly pro-German tilt which only later shifted in favor of the Atlantic states and that during the interwar period, Sweden abandoned neutrality in order to play a part in the League of Nations.

Abrahamson contends that during World War II Sweden's neutrality was markedly pro-Finnish and that it was only after the failure of several regional defense initiatives during the post-war period that Sweden again resorted to a policy of neutrality. Abrahamson concludes that the basis for this shift lies in "the Swedish view . . . that by joining a Western alliance world tension would only increase and possibly endanger the independence of Finland." In other words, a NATO membership by Sweden or the grant of base privileges to any foreign powers in any of the Scandinavian countries might encourage similar demands by the Soviet Union (1957:88).

Abrahamson's book provides a good illustration of the trend that emerged during the Cold War that analyzed Sweden's neutrality within the context of Great Power conflict. An additional concern of Abrahamson's study is that of small-state neutrality and its possible effects upon international trends. Abrahamson contends that Sweden has attempted to promote its own influence upon the international system through the maintenance of a high profile that includes serving as a mediator in world affairs. To Abrahamson, this role may be the small state's most important *raison d'être*.

Abrahamson attempts to analyze Sweden's foreign policy development through a focus upon the issue of neutrality. However, foreign policy and neutrality—though often closely intertwined—are not necessarily synonymous. In spite of its limited scope, Abrahamson's work provides a concise history of Sweden's neutrality policy. Certain areas of Swedish foreign policy—such as trade and foreign assistance—are not addressed by the author.

William Zartman (1954) takes a very different view of Sweden's role in the international arena. Writing from the perspective of the Cold War period, Zartman argues that Sweden fails to take a more active role in solving world problems in areas where the state could make substantial contributions. Instead, Sweden is regarded as primarily serving self interests to the detriment of its image as a mediator in the international arena.

The thrust of Zartman's article is mainly an analysis of the role of the Scandinavian states during the Cold War period in the promotion of global neutrality within the framework of an international movement. Zartman cites the active desire by Norway and Denmark to export a policy of neutrality as evidence of neutralism within these two states. Zartman asserts that this is not the case with Sweden, because Sweden's neutrality is based upon a wartime position. This form of neutrality is viewed as the attempt to maintain Sweden's own peace without any ambitions of extending neutrality to the international system. According to Zartman, Sweden's neutrality policy is based upon realism and national interest whereas neutralism rests upon utopian ideals and international concerns.

Zartman's conclusions directly contradict the image of Sweden's foreign policy which many Swedish policy makers publicly present. This is an important point. In Zartman's view, Sweden is not a value-promoting state. Rather, the policy of neutrality is based upon self interest and necessity.

The Era of Internationalization

In 1961, Prime Minister Tage Erlander met with President John F. Kennedy in the White House. Twenty-six years would elapse until a Swedish head of government would again officially visit the United States. During the Vietnam War, relations between the United States and Sweden cooled considerably until, finally, diplomatic relations were frozen in 1973 following the harsh criticism of the 1972 Christmas bombings by Prime Minister Olof Palme.

During this time, Sweden embarked upon a major foreign aid policy to promote development in Third World countries and assumed a new role as champion of solidarity. In the 1960s, Sweden elected not to build a nuclear arsenal and instead became active in the promotion of arms control. Sweden—it may be said—assumed the role of a moral voice in the spirit of the activist UN Secretary General Dag Hammarskjöld who died in the line of duty in 1961.

The era of internationalization marked the emergence of a so-called "active foreign policy" through which Sweden seeks to promote respect for international law and institutions, to achieve world solidarity, and to maintain its own high-profile in development assistance, international mediation, and disarmament. This era was also highlighted by the discussions concerning a possible Swedish membership in the EEC. In 1972, Sweden decided not to apply for membership in a decision that was primarily justified upon Sweden's concern about the maintenance of a credible neutrality.

The American discussions during this period range from an overview of Sweden's neutrality tradition by Joseph Board (1970) to discussions of specific policy questions by Martin Schiff (1969) and by Donald Hancock (1972). The period also includes a study of the internal mechanisms of Swedish foreign policy process by James Waite (1971) and a case study of Sweden's foreign policy during World War I by Steven Koblik (1972).

Joseph Board's 1970 study traces Sweden's shift toward a more active neutrality which led to increased strains within the domestic foreign policy consensus. Board notes that such strains may well result in additional party controversy and in modifications of existing foreign policy priorities.

Board focuses upon the major change in Sweden's neutrality during this time which, in his view, is its policies toward the developing states. Because Sweden is small and non-aligned, Board reasons that it is able to play an assertive role in the Third World. Whereas other states may spark resentment, Sweden—with its long tradition of neutrality—will not.

Board, however, contends that Sweden's involvement in the Third World may pose future dilemmas with respect to the United States. The only long-term impact of anti-U.S. sentiment sparked by the Vietnam War that Board foresees is to "deromanticize" the United States in the eyes of the Swedish people. He does not view the downgrading of diplomatic contacts between the two countries as being of lasting significance.

Board views Sweden as performing the role of balancer between the power blocs. Sweden's non-aligned status plays an important role in the promotion of systemic stability even though Sweden is ideologically linked to the West.

In Board's view, this balance has been achieved through both direct and indirect means—indirectly by the presence of the western military alliance which has stemmed Soviet expansion and directly through Sweden's policy of a strong defense. According to Board, this defense policy has served to raise the costs to potential aggressors upon Sweden and has turned the state into a kind of "international hedgehog."

Board contends that Sweden as a small state can do little to determine the course of events. However, he notes that once an event has occured, Sweden's long tradition of neutrality and its diplomatic skill may combine to provide effective policy making. Although Sweden's size and geographic profile restrict the range of available policy alternatives, Board observes that the state retains a remarkable array of technological, economic, and military resource capabilities. Though the broad course of action may be dictated by the Great Powers, it is still the province of the small state's policy makers to decide the specifics of the resultant reactions.

In a 1972 study, M. Donald Hancock maintains, like Board, that the Swedish post-war concept of neutrality does not preclude international activism. Neutrality—viewed as an integral part of Swedish foreign policy—embraces two tenets, namely: freedom from military alliance and active involvement in questions concerning international peace and solidarity. Whereas Sweden remains outside organizations such as NATO and the EEC, it nevertheless plays a vital role within "peace promoting" international bodies such as the United Nations, the U.N. Commission on Disarmament, and international foreign assistance organizations. Hancock does not view these positions as contradictory. He argues that neutrality is not merely a "prescription" for escaping conflict, but that it also seeks to preserve national interests during times of peace and to promote the peaceful development of the world, as well.

Hancock delves further into the questions surrounding the nature of Sweden's neutrality resulting from changes within the Nordic and European economic spheres. Historically, Sweden has promoted regional cooperation on several occasions after the breakup of the Norwegian union in 1905.

Hancock traces the development of regionalism from the establishment of the Nordic Interparliamentary Union in 1907 to the expansion of the European Free Trade Association (EFTA) during the 1960s. Hancock asserts that positive growth in Nordic cooperation in cultural and political matters occurred, although not within the military sphere. Whereas Nordic integration into a supranational union failed, inter-governmental agreements were achieved in the areas of customs regulations, passport control, welfare benefits, and the creation of a common Scandinavian labor pool. Hancock contends that such cooperation has led to regional stabilization and, hence, increased security. However, he considers the advent of the European Common Market to be a potential threat to this stability, because, unlike EFTA, the EEC maintains a supranational structure. Whereas EFTA affects only certain industrial tariffs, the EEC seeks to go much further in the development of a superstate. The Common Market constitutes a traditional, and significant, market for Nordic exports and, thus, cannot be ignored. A possible exclusion from this bloc could have profound effects upon the economies of Sweden and of the other Scandinavian states.

Hancock's review of Sweden's neutrality is, of course, only a portion of his study of Sweden's "politics of post-industrial change." His study testifies not only to the changes within Sweden's policy making, but in the American post-war analysis of Sweden's foreign policy as well. The focus here is concerned less with the historical antecedents of neutrality and more with the exploration of how the doctrine relates to developments within certain issue areas.

Hancock and Board both concentrate upon the domestic politics of Sweden. They only briefly review the aspects of foreign policy in general and neutrality in specific. This approach, however, is quite common in the American literature of the period that is fascinated with the development of post-industrial societies such as Sweden.

Using the Swedish position toward European economic integration as a departure point, Martin Schiff's 1969 dissertation traces the historical development of Sweden's neutrality policy and its relation to theories of political integration. Schiff analyzes Sweden's non-integration within the EEC from both the economic and political perspectives.

Schiff argues that before World War II the international system enabled Sweden to act somewhat independently of other states. During the period after the war, however, he notes that there has been a rapid growth in interstate military and economic actions.

Whereas Sweden's "active neutrality" was successful in the establishment of certain agreements with the Eastern bloc, as well as with the developing nations and with the U.N., there were several areas in which such a policy was incompatible with international developments.

In particular, Schiff cites several areas of defense related political integration in Europe. According to Schiff, the growth of international organizations, such as NATO, has made it difficult for Sweden to achieve the traditional "freedom from alliances." During the past, international organizations largely consisted of military treaties that Sweden as a neutral could avoid. Today, however, the increasing intimacy between the economic and the political dimensions of international organizations significantly raises the costs of non-participation.

Schiff views Sweden's neutrality of the post-war period as changing in character. To substantiate this observation, Schiff cites Sweden's new orientation toward the Soviet Union, more active role in international trade, and spirited participation in the United Nations (1969:142).

Schiff regards this new activism as evidence of a shifting ideological basis within Sweden's neutrality. The neutrality of the past that sought to remain free from alliances has now become an active neutrality that strives to shape international events. According to Schiff, this ideological shift is based upon "objective and independent evaluations" of the international system. However, he contends that this increased international activity could result in a conflict between internationalist and Swedish goals.

To substantiate this idea, Schiff offers the example of Sweden's possible membership within the EEC. He concludes that Sweden's neutrality would not be abandoned for the sake of an EEC membership and states further that there exists a rigidity between internal and external factors that direct the course of Sweden's foreign policy. In Schiff's view, this prevents Sweden from being actively integrated into the international system in a manner which would jeopardize the policy of neutrality.

Although Schiff's study focuses upon the particular case of Sweden and the EEC, it also presents a valuable analysis of the history, nature, and mechanisms of Sweden's neutrality policy. Schiff's work represents an early effort to examine both the economic restraints as well as the necessities associated with Swedish foreign policy in general and neutrality in particular.

Whereas Schiff's analysis reviews a specific issue area, James L. Waite (1971) investigates Sweden's foreign policy making process and studies its mechanisms in some detail. Waite examines not only Sweden's political structures and historical foreign policy developments, but the relationship of these factors to the international system as well. He separates Sweden's foreign policy into various internal and external inputs, outputs, and feedbacks, and associates these factors to specific decision-making criteria.

Waite contends that Sweden's domestic and foreign policies are tightly intertwined. In his view, one is often the staging area for effecting change within the other. Waite describes foreign policy as "being at one end of a continuum with domestic policy at the other," with the dividing line between the two being quite unclear (1971:48).

According to Waite, Swedish policy makers do not simply decide upon a particular policy direction. Instead, they formulate policies within the context of internal and external constraints which are especially prevalent in a small centralized state strongly integrated into the international system. Waite contends that Sweden has long practiced the "Machiavellian advice to small states," and has been squeezed between "a two-sided press, with independence on one side and integration on the other" (1971:51).

Waite asserts that Sweden's foreign policy scope is limited by ideological, economic, and political variables. Sweden cannot make policies that jeopardize its international standing or its own domestic structures. Rather, Sweden is compelled by its size to rely more upon political guile than upon force. Every internal and external variable must be carefully balanced in order to formulate policies that do not excessively strain the state. Sweden, unlike larger and more powerful states, cannot rely upon sheer force to dictate policy, but must exercise policy making skill in order to play a role in the international arena.

In Waite's view, Sweden must act abroad as a result of economic factors. Waite observes that the extent of Sweden's economic and technological base makes it of vital importance that "trade be carried out with major centers of power; yet in so doing the country's foreign policy becomes suspect" (1971:255). Waite attributes the need to somehow balance economic necessity with strategic objectives as a major reason for several of Sweden's foreign policy outcomes. To support this contention, Waite cites Sweden's controversial policies toward U.S. involvement in Vietnam and the contradictory Swedish stance in the EEC membership question. In Waite's view, Sweden's promotion of certain positions—such as condemnation of U.S. foreign policy—lends credibility to its own foreign policy in the view of its domestic constituents but, perhaps more importantly, in the Soviet Union and the Third World as well.

The dissertations of Waite and Schiff represent original attempts to provide a thorough analysis of the restraints which Swedish policy-makers must face in the pursuit of a policy of neutrality. It is unfortunate that these studies were never published, because they contain observations that may have been of real benefit to the national security debate within Sweden during the 1970s.

Steven Koblik (1972) also asserts that Sweden's foreign policy of neutrality is shaped by both external and internal variables. He focuses, however, upon an earlier period—Sweden's political position in 1917–18 toward the end of World War I. Koblik's study makes the point that Sweden's policy-making community lacked consensus during this time. Political maneuvering by various party leaders who were attempting to influence the policy making process dominated the foreign policy scene. The popular support that the policy of neutrality enjoyed at the outset of the war was diminished as the war progressed until, in 1916, the united front cracked.

Because Sweden lacked domestic consensus, Koblik asserts that its foreign policy during the World War I never became clearly defined. During Germany's control of the Baltic, Sweden's neutrality was benevolent toward the Axis powers.

When the tide of the war turned—marked with the withdrawal of Russia and an increased participation by the United States—Sweden's policy gravitated toward the West and away from Germany. In Koblik's view, the relative success of Sweden's neutrality policy was not so much the result of actual policy making as of the constraints placed upon it by the belligerent powers in certain economic, military, and political areas. Through his focus upon the domestic and the international dimensions of the neutrality issue, Koblik exposes the limitations of small power decision making.

Koblik's analysis characterizes Sweden's foreign policies of the period as being both passive and reactive in the sense that Sweden did not actively seek to shape the course of events. Koblik's study is unique in that it examines the foreign policy from the internal perspective. Instead of analyzing Swedish foreign policy as a concrete political reality, Koblik's study penetrates the façade of the Swedish consensus that surrounds neutrality and other foreign policy questions.

Eroding Boundaries

In 1976, forty years of uninterrupted Social Democratic Party rule came to an end through an election defeat at the hands of the non-socialist opposition. The change in government, however, did not result in any major change in foreign policy. The economic slowdown of the late 1970s dominated political discussion and resulted in budget cutbacks across the board including defense. In spite of the hard economic time, the decision was reached in 1982 to proceed with the development of a new and costly all-purpose aircraft—the JAS *Gripen*—and the traditional and costly commitment to development assistance was reaffirmed.

In October of 1981, a major foreign policy crisis occurred after a Soviet "Whiskey Class" submarine–possibly carrying nuclear weapons—went aground in the vicinity of a sensitive naval installation in Karlskrona. Since that time, numerous submarine incursions within Swedish territorial waters have been identified by the government which, after 1983, has refused to name a violator. The submarine issue and related matters has sparked an unusually significant domestic debate over Sweden's policies with the USSR. Naturally, during this period a debate developed over the level and direction of defense spending and its relationship to a credible neutrality.

In February 1986, Prime Minister Olof Palme was murdered while walking down the street in Stockholm. Two months later, Palme's successor—Prime Minister Ingvar Carlsson—visited Moscow. Carlsson added two more world capitals to his itinerary in 1987 when he visited Peking and Washington. In September, Prime Minister Carlsson met President Reagan at the White House during an official state banquet. During the spring of 1988, Carlsson toured Western European capitals. The post-Palme leadership continued the Swedish government's high-profile international travels.

American assessments of Sweden's foreign policy during this period range from Marquis Childs' traditional analysis of the moral and economic implications of foreign policy to John Boli's critique of Sweden's contradictory relationship with the Third World. The American analysis of Sweden's neutrality, however, changes significantly when the emphasis shifts from a preoccupation with political implications to that of strategic feasibility. The value of studying Sweden or any of the Scandinavian states is questioned by Marvin Rintala in a 1978 essay, whereas a number of more influential scholars—Canby (1981), Zakhem (1982), Taylor (1985), Cole (1986), and Leitenberg (1987)—assess the viability of Sweden's foreign policy in light of economic and strategic changes.

Marquis Childs, author of the 1930s classic, *Sweden: The Middle Way,* which focused upon Sweden's domestic structure, examines Sweden's international role in a sequel entitled *Sweden: The Middle Way on Trial* (1980). Childs focuses upon Sweden's humanitarian activism and credits Gunnar and Alva Myrdal with much of the country's activist international profile through their active role in disarmament and Third World issues. According to Childs, the Myrdals helped shape the Swedish conscience— Alva through her work in the United Nations and in the area of nuclear disarmament and Gunnar through his role as spokesman opposing the Vietnam War. In an era of world events increasingly dominated by superpowers which ignore the plight of the needy, Sweden—in Childs' view—has pursued a remarkably energetic policy of foreign aid. Sweden has participated in international programs that promote improved living conditions in developing countries and has achieved the one percent of GNP goal for combined multilateral and bilateral foreign assistance (Childs, 1980:150).

Whereas Childs' study illuminates Sweden's public policy making process, it reveals relatively little of the impact of external events upon the shaping of Sweden's foreign policy. In Childs' view, the leadership of charismatic individuals such as the Myrdals affects a particular policy much more than specific external variables such as the influence of the superpowers, of Sweden's trade partners, or of Sweden's own image as international mediator.

One scholar who does address some of these external factors is John Boli in a 1983 article. Boli rejects the standard view that Sweden— because it is a small and wealthy state—must join in the causes of other small states in order to promote a safer, more just, and more equal world system. In Boli's view, this approach overlooks Sweden's systemic role as a "subsidiary core power." Boli asserts that because Sweden is "a small nation in the core of the system," it is "highly exposed to and influenced by the ideological trends and political 'fashions' of the larger world" (1983:188). Sweden's proclaimed solidarity with other small states then is based less upon idealistic "utopian" notions than on activist policies developed from Sweden's own systemic position and historical antecedents.

The first section of Boli's study is primarily concerned with the role of Sweden as a member of the capitalist core group or a state highly involved in trade and capital formation within the Western capitalist economic system. In Boli's view, the achievement of Sweden's social democracy from the 1930s has been more to redistribute wealth and to eliminate poverty than to restructure the basic economy in a socialist direction (1983:193).

The second portion of Boli's work examines Sweden's economic development to a position as a sub-core state (*i.e.* a state closely integrated with the power states within the modern global economic structure). The third and final section addresses the role and impact of Sweden's neutrality upon its economy.

During World War II, Sweden's policy of accommodation enabled it to emerge with an "industrial power base which was completely unscathed and operating at full strength" (Boli, 1983:200). According to Boli, this factor has shaped Sweden's foreign policy during the post-war era and has signalled a distinct shift toward a policy of "active neutrality."

During the 1960s, the nature of this active policy shifted from an emphasis upon programs of international disarmament and cooperation to a concern for the problems of the developing states. Sweden became increasingly vocal in its statements concerning the Vietnam War and increased the amount of its financial support for the developing world. Through the promotion of "world system" policies, Sweden gradually began to oppose the policies of several large core powers including the United States and Great Britain. Boli asserts that Sweden, because of its own role as a sub-core power, may have been pursuing what was essentially a contradictory foreign policy.

Boli, however, argues that Sweden's sub-core status does not preclude action against the main core states. This position is, in fact, a privileged one within the economic structure because it "benefits from the structure established by the primary core but need not undertake the tasks necessary to maintain it." Boli also notes, however, that the sub-core state is "especially sensitive to the ideological and organizational trends generated by the world-system" (Boli, 1983:213). He contends that such a sensitivity may lead to a dependency by the sub-core states upon international political opinion. Boli concludes that "practically all of Swedish foreign policy has conformed, issue by issue, with the dominant sociological trends of the contemporary world system" (1983:216).

The study by John Boli is significant in that it focuses upon a dimension of Swedish foreign policy that is outside the spheres of neutrality and strategic issues. Boli's theoretical focus concerns Sweden's dual and, perhaps, contradictory identities within an international capitalist system.

Boli concludes that Sweden is perhaps more capitalistic and more closely linked to the West than is generally acknowledged.

Whereas Childs and Boli both consider Sweden to be a relevant international actor, Marvin Rintala (1978) regards Sweden and the Scandinavian states as of relatively little importance in an analysis of the international system. Rintala concentrates his analysis upon the geographic location, relative size, economic capability, and the degree of consensuality among four of the Nordic states. Rintala asserts that this region constitutes but a relatively tiny segment of the international environment. The generally divergent character of the separate foreign policies reduces their international impact. Rintala concludes that "political scientists generally ought not to stress northern Europe as a successful case of political integration, and that although comparative politics specialists might find value in a study of the area, its importance to students of international politics is minor" (1978:206).

Rintala's study overlooks important economic changes within Sweden during the late 1970s, as well as new strategic developments within the Baltic region. Some recent American studies of Sweden's foreign policy, however, have taken these changes into account. Stephen L. Canby's 1981 analysis assesses the impact of changes within Sweden's defense structure during the late 1970s. Canby considers some of the possible consequences that this development may have for the future of the Nordic balance including the possibility that Sweden may lose its critical role.

For Canby, the crucial question is not whether Sweden will continue a policy of neutrality, rather, can the policy continue in its present form. Canby doubts that Sweden can afford an "extrovert" defense strategy based upon sophisticated and expensive air force and naval high technologies. He postulates that Sweden will shift to a putatively cheaper "introvert" strategy based upon territorial defense (1981:117). Economic realities will necessitate Sweden's shift from an comprehensive defense system to one that emphasizes strength within certain key zones. Rather than prevent an all-out attack, the revised Swedish defense would merely attempt to thwart aggressors at certain strategic points. Canby asserts that Sweden's military planners face the twin dilemmas of escalating equipment replacement costs on the one hand and defense budget cuts necessitated by a constrained economy on the other.

Canby contends that Sweden can no longer afford the luxury of both a standing army and technologically advanced air and naval forces. He further argues that through an attempt to retain both, Sweden is becoming weaker. Sweden must choose between a dependence upon high technology for defense in specific areas or a reliance upon traditional forces that may, in turn, increase Sweden's dependence upon other states in the event of conflict. In Canby's view, this dilemma may even lead to a loss of Sweden's role as "equilibrator" within the Nordic balance (1981:123).

This dilemma is developed even further by Zov Zakhem in 1982. Although Zakhem's article doesn't primarily focus upon Sweden, it does address Sweden's increased economic and military dilemma and its potential impact upon NATO. Zakhem notes that an increased Soviet interest in the Baltic, together with the problem of selecting either an introvert or extrovert defense policy, could lead to a destabilization of the norther tier (1982:205). This, in turn, may result in a further increase in Soviet activity within the region and, consequently, create additional NATO security problems.

It is interesting to note that both Canby and Zakhem are defense experts working within the U.S. defense community. This may explain their interest in the Swedish defense capability and its relationship to NATO strategy and may, perhaps, signal an increased awareness of Sweden's strategic position by US military planners.

Primarily because of economic constraints, both Canby and Zakhem regard Sweden as no longer effectively performing its role as the fulcrum of the Nordic balance. These authors do not analyze the specific virtues of Sweden's foreign policy, nor do they attempt to explain the forces underlying the present dilemma. It is the strategic implications of the Swedish policy that constitutes the main focus of interest for these Washington, D.C.-based observers.

In another study by a strategic analyst, William J. Taylor connects the internal processes of Sweden's defense policy to the constraints that have led to Sweden's current strategic dilemma. Taylor asserts that neutrality is a widely-accepted principle and is not likely to become an issue within Swedish politics in the near future. His focus is not, therefore, concerned with the basic structure of neutrality, but with the relationship of the Swedish defense program to the general policy making arena. In Taylor's view, Sweden requires a defense that is strong, modern, and comprehensive. He contends that this sort of defense is essential to maintain the Nordic balance through the prevention of instabilities that may result in superpower confrontation within the region (Taylor, et. al., 1985:128).

Taylor's study is unusual in that he examines both the content and the process of Sweden's defense policy. The political, technological, and strategic constraints result in a decision-making process that is complex and—at times—contradictory. To illustrate this idea, Taylor examines the debate during the late 1970s over a replacement for the aging *Viggen* fighter aircraft. In Taylor's opinion, these drawn-out discussions affected not only Sweden's defense planning, but the future of Sweden's total defense policy as well. The debate centered upon the domestic production of a new fighter aircraft and several alternatives were considered. During the course of the deliberations, however, the decision was made to develop the all-purpose *JAS 39* which would be delivered by 1992.

Political, economic, and strategic considerations hindered the development of a clear policy line. In 1978, it was thought that the decision to develop a new aircraft had been virtually concluded. However, the issue became politicized after secret agreements between the non-socialist government and the defense contractor were revealed. Even the military became subject to inter-service rivalries with the navy, the army, and the air force competing for parts of the allotment. These rivalries have, in fact, increased during recent years in the face of budget constraints and political demands for clear priorities from the supreme commander.

In a 1987 study of Soviet submarine operations within Swedish waters, Milton Leitenberg describes these incidents in terms of Soviet military policy, rather than in terms of the possible implications for Sweden's defense policy. Leitenberg's book is primarily a case study of Soviet policy toward another state, whereas the internal Swedish discussion concerning the incidents is less important to his analysis.

The major portion of Leitenberg's controversial work presents a description of the submarine incursions over time. The author presents a chronology of events and suggests some possible policy outcomes, but he does not analyze in any systematic way the relevant Swedish foreign policy responses. Leitenberg assumes that the submarines are of Soviet origin and that Sweden's foreign policy is a clearly defined policy of neutrality. He links the failure to capture the submarines, in part, to a failure of this policy. Sweden's ineffective response to the submarine problem is linked to an inability to clearly face political realities, the smallness of the state, and the mistaken assumptions among certain policy-makers. Leitenberg reserves particular criticism for the late Olof Palme by describing his policies as "partial truths" and "dangerous political rot" (1987:116).

Leitenberg, however, does not regard Sweden as having a full range of policy options. Because of size limitations and domestic political constraints, Sweden is viewed as a classic "taker state." Sweden must pursue a non-active policy with regard to the submarines and cannot risk pressing the Soviet Union too hard lest Sweden further jeopardizes its already tenuous position vis-à-vis that state. Unlike many of the previous observers of Swedish foreign policy, Leitenberg views Sweden as a passive and weak state which neither can nor desires to change its strategic position. This pessimistic thesis follows in the tradition of Morgenthau (1939) and Zartman (1954) who were both writing during periods of tension in Europe.

Paul Cole (1986) also analyzes Sweden's changing strategic environment and its current relationship with the Soviet Union. Cole questions the viability of Sweden's post-war policy of neutrality and the capacity for this policy to succeed within a new security environment. Traditionally, Sweden has relied upon strong defense and "quiet diplomacy" to increase its policy options. However, in recent years this policy has become increasingly difficult to maintain as a result of the increased Soviet miltary presence in the Baltic.

According to Cole, the Soviets have made vast qualitative and quantitative improvements in its armed forces within the region since 1964. He connects the Soviet buildup to its increased activity within Sweden's territorial air and water space. Cole regards Sweden's inability to recognize the buildup as creating doubts in the West about the credibility of Sweden's defense. In the absence of a credible Swedish policy of neutrality, the future of the Nordic balance—within which Sweden has played an important role as an independent source of strength—is threatened. Within this context, Cole suggests the possiblity that Sweden may have to change its traditional security policy. Cole describes two extreme and unlikely possibilities.

> On the one hand, Sweden could abandon its neutrality and pursue closer ties with NATO. On the other, Sweden could conclude that the challenges that will emerge in the next decade are too great and the solutions too expensive for a small, independently minded nation (1986:25).

The problems surrounding Sweden's choice of a security policy are linked to both domestic and international constraints. Cole contends that Sweden's inability to maintain an independent armaments industry because of escalating costs will create domestic problems for a policy traditionally grounded in self-sufficient arms production. Without this production capability, Swedish industry as a whole may suffer and may—in turn— lead to a decline in other sectors of the economy as well. This problem has sparked domestic debates over the maintenance of a flexible industry based upon different threat perceptions. According to Cole, these debates have sometimes dragged on, as in the case of the JAS aircraft, and have led to policies which have not responded adequately to the actual threats.

A similar case may be that of the territorial violations that have plagued Sweden during the 1980s. Cole views Sweden's inability to capture submarines as an illustration of existing vulnerabilities of Sweden's military policy. Cole reasons that the lack of a domestic consensus over submarine incursions stems from a conflict between threat perceptions and domestic politics. These incidents are more serious than the Swedish government has publicly admitted. In fact, some U.S. commentators trace the lack of Swedish initiative to the idea that the Swedish people are "terrified" (Cole, 1986:29).

Cole is one of the few authors to examine Sweden's relationship with the US. A sensitive issue in the early 1980's was the US high-technology control program and the spectre of increased technological dependence upon the United States. Cole reasons that Sweden's closer economic ties to the US may lead to problems for Sweden's pursuit of a credible neutrality.

In Cole's view, the future of Sweden's foreign policy and national security is far from clear. Sweden's difficulty, then, is how to make its neutrality policy appear credible despite the erosion of two of the pillars of its defense policy, namely: technology and industrialization. Cole is convinced that the Soviets will continue to develop their military power and that part of that power will be directed toward the nations of northern Europe. Cole reasons that "the question for the immediate future is whether Sweden will continue to permit the domestic content of foreign policy to overshadow the shift in the balance of power in northern Europe." Cole adds that the stakes are high and may be "nothing less than the credibility of Swedish neutrality" (1986:38).

Swedish Neutrality: Commitment or Convenience?

The image of Swedish foreign policy in American scholarship has evolved from discussions of the policy as model to that of an analysis of policy efficacy. The early writings were concerned primarily with an analysis of how Sweden's neutrality actually functioned. During the time that neutrality was in vogue in the United States, the studies largely stressed Sweden's contribution to the League of Nations in a positive light. From the 1930s through World War II, questions arose as to how Sweden's neutrality functions during conflict. The discussions became more focused and specific, but, nevertheless, remained historical in nature. The case studies analyzing the war years were mostly concerned with the moral dimensions of Sweden's neutrality, rather than in the content of its foreign policy.

The article by Morgenthau, however, views Sweden's neutrality from the "Great Power" perspective. The focus is not on Swedish policy as such, but rather on neutrality's effect upon the balance of power. It is interesting to note that at the time of Morgenthau's contribution, he had only recently immigrated to the U.S. from Europe and had experienced first-hand the power of the mighty.

From the late 1940s through the 1950s, Sweden's foreign policy attracted increased interest. This development may have reflected the active debate—both within Sweden and internationally—regarding Sweden's relationship with NATO. The focus shifted from moralistic perspectives to an analysis of how neutrality functions during times of conflict. For example, Fox focused upon the impact that this policy had upon small states and discussed how these states can best respond within the context set by the Great Powers.

Surprisingly, there are no major published works on Sweden's foreign policy during the 1960s. This may result from an American fascination with Sweden's domestic politics. Perhaps, it may also reflect a time when Sweden was considered to be less strategically relevant to the U.S.

Interest in the relationship between the domestic and foreign policy arenas became evident during the seventies. An interesting example of this shift may be seen in a comparison of Marquis Childs' two works on Sweden. In the initial study, Childs ignores the matter of foreign policy and focuses instead upon Sweden's economy and the structure of the emerging welfare state. The second work, however, examines the problems of the mature welfare state and includes the subject of Sweden's foreign policy.

After the 1970s, the American interest in Sweden shifts from an analysis of neutrality's role as a model to an examination of its consequences to Sweden within a changed international environment. Several authors focus on the problems for neutrality that have been created by shifting economic conditions and increased interdependence. The writings of the early 1980s have concentrated upon changes to Sweden's strategic environment and the implications for its defense policies.

Whereas Sweden once may have been an interesting model, today it has become part of a vital region deserving of careful study. It may be reasonable to assert that this change in focus parallels the increased strategic significance of the North Atlantic and the Baltic regions to the US. To some extent, one may argue that the scope and interest in Sweden's foreign policy among American analysts reflects the political awareness of Sweden's strategic position.

It is likely that small states become interesting topics to study when they fall on the borderline of the spheres of influence of antagonistic "Great Powers." This mirrors the political reality of a world divided into blocs. An independent player that may possibly affect the balance between the blocs will likely prove to be an interesting topic for analysis.

Sweden has long been a subject for students of the welfare state. Numerous American social scientists have focused upon Sweden as an interesting case of advanced social engineering. Within the field of international politics, Sweden is also becoming the target of more intensive investigation. This is evidenced by the growing body of literature devoted to the strategic dilemma of Sweden—*the committed neutral.*

References

Abrahamson, Samuel (1957) *Sweden's Foreign Policy*. Washington, D.C.: Public Affairs Press.

Auslund, John C. (1986) *Nordic Security and the Great Powers*. Boulder, Colo.: Westview Press.

Bellquist, Eric C. (1929) "Some Aspects of the Recent Foreign Policy of Sweden." *University of California Publications,* Vol. 1, No. 3, pp. 251–378.

Board, Joseph B. (1974) "A New Look at Swedish Politics: Compromise and Change." *Scandinavian Studies,* Vol. 46, No. 1, pp. 1–19.

———. (1970) *The Government and Politics of Sweden*. Boston, Mass.: Houghton-Mifflin Co.

Boli, John (1983) "The Contradictions of Welfare Capitalism in the Core: The Role of Sweden in the World System." in Patrick McGowan and Charles W. Kegley, eds. *Foreign Policy and the Modern World System*. Vol. 8, Sage International Yearbook of Foreign Policy Studies. Beverly Hills, Calif.: Sage Publications, pp. 187–221.

Canby, Stephen L. (1981) "Swedish Defense," *Survival,* Vol. 108, 116–7.

Childs, Marquis W. (1936) *Sweden: The Middle Way*. New Haven, Conn.: Yale University Press.

———. (1980) *Sweden: The Middle Way on Trial*. New Haven, Conn.: Yale University Press.

Cole, Paul M. and Douglas M. Hart, eds. (1986) *Northern Europe: Security Issues for the 1990s*. Boulder, Colo.: Westview Press.

Fleisher, Frederick (1956) *The New Sweden—The Challenge of a Disciplined Democracy*. New York: David McKay Co.

Fleisher, Wilfrid (1956) *Sweden the Welfare State*. New York: The John Day Co.

Fox, Annette Baker (1959) *The Power of Small States—Diplomacy in World War II*. Chicago, Ill.: University of Chicago Press.

Hancock, M. Donald (1974) "Scandinavia and the Expanded European Community," *Scandinavian Studies,* Vol. 46, No. 4, pp. 319–30.

———. (1972) "Sweden, Scandinavia and the EEC," *International Affairs,* Vol. 48, pp. 424–37.

———. (1972) *Sweden: The Politics of Post-Industrial Change*. Hinsdale, Ill.: The Dryden Press.

———. (1974) "Swedish Elites and the EEC: Models of the Future," *Cooperation and Conflict,* Vol. 9, No. 4, pp. 225–45.

Haskel, Barbara (1976) *The Scandinavian Option*. Oslo: Universitetsfölaget.

Hedin, Naboth (1943) "Sweden: The Dilemma of a Neutral," *Foreign Policy Reports,* Vol. 14, No. 5, pp. 50–63.

Hinshaw, David (1949) *Sweden: Champion of Peace*. New York: G.P. Putnam's Sons.

Hopper, Bruce (1945) "Sweden: A Case Study in Neutrality," *Foreign Affairs,* Vol. 23, No. 3, pp. 435–49.

Jessup, Philip C. (1936) *Neutrality: Today and Tomorrow*. Morningside Heights, NY: Columbia University Press.

Joesten, Joachim (1945) "Phases in Swedish Neutrality," *Foreign Affairs,* Vol. 23, No. 2, pp. 324–329.

———. (1943) *Stalwart Sweden.* Garden City, NY: Doubleday, Doran and Co.

Johnson, Luther E. (1966) "Freedom from Alliances: Contemporary Swedish Views Toward International Relations," Ph.D. Dissertation. Washington, D.C.: The American University.

Jones, Samuel Shepard (1939) *The Scandinavian States and the League of Nations.* Princeton, NJ: Princeton University Press.

Koblik, Steven (1972) *Sweden: The Neutral Victor.* Lund: Lund Studies in International History.

———. (1984) "Sweden's Attempts to Aid Jews, 1939–45," *Scandinavian Studies,* Vol. 56, pp. 89–113.

———, ed. (1975) *Sweden's Development from Poverty to Affluence 1750-1970.* Minneapolis, Minn.: University of Minnesota Press.

Leitenberg, Milton (1987) *Soviet Submarine Operations in Swedish Waters 1980–86.* New York, NY: Praeger.

Lindgren, Raymond E. (1959) *Norway-Sweden—Union, Disunion, and Scandinavian Integration.* Princeton, NJ: Princeton University Press.

Morgenthau, Hans J. (1939) "The Resurrection of Neutrality in Europe," *American Political Science Review,* Vol. 23, No. 3, pp. 473–86.

Rintala, Marvin (1978) "Northern Europe in International Politics," *World Affairs,* Vol. 140, No. 3, pp. 206–16.

Sandler, Åke (1960) "Sweden's Postwar Diplomacy: Some Problems, Views, and Issues,"*The Western Political Quarterly,* Vol 13, pp. 924–33.

Schiff, Martin (1972) "Sweden and the European Economic Community,"*Scandinavian Studies,* Vol. 44, No. 1, pp. 43–51.

———. (1969) "Swedish Neutrality and European Integraton," Ph.D. Dissertation. New Brunswick, NJ: Rutgers University.

Scott, Franklin D. (1975) *Scandinavia.* Cambridge, Mass.: Harvard University Press.

———. (1951) "Scandinavia Today," *Foreign Policy Association,* Headline Series, No. 35.

———. (1978) *Sweden: The Nation's History.* Minneapolis, Minn.: University of Minnesota Press.

———. (1950) *The United States and Scandinavia.* Cambridge, Mass.: Harvard University Press.

Scheidenfaden, Erik (1948) "Scandinavia Charts a Course," *Foreign Affairs,* Vol. 26, No. 4, pp. 653–64.

Taylor, William J. (1982) "The Defense Policy of Sweden," in Murray, Douglas J. and Paul R. Viotti, eds. *The Defense Policies of Nations.* Baltimore, MD: Johns Hopkins University Press, pp. 299–322.

and Paul M. Cole, eds. (1985) *Nordic Defense: Comparative Decision Making.* Lexington, Mass.: Lexington Books.

Turlington, Edgar (1936) *Neutrality: The World War Period.* Morningside Heights, NY: Columbia University Press.

Waite, James L. (1971) "Contemporary Swedish Foreign Policy: A Systemic Analysis," Ph.D. Dissertation. Carbondale, Ill.: Southern Illinois University.

_____ . (1974) "The Swedish Paradox: EEC and Neutrality," *Journal of Common Market Studies,* Vol. 12, pp. 319–36.

West, John M. (1978) "The German–Swedish Transit Agreement of 1940," *Scandinavian Studies,* Vol. 50, No. 1, pp. 76–99.

Zakhem, Dov S. (1982) "NATO's Northern Front: Developments and Prospects," *Cooperation and Conflict,* Vol. 17, No. 4, pp. 193–205.

Zartman, William I. (1954) "Neutralism and Neutrality in Scandinavia," *The Western Political Quarterly,* Vol. 7, No. 3, pp. 125–60.

For Further Reading

Don Odom

The studies dealing with Swedish foreign relations cited below by no means comprise a complete English–language bibliography on the subject. This listing merely enables interested readers to proceed beyond the introductory overviews in this volume. The selection is limited to books and journal articles in English and a few significant studies in Swedish. More comprehensive listings can be found in *International Studies in the Nordic Countries,* a biannual newsletter published by the Nordic Cooperation Committee for International Politics, Box 1253, S–11182 Stockholm, Sweden. This publication is the best source to follow current research, workshops, conferences, and publications in the field.

Several English-language periodicals are devoted to the study of Scandinavia including Swedish foreign relations. A primary source is the quarterly *Cooperation and Conflict* published by the Nordic Cooperation Committee for International Politics since 1965. The Nordic Political Science Associations sponsor *Scandinavian Political Studies,* formerly a yearbook but since 1978 a quarterly. *Scandinavian Review* and *Scandinavian Studies* are the two major U.S. journals in the field. However, both titles are only to a very limited extent devoted to foreign policy issues.

Some major Scandinavian-language journals are also important. *Internasjonal Politikk* is published by the Norwegian Institute of International Affairs, *Internationella Studier* by the Swedish Institute of International Affairs and *Ulkopolitiikka* by the Finnish Institute of International Affairs. The official *Documents on Swedish Foreign Policy* is an annual English-language compilation of key Swedish foreign policy documents published by the Swedish Ministry of Foreign Affairs.

General Overviews

Albrecht, Ulrich, Burkhard Auffermann, and Perti Joenniemi. (1988) *Neutrality: The Need for Conceptual Revision.* Occasional Papers, No. 35, Tampere: Tampere Peace Research Institute.

Andrén, Nils. (1967) *Power-Balance and Non-Alignment: A Perspective on Swedish Foreign Policy.* Stockholm: Almquist & Wiksell.

"Anglo–Swede." (1939) "International Relations," in M. Cole and C. Smith, eds. *Democratic Sweden.* Published for New Fabian Research Bureau. New York: Greystone Press.

Archer, Clive and David Scrivener. (1983) "Frozen frontiers and resource wrangles: conflict and cooperation in Northern Waters." *International Affairs,* Vol. 59, No. 1, Winter, pp. 59–76.

Childs, Marquis. (1936) *Sweden: The Middle Way.* New Haven, Conn.: Yale University Press.

Cole, Paul M. and Douglas M. Hart, eds. (1986) *Northern Europe: Security Issues for the 1990s.* Boulder, Colo.: Westview Press.

Danspeckgruber, Wolfgang. (1986) "Armed Neutrality: Its Application and Future." in S. Flanagan and F. Hampson, eds. *Securing Europe's Future.* London: Croom Helm.

Foreign Policy-making in the Nordic Countries. (1984) Special Issue of *Cooperation and Conflict.* Vol. XIX, No. 2, pp. 87–164.

Friis, Henning, ed. (1950) *Scandinavia Between East and West.* Ithaca, NY: Cornell University Press.

Hakovirta, Harto. (1983) "The Soviet Union and the Varieties of Neutrality in Western Europe." *World Politics,* Vol. 35, No. 4, pp. 563–85.

Hakovirta, Harto. (1988) *East-West Conflict and European Neutrality.* Oxford: Oxford University Press.

Holst, Johan Jøorgen, ed. (1973) *Five Roads to Nordic Security.* Oslo: Universitetsforlaget.

Huldt, Bo and Atis Lejins, eds. (1986) *European Neutrals and the Soviet Union.* Conference Paper No. 6. Stockholm: Swedish Institute of International Affairs.

Höll, Otmar, ed. (1983) *Small States in Europe and Dependence.* The Laxenburg Papers, No. 6. Vienna: Braumüller.

Joenniemi, Pertti, ed. (1986) "Nordic Security." Special Issue of *Current Research on Peace and Violence,* Vol. 9, No. 1–2, Tampere, Finland: Tampere Peace Research Institute.

Jervas, Gunnar, ed. (1973) *Utrikespolitik i Norr.* Lund: Studentlitteratur.

Karsh, Efraim. (1988) *Neutrality and the Small State.* London: Routledge.

Lindahl, Ingemar. (1988) *The Soviet Union and the Nordic Nuclear-Weapons-Free-Zone Proposal.* London: Macmillan Press.

Neuhold, Hanspeter and Hans Thalberg, eds. (1984) *The European Neutrals in International Affairs.* Vienna: Braumüller.

Nordic Voices. (1984) Special Issue of *Daedalus.* Vol. 113, No. 2, Spring.

Papacosma, S. Victor and Mark Rubin, eds. (1988) *Europe's Neutral and Nonaligned States: Between NATO and the Warsaw Pact.* Wilmington, Del.: Scholarly Resources.

Sundelius, Bengt, ed. (1982) *Foreign Policies of Northern Europe.* Boulder, Colo.: Westview Press.

Sundelius, Bengt, ed. (1987) *The Neutral Democracies and the New Cold War.* Boulder, Colo.: Westview Press.

Tägil, Sven, et al. (1980) *Sweden in the World Society.* New York: Pergamon Press.

The Nordic Enigma. (1984) Special Issue of *Daedalus.* Vol. 113, No. 1. Winter.

Historical Works

Agrell, Wilhelm. (1985) "Sweden and the Cold War: The Structure of a Neglected Field of Research." *Scandinavian Journal of History.* Vol. 10, No. 3, pp. 239–53.

Barros, James. (1968) *The Åland Islands Question: Its Settlement by the League of Nations.* New Haven, Conn.: Yale University Press.

Bellquist, Eric C. (1929) "Some Aspects of the Recent Foreign Policy of Sweden," *University of California Publications,* Vol. 1, No. 3, pp. 251–378.

Blidberg, Kersti. (1987) *Just good friends—Nordic Social Democracy and Security Policy 1945–50. Forsvarsstudier* No. 5, Oslo: *Forsvarshistorisk forskningssenter.*

Böhme, Klaus-Richard. (1984) "The Principal Features of Swedish Defence Policy 1925-1945," *Neutrality and Defense: The Swedish Experience.* Stockholm: Swedish Commission on Military History.

Carlgren, Wilhelm. (1977) *Swedish Foreign Policy during the Second World War.* London: Ernest Benn.

Ekman, Stig. (1986) *Stormaktstryck och småstatspolitik.* Stockholm: Liber Förlag.

Gerner, Kristian. (1986) "The Swedish Defense Doctrine in the Postwar Era: Changes and Implications." *Scandia.* Vol. 52, No. 2, pp. 307–325.

Haskel, Barbara. (1976) *The Scandinavian Option: Opportunities and Opportunity Costs in Postwar Scandinavian Foreign Policies.* Oslo: Universitetsforlaget.

Koblik, Steven, ed. (1975) *Sweden's Development from Poverty to Affluence, 1750-1970.* Minneapolis, Minn.: University of Minnesota Press.

Johansson, Alf W. (1984) *Per Albin och kriget.* Stockholm: Tidens förlag.

Lundestad, Geir. (1980) *America, Scandinavia, and the Cold War 1945–1949.* Oslo: Universitetsforlaget.

Möller, Yngve. (1986) *Östen Undén: En biographi.* Södertälje: Norstedts.

Nevakivi, Jukka. (1984) "Scandinavian Talks on Military Cooperation in 1946–1947: A Prelude to the Decisions of 1948–1949," *Cooperation and Conflict.* Vol. XIX, No. 3, pp. 165–175.

Olsson, Ulf. (1982) "The State and Industry in Swedish Rearmament," in Martin Fritz, et. al. *The Adaptable Nation: Essays in the Swedish Economy during the Second World War.* Stockholm: Almquist and Wiksell.

Persson, Sune. (1979) *Mediation and Assassination: Count Bernadotte's Mission to Palestine.* London: Ithaca Press.

Schiller, Bernt. (1984) "At Gun Point: A Critical Perspective on the Attempt's of the Nordic Governments to Achieve Unity after the Second World War," *Scandinavian Journal of History.* Vol. 9, No. 3, pp. 221–38.

Scott, Franklin. (1977) *Sweden: The Nation's History.* Minneapolis: University of Minnesota Press.

Tingsten, Herbert. (1948) *The Debate on the Foreign Policy of Sweden 1918-1939.* Trans. by Jan Bulman. London: Oxford University Press.

Wahlbäck, Krister. (1986) *The Roots of Swedish Neutrality.* Stockholm: The Swedish Institute.

Security Policy

Agrell, Wilhelm. (1983) "Soviet Baltic Strategy and the Swedish Submarine Crisis." *Cooperation and Conflict.* Vol. XVIII, No. 4, pp. 269–281.

Agrell, Wilhelm. (1986) "Behind the Submarine Crisis: Evolution of the Swedish Defence Doctrine and Soviet War Planning," *Cooperation and Conflict,* Vol. XXI, No. 4, pp. 197–217.

Andrén, Nils. (1982) "Sweden's Defence Doctrines and Changing Threat Perceptions," *Cooperation and Conflict.* Vol. XVII, No. 1, pp. 29–40.

Bjøl, Erling. (1983) "Nordic Security." *Adelphi Paper No. 181.* London: International Institute for Strategic Studies.

Brodin, Katarina. (1978) "Surprise Attack: The Case of Sweden." *The Journal of Strategic Studies.* Vol. 1, No. 1, pp. 98–110.

Canby, Stephen. (1981) "Swedish Defense," *Survival,* May/June, pp. 116–123.

Cole, Paul. M. (1988) "Sweden's Security Policy in the 1980s," *SAIS Review.* Vol. 8, No. 1, Winter–Spring, pp. 231–227.

Defense Commission Report. (1985) "Sweden's Security Policy Entering the 1990s." *SOU,* No. 23. Stockholm: Ministry of Defense.

Dörfer, Ingemar. (1973) *System 37 Viggen.* Oslo: Universitetsforlaget.

Dörfer, Ingemar. (1982) "Nordic Security Today: Sweden," *Cooperation and Conflict,* Vol. XVII, No. 4, pp. 273–285.

Jervell, Sverre and Kare Nyblom, eds. (1986) *The Military Buildup in the High North.* Lanham, Md.: University Press of America.

Jönsson, Christer and Bo Petersson. (1985) "The Bear and the Mouse That Roared: Soviet Reactions to Public Swedish Criticism—Czechoslovakia and Vietnam," *Cooperation and Conflict.* Vol. XX, No. 2, pp. 79–90.

Leitenberg, Milton. (1987) *Soviet Submarine Operations in Swedish Internal Waters 1980-1986.* New York: Praeger.

Neutrality and Defence: The Swedish Experience. (1984) Stockholm: The Swedish Commission on Military History.

Oldberg, Ingemar. (1985) "Peace Propaganda and Submarines: Soviet Policy toward Sweden and Northern Europe." *Annals of the American Academy.* Vol. 481, September, pp. 51–60.

Peterson, Martin. (1980) "Stockholm: Nonaligned and Nervous." *The Washington Quarterly,* Summer, pp. 187–91.

Posen, Barry R. (1982) "Inadvertent Nuclear War? Escalation and NATO's Northern Flank." *International Security,* Vol. 7, No. 2, Fall, pp. 28–54.

Ries, Tomas. (1982) "The Nordic Dilemma in the 80s: Maintaining Regional Stability Under New Strategic Conditions." *PSIS Occasional Papers, No. 1.* Geneva: Programme for Strategic and International Security Studies.

Roberts, Adam. (1986) *Nations in Arms.* Second (Revised and Enlarged) Edition, Studies in International Security No. 18, London: Macmillan.

Salicath, Carl P. (1987) "Alien Submarines in Swedish Waters: The Method of Counting as a Political Instrument," *Cooperation and Conflict.* Vol. XXII, No. 1, pp. 49–55.

International Economic Relations

Adler-Karlsson, Gunnar. (1968) *Western Economic Warfare 1947-67*. Stockholm: Almquist & Wiksell.

Archer, Clive T. (1976) "Britain and Scandinavia: Their Relations Within EFTA." *Cooperation and Conflict*, Vol. 11, No. 1, pp. 1–24.

Bergquist, Mats. (1971) "Sweden and the EEC: A Study of Four Schools of Thought and Their Views on Swedish Common Market Policy in 1961–62." *Cooperation and Conflict*, Vol. 5, No. 1, pp. 39–55.

Boli, John. (1983) "The Contradictions of Welfare Capitalism in the Core: The Role of Sweden in the World–System," in Patrick McGowan and Charles W. Kegley, Jr., eds. *Foreign Policy and the Modern World System*. Beverly Hills, Calif.: Sage.

Carlsnaes, Walter. (1988) *Energy Vulnerability and National Security*. London: Pinter.

Cole, G. D. H. (1939) "Sweden in World Trade," in M. Cole and C. Smith, eds. *Democratic Sweden*. Published for New Fabian Research Bureau. New York: Greystone Press.

Dohlman, Ebba. (forthcoming) *National Welfare and Economic Interdependence: The Case of Sweden*. Oxford: Oxford University Press.

Hamilton, Carl B., ed. (1987) *Europa och Sverige*. Stockholm: SNS Förlag.

Hancock, M. Donald. (1972) "Sweden, Scandinavia and the EEC." *International Affairs*, Vol. 48, No. 3, July, pp. 424–37.

_____, ed. (1974) "Sweden and the European Community." Special issue of *Scandinavian Studies*, Vol. 46, No. 4.

_____. (1984) "Swedish Elites and the EEC: Models of the Future." *Cooperation and Conflict*, Vol. 9, No. 4, pp. 225–43.

Haskel, Barbara G. (1974) "Disparities, Strategies and Opportunity Costs: The Example of Scandinavian Economic Market Negotiations." *International Studies Quarterly*, Vol. 18, No. 1, pp. 3–30.

Martin, Andrew. (1984) "Trade Unions in Sweden; Strategic Responses to Change and Crisis." in Peter Gourevitch, et. al. *Unions and Economic Crisis: Britain, West Germany and Sweden*. Boston: Allen & Unwin.

Miljan, Toivo. (1977) *The Reluctant Europeans. The Attitudes of the Nordic Countries Towards European Integration*. London: C. Hurst and Co.

Mjøset, Lars. (1987) "Nordic economic policies in the 1970s and 1980s." *International Organization*, Vol. 41, No. 3, Summer.

Nordic relations within the European Community. (1973) Special Issue of *Scandinavian Political Studies*. Vol. 8.

Örvik, Nils. (1974) "Nordic Cooperation and High Politics." *International Organization*, Vol. 28, No. 1, pp. 61–88.

"Scandinavian and Western European Economic Integration." (1969) Special issue of *Cooperation and Conflict*, Vol. 4, No. 1.

Sjöstedt, Gunnar (1987) *Sweden's Free Trade Policy: Balancing Economic Growth and Security* Stockholm: The Swedish Institute.

Sundelius, Bengt. (1978) *Managing Transnationalism in Northern Europe.* Boulder, Colo.: Westview Press.

Waite, John. (1974) "The Swedish Paradox: EEC and Neutrality." *Journal of Common Market Studies,* Vol. 12, No. 3, pp. 319–36.

Development Assistance Policy

Andersson, Christian, Lars Heikensten, and Stefan de Vylder, eds. (1984) *Bistånd i kris.* Stockholm: LiberFörlag.

Barnes, Ian. (1980) "The Changing Nature of the Swedish Aid Relationship During the Social Democratic Period of Government." *Cooperation and Conflict,* Vol. 15, No. 3, pp. 141–50.

Beckman, Björn. (1979) "Aid and Investment: The Swedish Case," *Cooperation and Conflict.* Vol. XIV, No. 2-3, pp. 133–48.

Brundenius, Claes. (1978) *Foreign Investment and Technology: The Case of Swedish Manufacturing Subsidiaries in Brazil.* Lund: Research Policy Program, University of Lund.

Elgström, Ole. (1987) "Negotiating with the LDCs: Situation and Context." *Cooperation and Conflict,* Vol. XXII, No. 3, pp. 135–51.

Früling, Pierre, ed. (1986) *Swedish Development Aid in Perspective.* Stockholm: Almquist & Wiksell.

Jinadu, L. Adele. (1984) "The Political Economy of Sweden's Development Policy in Africa," *Cooperation and Conflict.* Vol. XIX, No. 3, pp. 177–96.

Hermele, Kenneth, and Karl-Anders Larsson. (1977) *Solidaritet eller imperialism. Om Sverige, världsordningen och tredje världen.* Stockholm: Liber.

Michanek, Ernst. (1977) *Role of Swedish Non-Governmental Organizations in International Development Cooperation.* Stockholm: SIDA.

Millwood, David and Helena Gazelius. (1985) *Good Aid: A Study of Quality in Small Projects.* Stockholm: SIDA.

Myrdal, Gunnar. (1960) *Beyond the Welfare State.* New Haven, Conn.: Yale University Press.

"Nordic Aid to Underdeveloped Countries." (1970) Special issue of *Cooperation and Conflict,* Vol. 5, No. 2.

Radetzki, Marian. (1981) *Sverige och den tredje världen.* Stockholm: Studieförbundet Näringlsliv och Samhälle.

Stokke, Olav. (1978) *Sveriges utvecklingsbistånd och biståndspolitik.* Uppsala, Sweden: Nordiska Afrikainstitutet.

"The Nordic Countries and the New International Economic Order." (1979) Special issue of *Cooperation and Conflict,* Vol. 14, Nos. 2–3.

Wohlgemuth, Lennart, ed. (1976) *Bistånd på mottagarens villkor.* Stockholm: SIDA.

Sources of Foreign Policy

Agrell, Wilhelm. (1985) *Alliansfrihet och atombomber: Kontinuitet och förändring i den svenska forsvarsdoktrinen från 1945 till 1982.* Stockholm: Liber.

Andrén, Nils and Einar Lyth. (1982) "Citizens in Arms: The Swedish Model," in Gwyn Harries–Jenkins, ed. *Armed Forces and the Welfare Societies: Challenges in the 1980s*. London: Macmillan, pp. 124–57.

Barnes, Ian R. (1974) "Swedish Foreign Policy: A Response to Geopolitical Factors." *Cooperation and Conflict*, Vol. 9, No. 4, pp. 243–62.

Birnbaum, Karl E. (1965) "The Formation of Swedish Foreign Policy: Some Points of Departure for an Inquiry," *Cooperation and Conflict*, Vol. 1, No. 1, pp. 6–31.

Dörfer, Ingemar. (1973) *System 37 Viggen: Arms, Technology and the Domestication of Glory*. Oslo: Universitetsforlaget.

Goldmann, Kjell, Sten Berglund, and Gunnar Sjöstedt. (1986) *Democracy and Foreign Policy: The Case of Sweden*. Hants, U.K.: Gower.

Hart, Thomas G. (1976) *The Cognitive World of Swedish Security Elites*. Stockholm: Esselte.

Heclo, Hugh C. and Henrik Madsen. (1987) *Policy and Politics in Sweden: Principled Pragmatism*. Philadelphia, Penn.: Temple University Press.

Holmström, Barry. (1972) *Koreakriget i svensk debatt*. Stockholm: Rabén & Sjögren.

Karvonen, Lauri and Bengt Sundelius. (1987) *Internationalization and Foreign Policy Management*. Hants, U.K.: Gower.

Petersson, Olof. (1982) *Väljarna och världspolitiken*. Stockholm: Norstedts.

Stenelo, Lars-Göran. (1972) *Mediation in International Negotiation*. Lund: Studentlitteratur.

Stenelo, Lars-Göran. (1984) *The International Critic*. Lund and Bromley: Studentlitteratur & Chartwell Bratt.

Sundelius, Bengt. (1984) "Interdependence, Internationalization and Foreign Policy Decentralization in Sweden," *Cooperation and Conflict*. Vol. XIX, No. 2, pp. 93–120.

Taylor, William and Paul M. Cole, eds. (1985) *Nordic Defense: Comparative Decision Making*. Lexington, Mass.: Lexington Books.

About the Contributors

Sverker Åström has been in public service since 1939, when he entered the Swedish diplomatic corps. Schooled under the legendary foreign minister Östen Undén, Ambassador Åström has been involved behind the scenes in most major Swedish foreign policy decisions of the postwar era. After early assignments in Moscow (1940–43) and Washington, D.C. (1946–48), he served in many high level positions, such as Assistant Secretary for Political Affairs (1956–64), Permanent Representative to the United Nations (1964–70), Permanent Under Secretary of Foreign Affairs (1971–77), and ambassador to France (1978–82). Ambassador Åström's interpretations of the requirements of neutrality have become the operational guidelines for Swedish politicians and diplomats alike.

Ebba Dohlman is Administrator in the Trade Directorate of the Organization for Economic Cooperation and Development (OECD) Paris. She has also worked as a consultant at the General Agreement on Tariffs and Trade (GATT) and the United Nations Commission on Trade and Development (UNCTAD) in Geneva. Her doctoral thesis at the London School of Economics is forthcoming from Oxford University Press as *National Welfare and Economic Interdependence: The Case of Sweden.*

Susan L. Holmberg is a graduate student in Political Science at the Massachusetts Institute of Technology. She holds a Master's Degree in International Relations from the Johns Hopkins University School of Advanced International Studies (SAIS), and spent 1983/84 as a Fulbright Scholar in Stockholm, researching Sweden's aid policy. Much of her scholarly work involves the study of comparative politics, the policy process, and development issues.

Joseph Kruzel is associate professor of political science and senior associate of the Mershon Center at Ohio State University. He has been a visiting scholar at the Swedish Institute of International Affairs. He is the author of numerous publications on security issues and is editor of *Between the Blocs: Problems and Prospects for Europe's Neutral and Nonaligned States.*

John Logue teaches political science at Kent State University. He has previously taught or held research positions at the Universities of Göteborg and Linköping in Sweden and at the Roskilde University Center in Denmark. His publications include *Socialism and Abundance: Radical Socialism in the Danish Welfare State* (1982), *Modern Welfare States: Politics and Policy in Social Democratic Scandinavia* with Eric S. Einhorn (1989), and numerous articles.

Don Odom, a graduate of the University of Maryland, received his graduate diploma in the social sciences from the International Graduate School of the University of Stockholm in 1988. His research interests include the study of comparative foreign policy with particular emphasis on the role of the small state in the international system. He is currently employed as an editor at the Stockholm International Peace Research Institute (SIPRI).

Mikael S. Steene, a graduate of Gustaphus Adolphus College, completed his graduate training in Scandinavian Studies at the University of Washington in 1987. He is now affiliated with the Elliott School of International Affairs, George Washington University, Washington, D.C.

Bengt Sundelius is director of the International Graduate School and associate professor of political science at the University of Stockholm. He has served on the faculties of Bradley University and the University of Washington and is an external research associate of the Swedish Institute of International Affairs. His previous publications with Westview Press include *Managing Transnationalism in Northern Europe, Foreign Policies of Northern Europe,* and *The Neutral Democracies and the New Cold War.*

Index

47 85